1991 BIENNIAL EXHIBITION

AF

1991 Biennial Exhibition

RICHARD ARMSTRONG
JOHN G. HANHARDT
RICHARD MARSHALL
LISA PHILLIPS

Whitney Museum of American Art
New York

IN ASSOCIATION WITH W.W. NORTON & COMPANY
NEW YORK, LONDON

EXHIBITION SCHEDULE

April 2 – June 16
SECOND FLOOR AND SECOND FLOOR FILM/VIDEO GALLERY

April 9 – June 23
FOURTH FLOOR AND LOBBY GALLERY

April 19 – June 30
THIRD FLOOR AND LOWER GALLERY

CONTENTS

The 1991 Biennial Exhibition is supported by
a grant from Emily Fisher Landau.

Additional funding has been provided by the
National Committee of the Whitney Museum.
Research for this exhibition and publication
was supported by income from an endowment
established by Henry and Elaine Kaufman,
The Lauder Foundation, Mrs. William A.
Marsteller, The Andrew W. Mellon Foundation,
Mrs. Donald Petrie, The Primerica
Foundation, The Samuel and May Rudin
Foundation, Inc., The Simon Foundation,
and Nancy Brown Wellin.

FOREWORD

David A. Ross, *Director*

In its continuing commitment to American art of the twentieth century, the Whitney Museum is proud heir to the patterns of patronage established in the early years of the century by its founder, Gertrude Vanderbilt Whitney. At the same time, this primary commitment, which defines and empowers the Museum, compels us to periodically construct a report on the vitality of American art in the form of a survey exhibition. In this, our sixty-sixth Annual or Biennial, the Museum presents an exhibition of one hundred artists working in a broad range of styles and from a diverse set of attitudes, who provide what we firmly believe to be a provocative and useful overview of American art today.

We recognize that no survey exhibition can ever be expected to offer a fair or objective picture of all current American art. In fact, this type of exhibition succeeds when its organizers express a collaborative, highly subjective response to American art and the current concerns of American artists. And though predictably opposed by those who are disengaged from the art of their time or are made anxious by the challenge and change inherent in the new art, the 1991 Biennial underscores this museum's willingness to consider and celebrate the new while acknowledging the continuing vitality and contribution of well-established artists. More significantly, this type of exhibition allows visitors to make connections among coexisting generations of American artists, among the various stylistic influences and vocabularies that constitute the American scene, and to grasp and, we hope, delight in the fertile complexity of American culture.

The 1991 Biennial is further distinguished by its use of a curatorial advisory committee. The Biennial was organized by Whitney Museum curators Richard Armstrong, John G. Hanhardt, Richard Marshall, and Lisa Phillips. They were assisted in their preliminary research by a group of distinguished colleagues representing seven regions of the United States: Cheryl Chisholm, Dana Friis-Hansen, Susanne Ghez, Kellie Jones, Lawrence Rinder, César Trasobares, and Marilyn Zeitlin. This new structure provided a valuable forum for curatorial debate and helped broaden considerably the exhibition's scope.

Nevertheless, the task of presenting the Biennial remains formidable, and it would be all but impossible without the dedicated work of the Museum's entire staff, and the support and understanding of the Museum's devoted Board of Trustees. Singular among the Board in respect to the 1991 exhibition is Emily Fisher Landau, who once again has provided a grant in support of the Biennial. Her courage and commitment to the Biennial is deeply appreciated by all who encourage and respect the Whitney Museum's ongoing engagement with the art of our time. I also acknowledge the continuing generosity of the Museum's National Committee, whose members have contributed additional funds needed to present this ambitious exhibition.

Clearly, we are grateful to the scores of lenders to this exhibition. But, finally, it is my privilege and honor to thank not only the Museum's curators, staff, and Trustees, but to acknowledge those American artists who continue to provide us with pleasure and provocation, and to whom we remain deeply indebted.

The 1991 Biennial Exhibition is the sixty-sixth event in the series of Annuals and Biennials begun by Gertrude Vanderbilt Whitney in 1932, shortly after the Museum was established. The historically stated purpose of these exhibitions, one of the longest continuous series on contemporary art in the United States, is "to represent in a broad way some of the most notable characteristics of American art today"—and they have successfully done that for almost sixty years. Frequent criticism to the contrary, these exhibitions offer a seriously considered and carefully selected survey of recent activities in American art. They have always been non-juried, invitational exhibitions restricted only to art produced within the previous two years—by artists of all ages, career levels, and styles. For the present Biennial, as for past surveys, the work of thousands of artists was reviewed and that of a few hundred closely examined before a final selection was made, a selection limited by the space needed to accommodate multiple examples by each artist. The 1991 Biennial Exhibition includes the work of one hundred painters, sculptors, photographers, and film and video artists, who reside in more than twenty cities and three countries and range in age from twenty-seven to seventy-one. When considering selections for the Biennial, the strength of the work of an established artist is evaluated both in relation to the entire oeuvre and to the recent production of contemporaries. With younger artists, achievement is measured in terms of the works' impact, influence, and introduction of new ideas and forms. Participation in previous Biennials as well as in recent or upcoming Whitney Museum exhibitions is also taken into account in order to avoid overexposure and repetition.

Because the Whitney Museum and a great number of American artists are New York-based, the exhibition is of course weighted toward this region as well

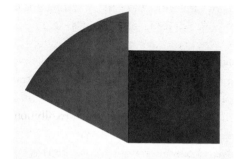

ELLSWORTH KELLY *Purple Panel with Blue Curve*, 1989

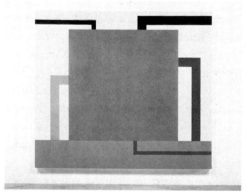

PETER HALLEY *Total Recall*, 1990

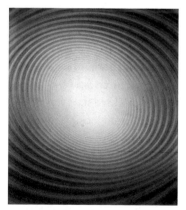

ADAM FUSS *Untitled*, 1989

as to New York's museum and gallery exhibitions of the past two years. Indeed, the Biennials were never intended to be nationwide surveys. The curators do attempt, however, to present the work of artists from other major centers in the United States, soliciting recommendations from artists, curators, and critics around the country. For the 1991 Biennial Exhibition, this practice was formalized for the first time. Seven art professionals from different regions of the country were invited to form an advisory committee. The members met individually with the Biennial curators in New York to make in-depth presentations of the work of ten to fifteen artists residing in their respective regions. The advisers' firsthand familiarity with these artists allowed them to present a fuller analysis of the works and their relation to those of regional contemporaries. A number of artists recommended by the advisers were then visited by the Biennial curators, and, as a result, the 1991 Biennial Exhibition has a high representation of artists working outside the New York area.

The Whitney Museum is now entering a new decade with new leadership, and in order to reinforce and substantiate its commitment to contemporary art, it was decided to expand the 1991 Biennial, devoting all the Museum's exhibition space to it. The consequent increase in the number of artists and art works necessitated a different organizational logic to ensure a clear and meaningful presentation. Accordingly, the installation of the exhibition on three successive floors of the Museum has been organized loosely by generations. Fifteen artists who came to prominence in the 1950s and 1960s—including Jasper Johns, Ellsworth Kelly, Joan Mitchell, Ed Moses, Philip Pearlstein, and Cy Twombly—are exhibited on the Second Floor; twenty-six artists who emerged in the 1970s and 1980s—among them Vito Acconci, Eric Fischl,

BRUCE NAUMAN *10 Heads Circle/In and Out* (detail), 1990

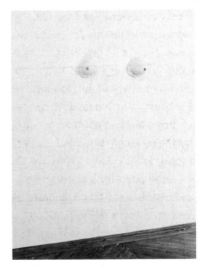

ROBERT GOBER *Two Breasts*, 1990

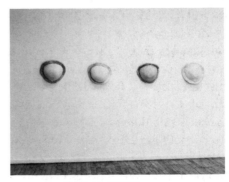

KIKI SMITH *Untitled I–IV*, 1990

Robert Gober, Luis Jimenez, Elizabeth Murray, and Cindy Sherman—are installed on the Third Floor; and twenty-nine younger artists, most of whom had their first shows in the late 1980s and have not been in previous Biennial Exhibitions, appear on the Fourth Floor; these include Nayland Blake, Felix Gonzalez-Torres, Mary Kelly, Cady Noland, Jim Shaw, Kiki Smith, and Jessica Stockholder. In addition, the Lobby Gallery will exhibit the *AIDS Timeline*, an installation by the artists' collaborative Group Material, which explores socio-political aspects of the disease and its ever-increasing and deadly effect on American society and culture.

The generational framework of the exhibition permits each floor of the Museum to have a distinct and compatible mood and impact, joining as it does artists of related accomplishment and aesthetic inclination. This type of organization makes apparent the way different generations of artists respond—through the form, format, and content of their art—to the changing attitudes about aesthetics, society, politics, and sexuality that have emerged over the last forty years. While this installation plan separates generations of artists, an overview of the exhibition allows us to recognize cross-generational aesthetic similarities during the last half of the twentieth century. Each successive generation expands upon certain formal and conceptual concerns that engaged artists in earlier generations, but reinterprets or refocuses the emphasis to respond to current aesthetic circumstances. For instance, the ongoing interest in a geometric abstraction that derives from and alludes to recognizable subject matter can be seen in the works of Ellsworth Kelly, Peter Halley, and Adam Fuss. Cross-generational affinities are also visible in the gestural abstract paintings of Joan Mitchell, Pat Steir, Ellen Phelan, and Rebecca Purdum, all of which exploit the

JASPER JOHNS *Untitled*, 1990

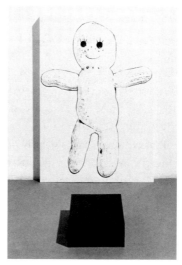

MIKE KELLEY *Empathy Displacement: Humanoid Morphology (2nd and 3rd Remove) #5*, 1990

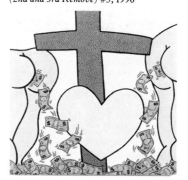

KEITH HARING *Purple Heart*, 1989

RICHARD MARSHALL

expressive gesture of paint to allude to landscape and natural phenomena. The focus on the human figure or body parts for both formal issues and surreal, psychological content can be observed in the works of artists such as Philip Pearlstein and Bruce Nauman no less than in those of Robert Gober and Kiki Smith, while a more emotionally detached and conceptually oriented use of the human form continues to engage artists as diverse as Chuck Close, John Coplans, and Jeanne Dunning. The continuous appeal of Pop imagery, especially cartoon-derived subject matter, is strongly in evidence in the latest work of senior artists Roy Lichtenstein and Jasper Johns, mid-career artists Mike Kelley, David Salle, and the late Keith Haring, and younger artists Larry Johnson and Jim Shaw. In sculptural expression, a younger generation of artists, including Nayland Blake, Cady Noland, and Jessica Stockholder, has revived the emphatic use of urban detritus, with its inherent cultural symbolism, which was introduced in the sculptural work of Robert Rauschenberg and Cy Twombly and continued by middle-generation artists Donald Lipski and Julian Schnabel.

The Biennial serves as one of the most significant forums for the observation, evaluation, and discussion of contemporary art. It provides a framework for better understanding the diverse creative vitality that characterizes the art of this period and acknowledges the crucial position that art holds in contemporary society.

ROBERT RAUSCHENBERG *Striped Spindle Glut*, 1989

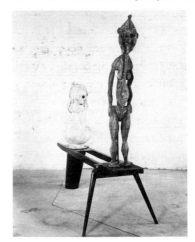

JULIAN SCHNABEL *George Washington Crossing the Delaware*, 1989

CADY NOLAND *Crate of Beer*, 1989

CIRCA 1991
Richard Armstrong

More than thirty years ago, Robert Rauschenberg prophetically announced that he wanted to work in the gap between art and life. If there is a single constant in the art exhibited here, it is to be found in the ongoing elaboration of the taste for quotidian imagery and techniques—for the recontextualized over the purely invented. Signs and symbols of the real world appear regularly in all sections of the 1991 Biennial Exhibition. Representationalism, mechanical reproduction, and assemblage predominate. This predominance can be measured, to a large extent, by age: the younger the artist, the less prevalent are non-objective painting and abstract sculpture. Although different artists use the repertory of externalized images in varied ways, it is clearly the preferred vernacular of contemporary American art.

Despite their shrinking number, the abstract artists here often form an important link to the zeal and ethical conviction of the original New York School. Such gestural painters as Joan Mitchell, Ed Moses, and Joseph Glasco have sustained the limitless promise of automatism—far from New York. Similarly, the expatriate Cy Twombly has extended Abstract Expressionism into a calligraphic realm. The poetic associations of his work reconnect his "written" paintings and additive sculpture to the mythic sources that first emboldened abstract artists in the 1940s. Frank Stella has deliberately sought to reinvigorate recent abstraction, citing the spatial richness of Baroque art as inspiration. Over the years, his paintings became progressively more three dimensional until they reached their present status as freestanding reliefs. By contrast, Ellsworth Kelly has refined his spare combinations of color and form, insisting on overcoming the essential flatness of painting by force of color. In their various ways, all these artists are rooted in conceptions of abstract art that predate the appearance of Pop.

The viability of Pop, its ironic recontextualization of found imagery, is confirmed in the recent work of Jasper Johns, Roy Lichtenstein, and Robert Rauschenberg. Yet the art of Johns and Lichtenstein, more so than that of Rauschenberg, remains apolitical, almost chaste in its relatively formal preoccupations. The work of younger artists during the past two decades, while preserving the ubiquity of Pop, has assumed a more forthright and responsive relationship to society. Ironic detachment has long since been abandoned in favor of overtly social discourses, from the sinister rearrangements of the symbols of adolescent fantasy that fuel Mike Kelley's and Jim Shaw's pieces to the reordering of physical detritus common to the works of Allen Ruppersberg, Donald Lipski, Cady Noland, and Jessica Stockholder. Each seeks forms that confer meaning while compulsively disrupting the associative significance of assembled sculpture and installation. As sculptors, their works populate and define space, obliging it to participate in a narrative other than the ostensibly neutral one of the exhibition site.

Like these sculptors, the majority of other artists here resort to narration to structure their work. Modern narration is conducted through the media and is therefore largely defined by it. Photography and photographic techniques necessarily loom large in this process, carrying the loaded social messages of Cindy Sherman, Laurie Simmons, and Richard Misrach. A particular kind of semiotic narration prevalent in contemporary art theory so intrigues Mark Tansey that his precisely rendered panoramas (and his unique wheel of disembodied phrases) satirize their own figurative-linguistic components, with every square foot legible and accessible for decoding. The same concern for accessibility is demonstrated in such otherwise disparate artists as Mary Kelly, Glenn Ligon, Larry Johnson, and Jessica Diamond, all of whom use narration as a means for considering identity as it is constructed by language. A symbiosis of word and image also characterizes the paintings and drawings of both David Wojnarowicz and Tim Rollins + K.O.S., as well as the photograph and text combinations of Carrie Mae Weems, Celia Alvarez Muñoz, and the Group Material *AIDS Timeline* installation. By adopting the look of popular culture, the work of Thomas Lanigan Schmidt, Luis Jimenez, and Keith Haring forces a reconsideration of the traditional separation between high and so-called low art. An unmuffled cry for art to somehow connect with everyday existence empowers all these works, giving voice to a generational desire to make widely legible, socially instructive art. Adapting the found and appropriated imagery and materials of Pop, sometimes combining it with a textual bias partly derived from Conceptualism, these artists hybridize at will.

A comparable hybridization, this one aimed at infusing abstraction with emotive as well as formal values, began in the 1970s in the early paintings of Pat Steir, Elizabeth Murray, and Jennifer Bartlett, and it continues today. Their careers commenced during the long reign of Minimalist and Postminimalist sculpture (unrepresented here, save for Bruce Nauman) and marked a widespread resurgence of painting as a credible expression. It was a revival that flourished and reached a public climax in the early 1980s with the appearance of Julian Schnabel, David Salle, and Eric Fischl, whose works introduced the ambitious storytelling that was to mark so much painting of that decade. The recent work of these three still

ROBERT RAUSCHENBERG *Bed*, 1955. Oil and pencil on pillow, quilt, sheet, on wood supports, 75¼ x 31½ x 8 (191.1 x 80 x 20.3) Collection, The Museum of Modern Art, New York. Fractional gift of Leo Castelli in honor of Alfred H. Barr, Jr.

highly influential artists demonstrates the continuing strength of their rich—even exotic—representational fables.

The documentary photographers Sally Mann, Alex Webb, and John Coplans could be considered the only realists in the exhibition. But each of them editorializes in ways that are at once obvious and invoke our empathy. The possibility that a photograph can be objective is so discredited that such ostensibly straightforward expositions as those of McDermott and McGough or Adam Fuss subvert supposedly factual aspects of the medium—in the former, its chronological accuracy, in the latter, the fabrication of subject matter.

The painters who work from direct observation, mostly of figures and landscape, are no less subjective. Thirty-five years of relentless scrutiny have imparted a palpable personality to the paintings of Alex Katz and Philip Pearlstein. Rooted in concrete and sensate data, their work revitalizes once discounted formal values. A related scrutiny also distinguishes Chuck Close's metaportraits, in which he particularizes the universals of facial anatomy to almost abstract conclusions. Other painters, such as Ellen Phelan, Rebecca Purdum, and Joseph Santore, likewise supersede the constraints of realism, espousing newly credible ideas of impressionist rendering. Two figurative sculptors, Robert Gober and Kiki Smith, also demonstrate a common urge to impart poetic force to so previously disdained a form as the human body. Their efforts are symptomatic of a widespread desire to foster wider, metaphoric meanings, partly in response to a stark recognition of mortality in the face of AIDS. This same desire for metaphoric power informs the work of Peter Halley, Carroll Dunham, and Philip Taaffe. Using external models such as architecture or biomorphic abstraction, they join the found and the imaginary in prescient fusions. Their revisionist efforts may lead somewhere new. If the decade of the 1980s, with its burgeoning art production, market, and attendant hyperbole, came to resemble the 1960s, will the 1990s recall the subtle hybridization of abstraction and expressionism of the 1970s, or even that of the 1950s?

RICHARD ARMSTRONG

CULTURE UNDER SIEGE
Lisa Phillips

In the past two years, the bubble of a boom economy burst and with it many things that had come to signify the excesses of American life in the eighties. Down went the dollar, savings and loan institutions, fast-won razzle-dazzle real estate empires, and junk-bond kings. All markets softened, the art market no exception. The decade shut down rapidly with a bad case of burnout and a need to reassess values.

Those who felt disempowered and abandoned by a decade of the economic and social dislocations of the Reagan era began to demand payback. Their quiet despair and pent-up resentments turned into rage as poverty, homelessness, racism, and the AIDS crisis escalated. The disenfranchised started to take political action, which others, fearful of losing their corner of power, tried to squelch. Neo-Conservatives and evangelical fundamentalists preached a new morality under the guise of patriotism, declaring unpatriotic anyone who departed from their views.

With rising economic uncertainty and social unrest, a scapegoat was needed. And with the cold war over and the Communist peril all but extinct, art and progressive culture became one of the convenient targets for the reactionary right, a site where unfocused anxieties could be directed. In the realm of culture, pornography and obscenity replaced Communism as the new threat to American values. The increased money, power, and media attention artists attained in the eighties only subjected them to more intense scrutiny as they entered the mainstream. Beginning in 1989, a series of vicious attacks was launched against artists, cultural institutions, and the NEA, intensifying into a heated public and political debate on magazine covers and in editorial pages—at least until the invasion of Kuwait last August, when Saddam Hussein became the new symbol of evil. The cultural community has been both shaken to its foundations and mobilized by the events of the past two years, events whose chilling effects will be felt for years to come.

This essay reviews the controversy that raged while the art in the 1991 Biennial Exhibition was being made. Though much of what follows may be familiar, its purpose here is to provide a backdrop, a partial socio-political context for much of the art on view. It is also an occasion for the reader to reflect on the shifting ground and volatile terms of the debate. The crisis of culture under siege helped re-politicize the art world and link art making to other areas of social responsibility. With restrictions imposed, artists had clear limits to test. There is ample evidence of this in the 1991 Biennial, and many artists, from Group Material and David Wojnarowicz to Jennie Livingston, clearly put themselves at risk with their brutally honest statements. And there are many other artists and collaborative groups such as Gran Fury and Boys with Arms Akimbo who have chosen to work outside institutional frameworks.

Art institutions, which determine to a great extent what and how art is seen, have had to be more sensitive to the implications of their programs and funding decisions. Some have been cowed by the inquisitors, self-censoring anything potentially inflammatory, while many others have taken direct action to combat and historically contextualize the recent attacks on culture. Among the latter was Joseph Kosuth's brilliant 1990 installation at The Brooklyn Museum, "The Play of the Unmentionable," in which he combined art and objects from every department of the museum with texts from a wide range of sources. The result was a running commentary on the changing perception of art across time and geography and the culturally mutable nature of ideas about sex, religion, and politics. Another fine exhibition, "Degenerate Art: The Fate of the Avant-Garde in Nazi Germany," was organized by the Los Angeles County Museum. The installation recreates the infamous Nazi exhibition of "entartete Kunst," where scores of artists, writers, and musicians were singled out for scorn and vilification.

Early warning signs of a conservative cultural backlash appeared ten years ago when Reagan attempted to abolish or perilously slash the NEA budget. A change in the public attitude toward the arts subsequently erupted in the highly publicized controversy surrounding Richard Serra's *Tilted Arc*, a permanent, site-specific sculpture commissioned in 1979 by the General Services Administration for 26 Federal Plaza in Lower Manhattan. Though the work was selected through an established, legitimate process by a GSA-appointed panel of experts and exhaustively reviewed for two years before its installation in 1981, *Tilted Arc* aroused hostilities soon after it went up. Many of the federal employees working in and around the building felt that Serra's work—a massive, curving, tilted plane of Cor-ten steel bisecting the outdoor plaza—was ugly, threatening, and mean-spirited, epithets frequently hurled at avant-garde art at its inception. *Tilted Arc* was praised and passionately defended on aesthetic grounds by many in the art community, who pointed out that challenging work often needs time before its artistic language can be appreciated and understood by a broader public.

Unwilling to bridge the gap between the art community and a larger public, and afraid to be the target of public acrimony, the GSA began to consider "relocating" the work. In 1985, after much petitioning and testimony on both sides in pro forma public hearings (presided over by the GSA and hardly impartial), *Tilted Arc* was ordered removed. The previously "silent majority" had made its point: it would not be subjected to what it perceived as the elitist and often arrogant attitudes of the art world, especially when its environment and hard-earned tax dollars were at stake. The GSA had also made its point: it would not stand for any work (or artist) that posed a threat to its authoritarianism. The decision to remove *Tilted Arc* set a dangerous precedent for government censorship of art and challenged the legitimacy of the art community's professional standing. It also posed larger questions: how public money should be spent on works of art and who should decide what is best for the "public"—specialists (i.e., art professionals), popular opinion, or government authorities?

In the spring of 1989, just as *Tilted Arc* was finally being dismantled, the outcry against public support for the arts took a new turn. Reverend Donald Wildmon, an evangelical minister from Mississippi and head of the American Family Association (AFA), had a fateful encounter with a photograph. Wildmon had been noted for his attacks against film (*The Last Temptation of Christ*) and television, calling for sponsors of certain objectionable programs to withdraw their funding or face boycotts. In an *Awards for the Visual Arts* exhibition catalogue, supported by a grant from the National Endowment for the Arts and the Equitable Life Assurance Society, he came across *Piss Christ*, a photograph by Puerto Rican-born artist Andres Serrano that depicted a crucifix submerged in urine. Wildmon saw red and the witch-hunt was on against Serrano, the NEA, and other blasphemous artists and their supporters. "Degenerate," he called them, the very term used by the Nazis to purge Germany of progressive or oppositional culture. Wildmon organized a massive letter-writing campaign against Equitable, and after receiving several thousand complaints from policyholders the company withdrew its decade-long sponsorship of the AVA program. Wildmon also alerted several friends in Congress, notably Jesse Helms, Republican Senator from North Carolina.

At about the same time, a young African-American artist, Dread Scott, came under fire for an installation at the School of The Art Institute of Chicago that forced visitors to walk on the American flag as they entered his work. This was simply too much for some people to tolerate. The State of Illinois cut support to the school and George Bush tried, unsuccessfully, to pass an amendment to the Constitution making flag desecration a federal offense.

Finally, on June 13, 1989, sensing the groundswell of hostility in Washington to controversial culture, Christina Ohr-Cahall, director of The Corcoran Gallery of Art, made the precipitous decision to cancel the now notorious exhibition "Robert Mapplethorpe: The Perfect Moment"—just days before its scheduled opening. The political firestorm ignited by her action culminated the following year in a showdown in Cincinnati, where museum director Dennis Barrie was indicted for hosting the exhibition at the Contemporary Arts Center.[1] Mapplethorpe's frankly erotic work was used by Wildmon, Helms, New York Senator Alfonse D'Amato, and others to illustrate their charges that decay and depravity permeated culture and that the NEA in funding such "immoral trash," was flagrantly disregarding public decency.[2] A Wildmon AFA press release on Mapplethorpe offered the following denunciation: "The exhibit of photographs by Mapplethorpe, a homosexual who died of AIDS earlier this year, contains homoerotic photos that are nothing less than taxpayer-funded homosexual pornography."[3]

Wildmon's extremism gained power from the absence of contesting voices: the art world, stunned by his air of irrefutability but caught off guard, was

ANDRES SERRANO *Piss Christ*, 1987

ROBERT MAPPLETHORPE *Man in Polyester Suit*
© 1980, The Estate of Robert Mapplethorpe

slow to organize a response. And it was also divided between grant-protective "Corcoranists" and those committed to freedom of expression at any cost.[4] Wildmon's strategy of marginalizing the opposition and then accusing it of immorality was an old one, practiced by McCarthy in the 1950s and others before. His attack against Mapplethorpe as a child molester, child pornographer, and sexual deviant is a fabrication that plays on the public's fears about homosexuality and the spread of AIDS. A full-fledged sex panic was underway, allowing demagogues to manipulate entrenched anxieties about change, difference, and the explicitly sexual.[5] And it was part of a larger right-wing attempt to regulate public expression of identity, most evident in denying women freedom of choice, and to diminish challenges to religious and governmental authorities. It's also no accident that gay, lesbian, black, and Hispanic artists are the primary targets in this crusade against culture. The Neo-Conservative position was perhaps best summarized by Irving Kristol in his *Wall Street Journal* editorial of August 7: "What the 'arts community' is engaged in is a politics of radical nihilism. . . . What they do, in fact, is powerfully shaped by certain radical ideological currents; radical feminism, homosexual and lesbian self-celebration and black racism are among them."[6]

In July 1989, one month after the Mapplethorpe show was canceled at the Corcoran, Jesse Helms took advantage of a near-empty Senate session to sneak through his now infamous amendment prohibiting the use of public funds (i.e., the NEA) for works that include "depictions of sadomasochism, homoeroticism, the sexual exploitation of children, or individuals engaged in sex acts and which, when taken as a whole, do not have serious literary, artistic, political or scientific value."[7] All 1990 NEA grant recipients were then required to sign this anti-obscenity pledge.

A handful of highly publicized organizations and individuals spurned NEA grants, refusing to sign the oath, and others sued the agency for infringement of first amendment rights.[8] The NEA was caught in the crossfire between its conflicting constituencies: grantees (artists, cultural institutions) and the "public interest" (politicians who authorize the NEA budget and guidelines). In October 1989, Artists Space, a respected New York alternative space, was about to open an exhibition about AIDS called "Witnesses: Against Our Vanishing." It became the first test case for the new language restrictions imposed on NEA grants and the first major challenge for John Frohnmayer, the newly appointed head of the embattled agency. In October, the director of Artists Space brought the show to the Endowment's attention because of the sensitive material in it. Based on a look at the catalogue alone, Frohnmayer revoked the $10,000 NEA grant Artists Space had received. But in November, after much protest from the art community, he traveled to New York to view the show and reversed his decision, reinstating the grant with the proviso that the money could not be used for the catalogue, which contained what he found to be offensive indictments against Helms and Cardinal O'Connor by David Wojnarowicz, an artist living with AIDS. Subsequently, on July 2, 1990, Frohnmayer vetoed four grants by lesbian, gay, and feminist performance artists Karen Finley, Holly Hughes, Tim Miller, and John Fleck for being "too political" (they filed a suit when their appeal was rejected in August 1990).

The dissension that began in early 1989 weakened the NEA and posed a real threat to its continued existence, if not its credibility. Many, like Kristol, argued that it should be abolished altogether. Others favored slashing the NEA budget and imposing stricter content restrictions on grants or restructuring the agency and the peer panel review system. Still others wondered if avant-garde art—which has traditionally assaulted mainstream values—should be funded by a government agency at all. Amidst this wrangling, in the fall of 1989, the NEA received congressional appropriation for the fiscal year 1990 with the restrictive language appended. Congress reduced the budget by a symbolic amount equivalent to the cost of the Serrano and Mapplethorpe projects and, as a punitive measure, considered denying the Southeast Center for Contemporary Art and the Institute of Contemporary Art in Philadelphia, the institutions that had organized these projects, federal subsidies for five years. Though this provision was negotiated out, the ICA and SECA were placed on a "watch list" for one year and required to have NEA-approved grants reviewed by Congress.

Frohnmayer began to work with the White House and congressional leaders on compromises and internal changes at the Endowment that would forestall future conflicts. This past fall, the NEA was reauthorized for a three-year term instead of the usual five-year term, but with no restrictions. (It was decided that obscenity should be determined by the courts and that any grantee convicted of obscenity be required to return the grant money.[9]) Twelve million dollars was shifted from the direct grant programs to state arts councils, and each panel was required to include at least one lay member. The impact of these reforms has not yet been felt in the art community.

The controversy over federal funding for the arts not only reflects a growing conservatism but also the nation's endemic anti-intellectualism, anti-elitism, and mistrust of artists. For decades, culture in America meant something imported—usually from Europe, where there is a long, honored tradition of cultural support. The Endowment budget ($174 million) is embarrassingly slight compared to the allocations that most European countries make to the arts (France's budget for the Ministry of Culture in 1989 was $1.58 billion and West Germany's was comparable). If each American taxpayer's share of the Endowment budget was calculated on a per capita basis it would amount to less than 77 cents (compared to the

TIM ROLLINS + K.O.S. *The Animal Farm (Jesse Helms)*, 1984–87

JOSEPH KOSUTH *The Play of the Unmentionable*, installation at The Brooklyn Museum, 1990

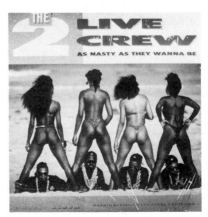

2 LIVE CREW *As Nasty As They Wanna Be*, 1990

90 cents that goes to military marching bands).[10]

If the art world felt increasingly alienated from the "public," Dennis Barrie's indictment in Cincinnati was experienced as a violation of art's traditional sanctuary in the museum and underscored the art community's degree of estrangement from mainstream society. No one, least of all Barrie, could predict the outcome of his trial with confidence. Who or what was this ambiguous public and did it really speak through the legislators? Barrie faced a jury in early October 1990—on obscenity charges for hosting the Mapplethorpe exhibition. The current obscenity laws are based on the *Miller v. California* 1973 ruling that defines obscenity by an affirmative response to the following three questions: Would "an average person, applying contemporary community standards . . . find that the work, taken as a whole, appeals to prurient interest?" Does the work depict or describe, "in a patently offensive way, sexual conduct specifically defined by the applicable state law?" And, does "the work, taken as a whole, lack serious literary, artistic, political, or scientific value?"

Though jurors may find the first two questions readily definable by community standards, the third question gets sticky. Who defines serious art? Wouldn't someone like Dennis Barrie know serious art when he sees it? Other art experts fanned the fire by publicly expressing doubts about Mapplethorpe's seriousness. Robert Hughes called him "overrated" and Hilton Kramer asked, "Are these disputed pictures works of art? Alas, I suppose they are, but they do not belong to the highest levels of art." Who is the more reasonable judge, Dennis Barrie or the two critics? In the trial, the defense called art experts to testify to Mapplethorpe's standing as a serious artist. The prosecution did not present a single expert to counter that testimony. The jury—all working-class people, most of whom had never been to an art museum—found Barrie innocent.[11]

There are paradoxes in a pluralistic culture such as ours that the language of the law cannot accommodate. Cultural expressions outside the Western tradition make the *Miller v. California* test debatable: in black culture, for instance, the distinction between popular and serious art has long been rejected. Although Luther Campbell of the rap group 2 Live Crew was acquitted on appeal last October on obscenity charges for producing *As Nasty as They Wanna Be*, a Florida record store owner who sold the album was convicted.

Language has seemed inadequate in other ways too: why can't something be both serious art and pornographic? This and other questions raised by the events of the past months have dominated discussions in art circles and helped set the stage for art activities and political actions. Whose right is it to set the moral code for expressions of sexuality? Let's not forget that the definitions of indecency and obscenity are always shifting. In 1882, Walt Whitman's *Leaves of Grass* was banned in Boston; Theodore Dreiser's *An American Tragedy* was declared obscene by a Massachusetts court in 1930. Who decides what is art? What constitutes censorship? Have attention-winning controversies clouded judgments about "quality"? Can the merits of art works be discussed when freedom of expression is at stake? Is "quality" a relative, socially determined word—like obscenity— that needs redressing? Finally, how can we bridge the gap between art and the public's understanding of it? How can we organize to represent ourselves effectively in high-level politics? These are some of the issues artists are grappling with in their work and in their lives.

In this Biennial there is evidence of artists confronting social issues both head-on and obliquely.

LISA PHILLIPS

Homoerotic subjects are explicitly addressed by a number of artists, among them David Wojnarowicz, Keith Haring, Felix Gonzalez-Torres, and Nayland Blake. Group Material's *AIDS Timeline* is a probing examination of the history of that plague, through the words and images of artists, politicians, scientists, and the media, which documents the impact that homophobia, sexism, and racism have had on the formation of this critical chapter in public health policy. Tim Rollins + K.O.S. offer a visceral, poetic allegory about sex, death, and salvation based on Flaubert's *Temptation of Saint Antony*. Several artists—including Luis Jimenez, Carrie Mae Weems, Glenn Ligon, and Lorna Simpson—grapple with inherited social roles, explicitly dismantling racial stereotypes in works that offer incisive and often unpleasant lessons about American life. Others, such as Jessica Diamond in *No Inside, No Outside*, point to the inescapability of our toxic environment through a series of absurd and tragicomic descriptions. Bruce Nauman gives expression to a generalized feeling of anguish, mourning, and yearning for an inner state of peace. The disparate sensations that Nauman's spinning head and droning hum evoke—of dementia and serenity—are both a symptom of and protection from a hostile world where hysteria, lurking beneath the surface, can erupt without warning. In the past two years, we have witnessed attacks against culture most of us could never have imagined possible. It has been shocking and sobering to recognize that basic rights we take for granted are held in a fragile balance and require continual defense and vigilance. Moral ground is shifting, lines need to be redrawn. The sense of circularity and self-enclosure induced by the endless repetition in Nauman's work describes perfectly the claustrophobia and frustration we experience in trying to formulate answers which only lead to more questions.

NOTES

1. The exhibition was organized by the Institute of Contemporary Art, University of Pennsylvania, Philadelphia, and held there from December 9, 1988, to January 29, 1989. It then traveled to the Museum of Contemporary Art, Chicago; Washington (D.C.) Project for the Arts; Wadsworth Atheneum, Hartford; University Art Museum, University of California, Berkeley; and The Institute of Contemporary Art, Boston. The Washington Project for the Arts hosted the exhibition, to record crowds, when the Corcoran dropped out.

2. Jesse Helms, quoted in Cathleen McGuigan, "Arts Grants Under Fire," *Newsweek*, August 7, 1989, p. 23.

3. Quoted in Richard Bolton, "The Cultural Contradictions of Conservatism," *New Art Examiner*, 17 (June 1990), p. 26.

4. The term "Corcoranist" was first used by Peter Schjeldahl in "The Treason of Clerks," *7 Days*, August 2, 1989.

5. Carol Vance has introduced the sex panic theory, most notably in "Reagan's Revenge: Restructuring the NEA," *Art in America*, 78 (November 1990), pp. 49–55.

6. Irving Kristol, "It's Obscene But Is It Art?" *The Wall Street Journal*, August 7, 1990, p. A8.

7. This is the modified language of Helms' original proposal, which read, "None of the funds authorized to be appropriated pursuant to this Act may be used to promote, disseminate, or produce—(1) obscene or indecent materials, including but not limited to depictions of sadomasochism, homo-eroticism, the exploitation of children, or individuals engaged in sex acts; or (2) material which denigrates the objects or beliefs of the adherents of a particular religion or non-religion; or (3) material which denigrates, debases, or reviles a person, group, or class of citizens on the basis of race, creed, sex, handicap, age or national origin."

8. The constitutionality of the anti-obscenity clause in Endowment grants was challenged by groups including the Bella Lewitzky Dance Foundation, the Newport Harbor Art Museum, and The Rockefeller Foundation. On January 9, 1991, a federal judge in Los Angeles ruled the clause unconstitutional, finding that it interfered with the recipient's constitutional exercise of free speech. Another lawsuit brought against the Endowment by The New School for Social Research was terminated on February 20, 1991, when the Endowment agreed to drop the pledge requirement for all 1990 grant recipients.

9. This congressional action, concluded on October 25, 1990, followed the court victories of 2 Live Crew and the Contemporary Arts Center.

10. See Nicols Fox, "Cultural Cowardice, Conservative Clout," *New Art Examiner*, 17 (September 1989), p. 38, and Francesc Torres, "Cops and Robbers: Art, State Support and Political Reaction in the USA," *Lapiz*, no. 65 (February 1990), p. 38.

11. For more on the trial and *Miller v. California*, see Jeff Rosen, " 'Miller' Time," *The New Republic*, October 1, 1990, pp. 17–19.

Painting   Sculpture   Photography

An asterisk at the end of a caption indicates that the work illustrated is not in the exhibition. Complete descriptions of these works appear in the list beginning on p. 385.

Second Floor

CHUCK CLOSE

JOHN COPLANS

JOSEPH GLASCO

JASPER JOHNS

ALEX KATZ

ELLSWORTH KELLY

ROY LICHTENSTEIN

JOAN MITCHELL

ED MOSES

BRUCE NAUMAN

PHILIP PEARLSTEIN

ROBERT RAUSCHENBERG

PAT STEIR

FRANK STELLA

CY TWOMBLY

Third Floor and Lower Gallery

VITO ACCONCI

JENNIFER BARTLETT

CARROLL DUNHAM

ERIC FISCHL

BILL FONTANA

ROBERT GOBER

PETER HALLEY

KEITH HARING

RONI HORN

LUIS JIMENEZ

MIKE KELLEY

LOUISE LAWLER

DONALD LIPSKI

DAVID McDERMOTT AND

PETER McGOUGH

RICHARD MISRACH

ELIZABETH MURRAY

ELLEN PHELAN

ALLEN RUPPERSBERG

DAVID SALLE

JOSEPH SANTORE

THOMAS LANIGAN SCHMIDT

JULIAN SCHNABEL

CINDY SHERMAN

LAURIE SIMMONS

PHILIP TAAFFE

MARK TANSEY

Fourth Floor and Lobby Gallery

CARLOS ALFONZO

NAYLAND BLAKE

JESSICA DIAMOND

JEANNE DUNNING

DAWN FRYLING

ADAM FUSS

FELIX GONZALEZ-TORRES

GROUP MATERIAL

GARY HILL

WENDY JACOB

LARRY JOHNSON

MARY KELLY

GLENN LIGON

SALLY MANN

CHRISTIAN MARCLAY

JOHN MILLER

CELIA ALVAREZ MUÑOZ

CADY NOLAND

RONA PONDICK

REBECCA PURDUM

ALAN RATH

TIM ROLLINS + K.O.S.

JIM SHAW

LORNA SIMPSON

KIKI SMITH

PHILIP SMITH

JESSICA STOCKHOLDER

ALEX WEBB

CARRIE MAE WEEMS

DAVID WOJNAROWICZ

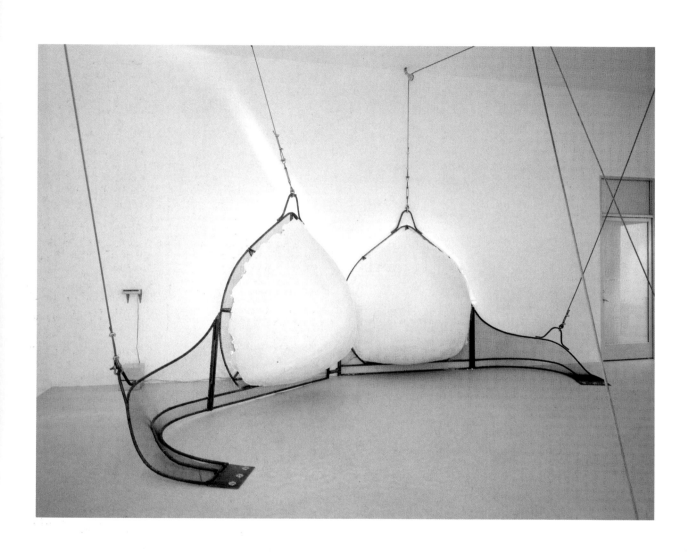

VITO ACCONCI

Adaptable Wall Bra   1990 *

Born in New York, 1940; studied at Holy Cross College, Worcester, Massachusetts (BA, 1962), University of Iowa, Iowa City (MFA, 1964); lives in New York.

ONE-ARTIST EXHIBITIONS

1971

112 Greene Street
New York

1972

Sonnabend Gallery
New York

1977

The Clocktower, Institute for Art and Urban Resources
New York

1978

Stedelijk Museum
Amsterdam

1979

CAPC Musée d'Art Contemporain
Bordeaux

1980

Museum of Contemporary Art
Chicago

1987

La Jolla Museum of Contemporary Art
(traveled)

1988

Brooke Alexander Gallery
New York

The Museum of Modern Art
New York

Rhona Hoffman Gallery
Chicago

1989

Barbara Gladstone Gallery
New York

1990

James Corcoran Gallery
Santa Monica

GROUP EXHIBITIONS

1977

Institute of Contemporary Art, University of Pennsylvania
Philadelphia
"Improbable Furniture"
(traveled)

1979

Museum of Contemporary Art
Chicago
"Concept/Narrative/ Document: Recent Photographic Works from the Morton Neumann Family Collection"

1981

Whitney Museum of American Art
New York
"1981 Biennial Exhibition"

1982

Stedelijk Museum
Amsterdam
"'60-'80: Attitudes/ Concepts/Images—A Selection from Twenty Years of Visual Arts"

1984

Hayden Gallery, Massachusetts Institute of Technology
Cambridge
"Visions of Paradise: Installations by Vito Acconci, David Ireland, and James Surls"

Hirshhorn Museum and Sculpture Garden, Smithsonian Institution
Washington, D.C.
"Content: A Contemporary Focus, 1974-1984"

1988

The World Financial Center
New York
"The New Urban Landscape"

1989

Whitney Museum of American Art
New York
"Image World: Art and Media Culture"

BIBLIOGRAPHY

Cone, Michèle
"Vito Acconci/Carpenter & Hochman." FLASH ART, no. 122 (April–May 1985), pp. 38-39.

Foster, Hal
"For a Concept of the Political in Art." ART IN AMERICA, 72 (April 1984), pp. 17-23.

Lotringer, Sylvère
"Vito Acconci: House Trap." FLASH ART, no. 147 (Summer 1989), pp. 124-28.

Onorato, Ronald J.
"Real Time—Actual Space." In SITINGS (exhibition catalogue). La Jolla: La Jolla Museum of Contemporary Art, 1986, pp. 25-30.

Onorato, Ronald J.
VITO ACCONCI: DOMESTIC TRAPPINGS (exhibition catalogue). La Jolla: La Jolla Museum of Contemporary Art, 1987.

Phillips, Patricia C.
"Vito Acconci." ARTFORUM, 23 (February 1985), pp. 89-90.

Shearer, Linda
VITO ACCONCI: PUBLIC PLACES (exhibition catalogue). New York: The Museum of Modern Art, 1988.

Weissman, Benjamin
"Vito Acconci: James Corcoran Gallery." ARTFORUM, 19 (October 1990), pp. 177-78.

VITO ACCONCI

Convertible Clam Shelter 1990*

Convertible Clam Shelter   1990

CARLOS ALFONZO

Cimetière Marin   1990

Born in Havana, 1950; studied at the Academia San Alejandro (MFA, 1973), University of Havana (1974-77); died in Miami, 1991.

ONE-ARTIST EXHIBITIONS

1977

Museo Nacional de Bellas Artes
Havana

1984

Galeria Ocho
Miami

1988

Bacardi Gallery
Miami

Frances Wolfson Art Gallery, Miami-Dade Community College, Wolfson Campus
Miami

1989

Greene Gallery
Coral Gables, Florida

Lannan Museum
Lake Worth, Florida

McMurtry Gallery
Houston

1990

Bass Museum of Art
Miami Beach

Greene Gallery
Coral Gables, Florida

Osuna Gallery
Washington, D.C.

GROUP EXHIBITIONS

1975

Museo de Arte Moderno
Mexico City
"Panorama del arte cubano de la colonia a nuestros días"

1985

The Southeastern Center for Contemporary Art
Winston-Salem, North Carolina
"The Art of Miami"

1986

Frances Wolfson Art Gallery, Miami-Dade Community College, Wolfson Campus
Miami
"Abstraction: Four from Latin America"

Museum of Contemporary Hispanic Art
New York
"Caribbean Art: African Currents"

1987

Jane Voorhees Zimmerli Art Museum, Rutgers, The State University of New Jersey
New Brunswick
"Outside Cuba/Fuera de Cuba: Contemporary Cuban Visual Artists" (traveled)

The Museum of Fine Arts
Houston
"Hispanic Art in the United States" (traveled)

1989

The Corcoran Gallery of Art
Washington, D.C.
"The 41st Biennial Exhibition of Contemporary American Painting"

University of South Florida, USF Art Museum
Tampa
"Made in Florida" (traveled)

1990

Museum of Contemporary Hispanic Art, The New Museum of Contemporary Art, and The Studio Museum in Harlem
New York
"The Decade Show: Frameworks of Identity in the 1980s"

BIBLIOGRAPHY

Blanc, Giulio V.
CARLOS ALFONZO: NEW WORK (exhibition catalogue). Miami Beach: Bass Museum of Art, 1990.

Blanc, Giulio V.
"The Enigmatic Carlos Alfonzo." ARTS MAGAZINE, 64 (October 1989), pp. 13-14.

THE DECADE SHOW: FRAMEWORKS OF IDENTITY IN THE 1980s (exhibition catalogue). New York: Museum of Contemporary Hispanic Art, The New Museum of Contemporary Art, and The Studio Museum in Harlem, 1990.

Fuentes-Pérez, Ileana, and Ricardo Pau-Llosa
OUTSIDE CUBA/FUERA DE CUBA: CONTEMPORARY CUBAN VISUAL ARTISTS (exhibition catalogue). New Brunswick: Jane Voorhees Zimmerli Art Museum, Rutgers, The State University of New Jersey, 1987.

Gladstone, Valerie
"Ten for the '90s: Miami Beach, Carlos Alfonzo." ART NEWS, 89 (April 1990), p. 148.

Livingston, Jane, John Beardsley, and Octavio Paz
HISPANIC ART IN THE UNITED STATES (exhibition catalogue). Houston: The Museum of Fine Arts, 1987.

Lurie, Sheldon
THE ART OF CARLOS ALFONZO (exhibition catalogue). Miami: Frances Wolfson Art Gallery, Miami-Dade Community College, Wolfson Campus, 1988.

CARLOS ALFONZO   *Told*   1990 *

Figurat 1990

JENNIFER BARTLETT

Earth   1990

Born in Long Beach, California, 1941; studied at Mills College, Oakland, California (BA, 1963), School of Art and Architecture, Yale University, New Haven (BFA, 1964; MFA, 1965); lives in New York and Paris.

ONE-ARTIST EXHIBITIONS

1970

119 Spring Street
New York

1972

Reese Palley Gallery
New York

1974

Paula Cooper Gallery
New York

1978

Hansen Fuller Gallery
San Francisco

San Francisco Museum of
Modern Art

1979

The Clocktower, Institute
for Art and Urban Resources
New York

1982

The Tate Gallery
London

1985

Walker Art Center
Minneapolis (traveled)

1988

The Seibu Museum of Art
Tokyo

Milwaukee Art Museum

1990

John Berggruen Gallery
San Francisco

Paula Cooper Gallery
New York

GROUP EXHIBITIONS

1971

The Museum of Modern Art
New York
"Seven Walls"

1972

Walker Art Center
Minneapolis
"Painting: New Options"

Whitney Museum of
American Art
New York
"1972 Annual Exhibition:
Contemporary American
Painting"

1977

Kassel, West Germany
"Documenta 6"

1978

Whitney Museum of
American Art
New York
"New Image Painting"

1980

Contemporary Arts Museum
Houston
"Extensions: Jennifer
Bartlett, Lynda Benglis,
Robert Longo, Judy Pfaff"

The Museum of Modern Art
New York
"Printed Art: A View
of Two Decades"

1981

Hayden Gallery,
Massachusetts Institute
of Technology
Cambridge
"Body Language: Figurative
Aspects of Recent Art"
(traveled)

Whitney Museum of
American Art
New York
"1981 Biennial Exhibition"

1986

Whitney Museum of
American Art
New York
"Three Printmakers: Jennifer
Bartlett, Susan Rothenberg,
Terry Winters"

1989

Cincinnati Art Museum
"Making Their Mark:
Women Artists Move into
the Mainstream, 1970-85"
(traveled)

BIBLIOGRAPHY

Bartlett, Jennifer
HISTORY OF THE UNIVERSE.
New York: Moyer Bell
Limited and Nimbus
Books, 1985.

Francis, Richard
JENNIFER BARTLETT: AT THE
LAKE, UP THE CREEK, IN THE
GARDEN (exhibition
catalogue). London: The
Tate Gallery, 1982.

Galligan, Gregory
JENNIFER BARTLETT
(exhibition catalogue).
Tokyo: The Seibu Museum
of Art, 1988.

Goldman, Judith
THREE PRINTMAKERS:
JENNIFER BARTLETT, SUSAN
ROTHENBERG, TERRY
WINTERS (exhibition
brochure). New York:
Whitney Museum of
American Art, 1986.

Goldwater, Marge, Roberta
Smith, and Calvin Tomkins
JENNIFER BARTLETT
(exhibition catalogue).
Minneapolis: Walker Art
Center, 1985.

Marshall, Richard
NEW IMAGE PAINTING
(exhibition catalogue). New
York: Whitney Museum of
American Art, 1978.

Smith, Roberta
RHAPSODY. New York:
Harry N. Abrams, 1985.

JENNIFER BARTLETT   *Fire*   1990

NAYLAND BLAKE

Born in New York, 1960; studied at Bard College, Annandale-on-Hudson, New York (BFA, 1982), the California Institute of the Arts, Valencia (MFA, 1984); lives in San Francisco.

ONE-ARTIST EXHIBITIONS

1985

New Langton Arts
San Francisco

1986

3735 Gallery
San Francisco

1987

Media Gallery
San Francisco (traveled)

San Francisco Camerawork
Bookstore

1988

Media Gallery
San Francisco

Public installation on
Mission Street
San Francisco

1989

Matrix Gallery, University
Art Museum, University of
California, Berkeley

Mincher/Wilcox Gallery
San Francisco

Richard Kuhlenschmidt
Gallery
Los Angeles

1990

Petersburg Gallery
New York

GROUP EXHIBITIONS

1988

American Fine Arts
New York

Hallwalls
Buffalo
"The Other Sex"

LACE
Los Angeles
"Against Nature: A Show
by Homosexual Men"

San Francisco Art Institute
"Assemblage '88: The
Recontextualized Object"

303 Gallery
New York
"Nayland Blake, Liz Larner,
Richard Morrison, Charles
Ray"

1989

White Columns
New York
"Remainders"

Whitney Museum of
American Art
New York
"Image World: Art and
Media Culture"

1990

Galeries Daniel Buchholz,
Gisela Capitain, Tanja
Grunert, Max Hetzler,
Jablonka, Isabella Kacprzak,
Esther Schipper, Monika
Sprüth, Sophia Ungers
Cologne
"Nachschub/Supply:
The Köln Show"

San Francisco Museum of
Modern Art
"New Work: A New
Generation"

Simon Watson Gallery
New York
"The Clinic"

Whitney Museum of
American Art
New York
"Mind Over Matter:
Concept and Object"

BIBLIOGRAPHY

Armstrong, Richard
MIND OVER MATTER:
CONCEPT AND OBJECT
(exhibition catalogue). New
York: Whitney Museum of
American Art, 1990.

Baker, Kenneth
"Objects at Media Gallery."
SAN FRANCISCO CHRONICLE,
February 24, 1987, p. 62.

Berkson, Bill
"San Francisco, Nayland
Blake, Media." ARTFORUM,
25 (May 1987), p. 157.

Bonetti, David
"Portrait of the Artist as a
Dandy." SAN FRANCISCO
EXAMINER, October 29,
1989, pp. E1, E6.

Porges, Maria F.
"The New Narratology."
CONTEMPORANEA, 2
(September 1989),
pp. 87-89.

Porges, Maria F.
THE NEW NARRATOLOGY:
EXAMINING THE NARRATIVE
IN IMAGE-TEXT ART (exhibition
catalogue). San Francisco:
San Francisco Artspace
Annex, 1989.

Rinder, Lawrence
NAYLAND BLAKE (exhibition
brochure). Berkeley: Matrix
Gallery, University Art
Museum, University of
California, Berkeley, 1989.

Weissman, Benjamin
"Nayland Blake, Richard
Kuhlenschmidt Gallery."
ARTFORUM, 28 (September
1989), pp. 154-55.

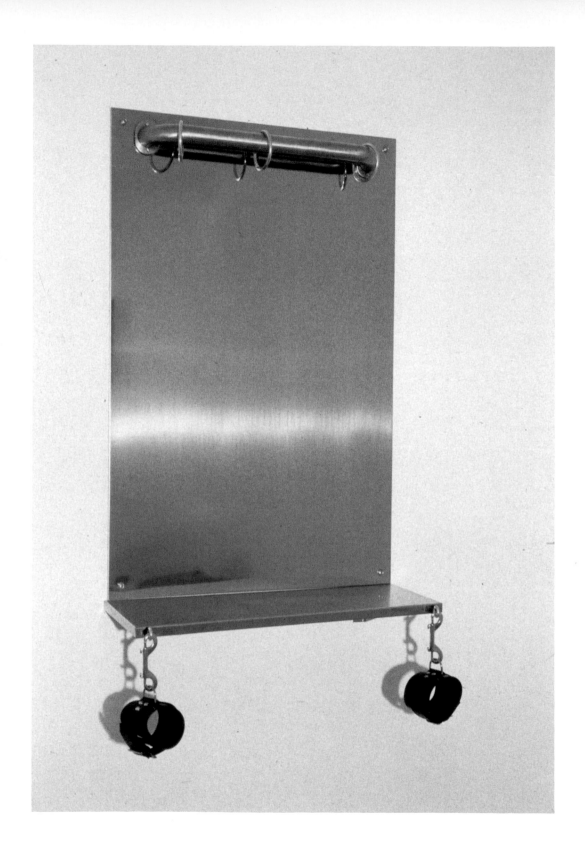

NAYLAND BLAKE   *Restraint #6 (Ankle, Shelf, Mirror)*   1989

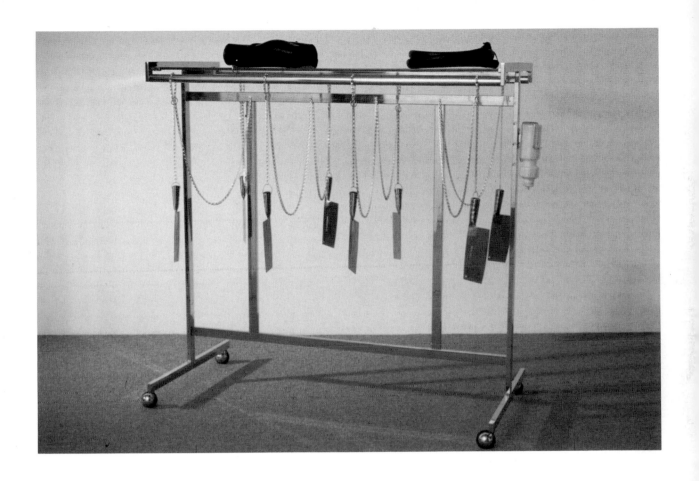

Work Station #5   1989

CHUCK CLOSE

Judy   1989–90 *

Born in Monroe, Washington, 1940; studied at the University of Washington, Seattle (BA, 1962), Yale Summer School of Music and Art, Norfolk, Connecticut (1961), Yale University School of Art and Architecture, New Haven (BFA, 1963; MFA, 1964), Akademie der Bildenen Künste, Vienna (1964-65); lives in New York.

ONE-ARTIST EXHIBITIONS

1967

University of Massachusetts Art Gallery
Amherst

1970

Bykert Gallery
New York

1971

Los Angeles County Museum of Art

1973

The Museum of Modern Art
New York

1975

Edwin A. Ulrich Museum of Art
Wichita State University
Kansas (traveled)

1977

The Pace Gallery
New York

1979

Musée National d'Art Moderne, Centre Georges Pompidou
Paris

1980

Walker Art Center
Minneapolis (traveled)

1985

Contemporary Arts Museum
Houston

Fraenkel Gallery
San Francisco

1988

The Pace Gallery
New York

GROUP EXHIBITIONS

1969

Whitney Museum of American Art
New York
"1969 Annual Exhibition: Contemporary American Painting"

1970

Allen Memorial Art Museum, Oberlin College
Oberlin, Ohio
"Three Young Americans"

1972

Kassel, West Germany
"Documenta 5"

1979

Whitney Museum of American Art
New York
"1979 Biennial Exhibition"

1980

Whitney Museum of American Art
New York
"The Figurative Tradition and the Whitney Museum of American Art: Paintings and Sculpture from the Permanent Collection"

1981

Pennsylvania Academy of the Fine Arts
Philadelphia
"Contemporary American Realism Since 1960"

Stedelijk Museum
Amsterdam
"Instant Photography"

1983

The Museum of Contemporary Art
Los Angeles
"The First Show: Painting and Sculpture from Eight Collections, 1940-1980"

1988

Whitney Museum of American Art, Downtown at Federal Reserve Plaza
New York
"Identity: Representations of the Self"

BIBLIOGRAPHY

Battcock, Gregory, ed. SUPER REALISM: A CRITICAL ANTHOLOGY. New York: E.P. Dutton, 1975.

Close, Chuck KEITH/SIX DRAWINGS/1979. New York: Lapp Princess Press, 1979.

Hills, Patricia, and Roberta K. Tarbell THE FIGURATIVE TRADITION AND THE WHITNEY MUSEUM OF AMERICAN ART: PAINTINGS AND SCULPTURE FROM THE PERMANENT COLLECTION (exhibition catalogue). New York: Whitney Museum of American Art, 1980.

Johnson, Ellen H., ed. AMERICAN ARTISTS ON ART FROM 1940 TO 1980. New York: Harper and Row, 1982.

Kertess, Klaus CHUCK CLOSE: NEW PAINTINGS (exhibition catalogue). New York: The Pace Gallery, 1988.

Lyons, Lisa, and Martin Friedman CLOSE PORTRAITS (exhibition catalogue). Minneapolis: Walker Art Center, 1980.

Lyons, Lisa, and Robert Storr CHUCK CLOSE. New York: Rizzoli International Publications, 1987.

CHUCK CLOSE

Bill 1990

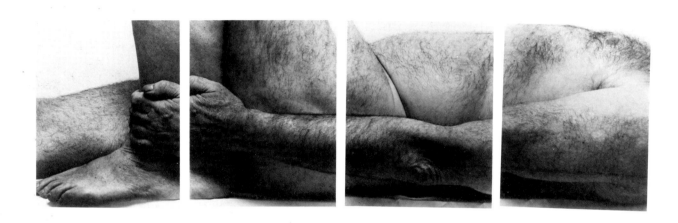

JOHN COPLANS

Self-Portrait 1990

Born in London, 1920; lives in New York.

ONE-ARTIST EXHIBITIONS

1981

The Art Institute of Chicago

Daniel Wolf Gallery
New York

1984

Pace/MacGill Gallery
New York

1985

The Fine Arts Gallery, University of California, Irvine

1986

Pace/MacGill Gallery
New York

1987

Blum Helman Gallery
Los Angeles

1988

Dart Gallery
Chicago

San Francisco Museum of Modern Art (traveled)

1989

Galerie Lelong
New York

1990

Galerie Lelong
New York

GROUP EXHIBITIONS

1984

Institute of Contemporary Art, University of Pennsylvania
Philadelphia
"Face to Face: Recent Portrait Photography"

1985

MIT List Visual Arts Center
Cambridge, Massachusetts
"Nude, Naked, Stripped"

1987

The New Museum of Contemporary Art
New York
"The Other Man: Representations of Masculinity"

1988

Institute of Contemporary Arts
London
"Another Objectivity: Recent International Photography"

National Portrait Gallery, Smithsonian Institution
Washington, D.C.
"The Instant Likeness: Polaroid Portraits"

1989

Frankfurter Kunstverein
Frankfurt
"Prospect Photographie"

International Museum of Photography at George Eastman House
Rochester, New York
"New Acquisitions, New Work, New Directions"

National Museum of American Art, Smithsonian Institution
Washington, D.C.
"The Photography of Invention: American Pictures of the 1980s"

1990

International Center of Photography Midtown
New York
"The Indomitable Spirit" (traveled)

Museum of Contemporary Hispanic Art, The New Museum of Contemporary Art, and The Studio Museum in Harlem
New York
"The Decade Show: Frameworks of Identity in the 1980s"

BIBLIOGRAPHY

Decter, Joshua
"New York in Review." ARTS MAGAZINE, 64 (April 1990), pp. 107-08.

Grundberg, Andy
"Hands Pose for Their Portraits." THE NEW YORK TIMES, January 29, 1989, p. H35.

Grundberg, Andy
"When Photographers Aim Their Cameras at Themselves." THE NEW YORK TIMES, November 18, 1985, section 2, p. 32.

Hagen, Charles
"New York: John Coplans." ARTFORUM, 27 (April 1989), p. 158.

"John Coplans: Body Images." APERTURE, no. 114 (Spring 1989), pp. 2-3.

Naef, Weston J.
THE GALLERY OF WORLD PHOTOGRAPHY: NEW DIRECTIONS. Tokyo: Shueisha Publishing Company, 1984.

Rubinstein, Meyer Raphael
"New York: John Coplans." FLASH ART, no. 146 (May-June 1989), p. 115.

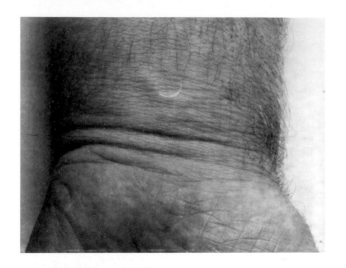

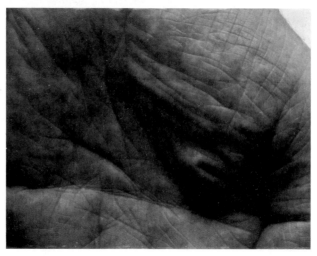

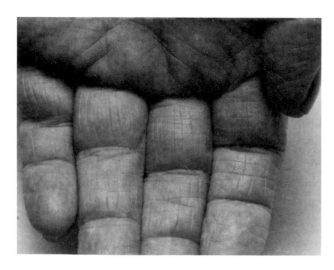

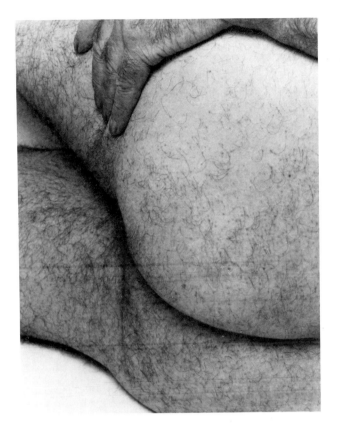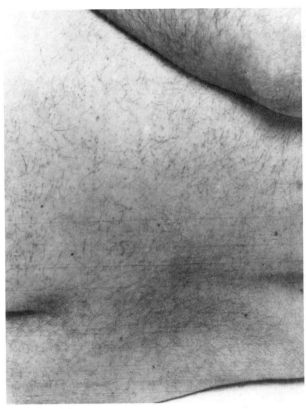

Self-Portrait   1990 *

JESSICA DIAMOND

Food for Thought   1990*

Born in New York, 1957; studied at the School of Visual Arts, New York (BFA, 1979), Columbia University, New York (MFA, 1981); lives in New York.

ONE-ARTIST EXHIBITIONS

1985

Hallwalls
Buffalo

1989

American Fine Arts
New York

1990

American Fine Arts
New York

Artspace Annex
San Francisco

Standard Graphik
Cologne

GROUP EXHIBITIONS

1983

The Drawing Center
New York
"Selections 22"

1984

Artists Space
New York
"Selections from the Artists File"

Damon Brandt Gallery
New York
"Livin' in the U.S.A."

1985

Nature Morte Gallery
New York
"Infotainment" (traveled)

1986

The New Museum of
Contemporary Art
New York
"On View"

1988

The Clocktower,
Institute for Art and
Urban Resources
New York
"The Pop Project:
Nostalgia as Resistance"

1989

Real Art Ways
Hartford
"The Elements: Sex, Politics,
Money, and Religion"

1990

Interim Art
London
"Jessica Diamond, Mike
Kelley"

Galeries Daniel Buchholz,
Gisela Capitain, Tanja
Grunert, Max Hetzler,
Jablonka, Isabella Kacprzak,
Esther Schipper, Monika
Sprüth, Sophia Ungers
Cologne
"Nachschub/Supply: The
Köln Show"

The New Museum of
Contemporary Art at
Marine Midland Bank
New York
"Spent: Currency, Security,
and Art on Deposit"

Rosamund Felsen Gallery
Los Angeles
"Just Pathetic"

Tom Cugliani Gallery
New York
"Jessica Diamond,
Douglas La Tourrette,
David Robilliard, Felix
Gonzalez-Torres"

BIBLIOGRAPHY

Diamond, Jessica
"Making Art, Making
Money: 13 Artists
Comment." ART IN
AMERICA, 78 (July 1990),
p. 139.

Dona, Lydia
"The Memo on the Wall:
Recent Work by Jessica
Diamond." ARTS MAGAZINE,
65 (October 1990), pp. 62-63.

Graw, Isabelle, et al.
NACHSCHUB/SUPPLY: THE
KÖLN SHOW (exhibition
catalogue). Cologne:
Galeries Daniel Buchholz,
Gisela Capitain, Tanja
Grunert, Max Hetzler,
Jablonka, Isabella
Kacprzak, Esther Schipper,
Monika Sprüth, Sophia
Ungers, 1990.

Lawson, Thomas
"Nostalgia as Resistance." In
MODERN DREAMS: THE RISE
AND FALL AND RISE OF POP
(exhibition catalogue). New
York: The Clocktower,
Institute for Art and Urban
Resources, 1988, pp. 151-70.

Lawson, Thomas, and
George W.S. Trow
INFOTAINMENT (exhibition
catalogue). New York:
Nature Morte Gallery, 1985.

Smith, Roberta
"Jessica Diamond." THE NEW
YORK TIMES, June 1, 1990,
p. C22.

Wallis, Brian, ed.
DEMOCRACY: A PROJECT
BY GROUP MATERIAL.
New York: Dia Art
Foundation, 1990.

Zinsser, John
"Jessica Diamond at
American Fine Arts."
ART IN AMERICA, 77
(November 1989), p. 190.

JESSICA DIAMOND

New Economic Shorthand: What Money?   1990

New Economic Shorthand: Totally Unequal   1990

CARROLL DUNHAM   *Shape with Incline*   1990*

Born in New Haven, 1949; studied at Trinity College, Hartford (BA, 1972); lives in New York.

ONE-ARTIST EXHIBITIONS

1981

Artists Space
New York

1985

Baskerville + Watson
New York

Daniel Weinberg Gallery
Los Angeles

The Institute of
Contemporary Art
Boston

1986

Barbara Krakow Gallery
Boston

Baskerville + Watson
New York

1987

Daniel Weinberg Gallery
Los Angeles

Jay Gorney Modern Art
New York

1988

Galerie Fred Jahn
Munich

Tyler Gallery, Tyler School
of Art, Temple University
Elkins Park, Pennsylvania

1989

Sonnabend Gallery
New York

1990

Jablonka Gallery
Cologne

GROUP EXHIBITIONS

1981

Hayden Gallery,
Massachusetts Institute
of Technology
Cambridge
"Four Painters"

1985

Whitney Museum of
American Art
New York
"1985 Biennial Exhibition"

1986

Margo Leavin Gallery
Los Angeles
"Paravision"

1988

The Saatchi Collection
London
"NY Art Now: The Saatchi
Collection (Part II)"

Whitney Museum of
American Art
New York
"Vital Signs: Organic
Abstraction from the
Permanent Collection"

1989

Museum des 20
Jahrhunderts
Vienna
"Sigmund Freud—Heute"

Stedelijk Museum
Amsterdam
"Horn of Plenty: Sixteen
Artists from NYC"

Walker Art Center
Minneapolis
"First Impressions: Early
Prints by Forty-six
Contemporary Artists"

1990

Albertina Museum
Vienna

Tony Shafrazi Gallery
New York
"The Last Decade: American
Artists of the 80's"

BIBLIOGRAPHY

Cameron, Dan
"Neo-Surrealism: Having It
Both Ways." ARTS
MAGAZINE, 59 (November
1984), pp. 68-73.

Carlson, Prudence
"Carroll Dunham: Drawings
1982-1983." MEANING (May
1989), p. 45.

Carlson, Prudence
CARROLL DUNHAM:
ZEICHNUNGEN—DRAWINGS
1982-1983 (exhibition
catalogue). Munich: Galerie
Fred Jahn, 1988.

Collins & Milazzo and
Robert Pincus-Witten
THE LAST DECADE:
AMERICAN ARTISTS OF THE
80's (exhibition catalogue).
New York: Tony Shafrazi
Gallery, 1990.

Colombo, Paolo
CARROLL DUNHAM:
SELECTED DRAWINGS
(exhibition catalogue).
Elkins Park, Pennsylvania:
Tyler School of Art, Temple
University, 1988.

Kertess, Klaus
"Carroll Dunham: Painting
Against the Grain—
Painting with the Grain."
ARTFORUM, 21 (June 1983),
pp. 53-54.

O'Brien, Glenn
"Psychedelic Art: Flashing
Back." ARTFORUM, 22
(March 1984), pp. 73-79.

Saltz, Jerry
"Carroll Dunham's Untitled
(1987)." ARTS MAGAZINE, 62
(January 1988), pp. 58-59.

Schjeldahl, Peter
"The New Low." THE
VILLAGE VOICE, November
13, 1990, p. 97.

Smith, Roberta
"Abstraction That Opens a
Window on the Psyche."
THE NEW YORK TIMES,
February 17, 1989.

CARROLL DUNHAM   *Floating Shape*   1989–90

Shape with Entrance   1990

JEANNE DUNNING

Neck   1990

Born in Hartford, 1960; studied at Oberlin College, Oberlin, Ohio (BA, 1982), The Art Institute of Chicago (MFA, 1985); lives in Chicago.

ONE-ARTIST EXHIBITIONS

1987

Feature
Chicago

1988

Feature
Chicago

1989

Feature
New York

1990

Feature
New York

Real Art Ways
Hartford

Roy Boyd Gallery
Santa Monica

GROUP EXHIBITIONS

1986

Randolph Street Gallery
Chicago
"Dull Edge"

1987

Illinois State University
Art Gallery
Normal
"Anxious Objects"

P.S. 1, Institute for Art
and Urban Resources
Long Island City, New York
"The Hallucination of Truth"

1989

CEPA
Buffalo
"Materiality"

Dayton Art Institute
Ohio
"A Certain Slant of Light:
The Contemporary
American Landscape"

John Michael Kohler
Arts Center
Sheboygan, Wisconsin
"The Unconventional
Landscape"

National Museum of
American Art,
Smithsonian Institution
Washington, D.C.
"The Photography of
Invention: American
Pictures of the 1980s"

1990

Art Against AIDS
(a public project for
Chicago buses)
Chicago
"On the Road"

Carnegie-Mellon
University Art Gallery
Pittsburgh
"New Generations: Chicago"

Feigen Gallery
Chicago
"Sarah Charlesworth,
Jeanne Dunning, Annette
Messager, Adrian Piper,
Laurie Simmons"

BIBLIOGRAPHY

Bonesteel, Michael
"Medium Cool: New
Chicago Abstraction."
ART IN AMERICA, 75
(December 1987),
pp. 138-47.

Bulka, Michael
"Hirsch Perlman, Jeanne
Dunning." NEW ART
EXAMINER, 14 (June 1987),
p. 45.

Corbin-Pardee, Linda
"The Unconventional
Landscape." NEW ART
EXAMINER, 17 (January
1990), pp. 47-48.

Decter, Joshua
"Jeanne Dunning." ARTS
MAGAZINE, 63 (Summer
1989), p. 93.

Heartney, Eleanor
"Second To What?" NEW ART
EXAMINER, 15 (May 1987),
pp. 22-26.

Hixson, Kathryn
"Cool, Conceptual,
Controversial." NEW ART
EXAMINER, 15 (May 1988),
pp. 30-33.

Humphrey, David
"Hair Piece." ART ISSUES,
no. 9 (February 1990),
pp. 17-20.

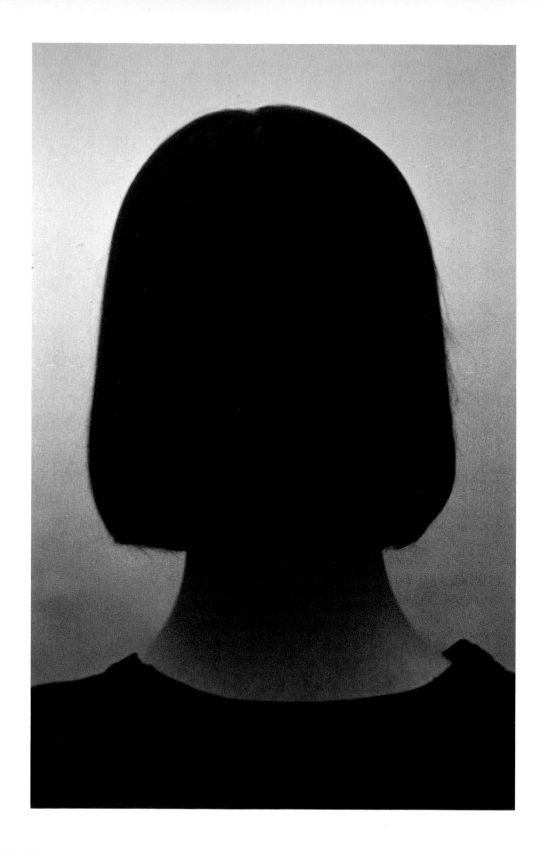

JEANNE DUNNING

Head 6 1989

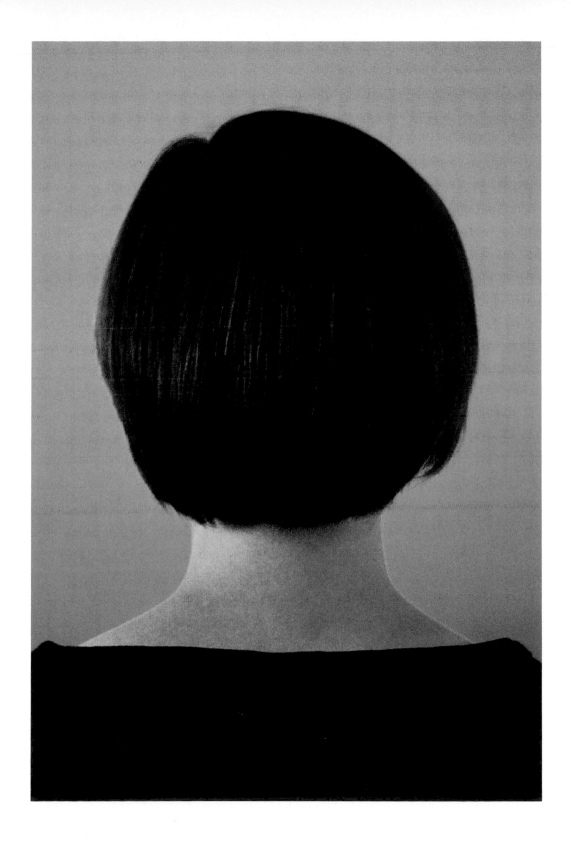

Head 10   1990

ERIC FISCHL

In the Temple 1989

Born in New York, 1948; studied at the California Institute of the Arts, Valencia (BFA, 1972); lives in New York.

ONE-ARTIST EXHIBITIONS

1980

Edward Thorp Gallery
New York

1983

Larry Gagosian Gallery
Los Angeles

Galleria Mario Diacono
Rome

1984

Mary Boone Gallery
New York

1985

Mendel Art Gallery
Saskatoon, Saskatchewan
(traveled)

1990

Mary Boone Gallery
New York

Walker Art Center
Minneapolis

GROUP EXHIBITIONS

1983

Whitney Museum of
American Art
New York
"1983 Biennial Exhibition"

1984

The Museum of Modern Art
New York
"An International Survey of
Recent Painting and
Sculpture"

Venice
"XLI Biennale di Venezia"

1985

Museum of Art,
Carnegie Institute
Pittsburgh
"1985 Carnegie International"

Whitney Museum of
American Art
New York
"1985 Biennial Exhibition"

1986

The Museum of
Contemporary Art
Los Angeles
"Individuals: A Selected
History of Contemporary
Art, 1945-1986"

Museum Ludwig
Cologne
"Europa/Amerika"

1987

Kassel, West Germany
"Documenta 8"

Los Angeles County
Museum of Art
"Avant-Garde in the
Eighties"

Walker Art Center
Minneapolis
"Past/Imperfect: Eric Fischl,
Vernon Fisher, Laurie
Simmons" (traveled)

1989

Museum Ludwig
Cologne
"Bilderstreit: Widerspruch,
Einheit und Fragment in
der Kunst seit 1960"

1990

Museum of Contemporary
Hispanic Art, The New
Museum of Contemporary
Art, and The Studio
Museum in Harlem
New York
"The Decade Show:
Frameworks of Identity in
the 1980s"

BIBLIOGRAPHY

Danto, Arthur C.
"Art: Eric Fischl." THE
NATION, May 31, 1986,
pp. 769-72.

Ferguson, Bruce W., Jean-
Christophe Ammann, and
Donald B. Kuspit
ERIC FISCHL: PAINTINGS
(exhibition catalogue).
Saskatoon, Saskatchewan:
Mendel Art Gallery, 1985.

Grimes, Nancy
"Eric Fischl's Naked
Truths." ART NEWS, 85
(September 1986),
pp. 70-78.

Lawson, Thomas
"Too Good to Be True."
REAL LIFE MAGAZINE, no. 7
(Autumn 1981), pp. 2-7.

Liebmann, Lisa
"Eric Fischl's Year of the
Drowned Dog: Eight
Characters in Search of an
Autumn." ARTFORUM, 22
(March 1984), pp. 67-69.

Linker, Kate
"Eric Fischl: Involuted
Narratives." FLASH ART,
no. 115 (January 1984),
pp. 56-58.

Schjeldahl, Peter
"Post-Innocence: Eric Fischl
and the Social Fate of
American Painting."
PARKETT, no. 5 (June 1985),
pp. 31-43.

Schjeldahl, Peter, and
David Whitney
ERIC FISCHL. New York: Art
in America and Stewart,
Tabori & Chang, 1988.

Storr, Robert
"Desperate Pleasures." ART
IN AMERICA, 72 (November
1984), pp. 124-30.

ERIC FISCHL

On the Stairs of the Temple   1989

The Tire Store   1989*

BILL FONTANA   Niagara Falls   1991

Born in Cleveland, 1947; studied at The New School for Social Research (BA, 1970); lives in Emeryville, California.

Vertical Water uses sound as a sculptural form to delineate the physical dimensions of the Whitney Museum. Sounds recorded at Niagara Falls are

Wave Cannon loudspeakers (A and B), placed in the Sculpture Court. Two parallel rows of smaller BOSE 102 series loud-speakers are mounted on the undersides of the lower two overhangs above the court: loudspeakers C to F play lower mid-range frequencies, and G to J play higher mid-range and high frequencies. This architectural definition of the various frequen-cies in the sound spectrum creates a wall of sound that mimics the height of the Falls. The higher frequencies of this apparent wall of sound will ascend the building, while the lower frequencies will echo within the parallel concrete walls of the Sculpture Court. The acoustic perception of a wall of water at the intersection of 75th Street and Madison Avenue is de-signed to mask the intense sound of traffic.

ONE-ARTIST EXHIBITIONS

1978

National Gallery of Victoria
Melbourne

1980

Newport Harbor Art Museum
Newport Beach, California

American Art
New York

1987

Museum Ludwig
Cologne

San Francisco Museum of
Modern Art

1988

University Art Museum,
University of California,
Berkeley

1989

Galerie Vorsetzen
Hamburg

Japanese Cultural Institute
Cologne

GROUP EXHIBITIONS

1979

Los Angeles Institute of
Contemporary Art
"Sound"

1980

Akademie der Künste
West Berlin
"Für Augen und Ohren"

Musée d'Art Moderne de
la Ville de Paris
"Écouter par les yeux"

1981

Neuberger Museum,
State University of New
York, College at Purchase
"Soundings"

1984

International
Bauausstellung Berlin

1988

Art Gallery of
New South Wales
Sydney
"The 7th Biennale of Sydney"

1989

Brucknerhaus
Linz, Austria
"ARS Electronica"

1990

San Francisco Museum of
Modern Art
"Bay Area Media"

University Art Museum,
University of California,
Santa Barbara
"Pulse 2"

BIBLIOGRAPHY

BROOKLYN BRIDGE SOUND
SCULPTURE (exhibition
catalogue). West Berlin:
Amerika Haus, 1983.

Fontana, Bill
"Entfernte Züge und Klang
Recycling Skulptur." In
ALLES UND NOCH VIEL
MEHR: DAS POETISCHE ABC
(exhibition catalogue).
Kunstmuseum Bern, 1984,
pp. 46-48.

Fontana, Bill
"Thoughts on Sound." In
SOUND (exhibition
catalogue). Los Angeles
Los Angeles Institute of
Contemporary Art, 1
pp. 39-40.

Hanhardt, John
BILL FONTANA

29).
y Museum
1986.

RE: BILL
FONTANA (exhibition
catalogue). Melbourne:
National Gallery of
Victoria, 1978.

BILL FONTANA

Bill Fontana recording sound on a beach in Okinawa for his sound sculpture
Acoustical Journey   1987

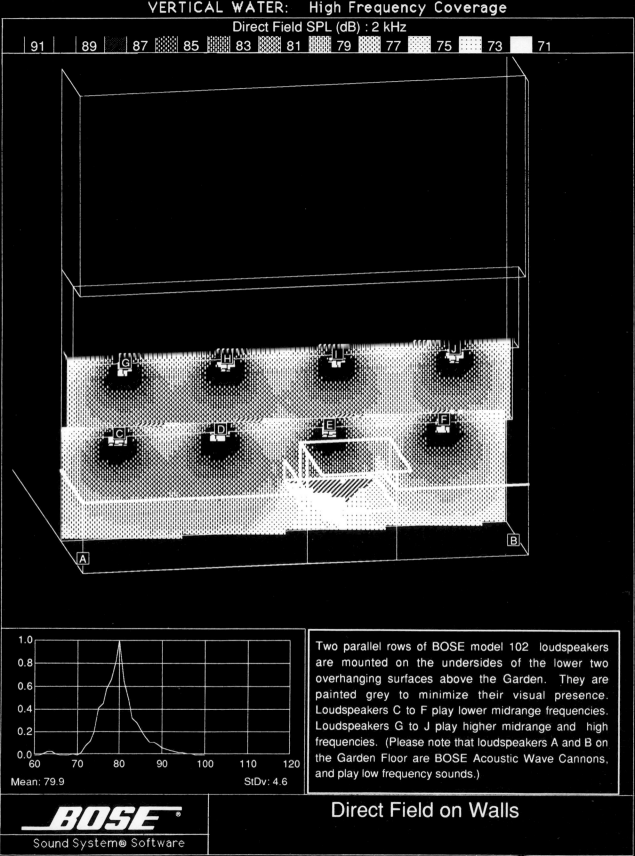

VERTICAL WATER: High Frequency Coverage
Direct Field SPL (dB) : 2 kHz

| 91 | | 89 | | 87 | | 85 | | 83 | | 81 | | 79 | | 77 | | 75 | | 73 | | 71 |

Mean: 79.9   StDv: 4.6

Two parallel rows of BOSE model 102 loudspeakers are mounted on the undersides of the lower two overhanging surfaces above the Garden. They are painted grey to minimize their visual presence. Loudspeakers C to F play lower midrange frequencies. Loudspeakers G to J play higher midrange and high frequencies. (Please note that loudspeakers A and B on the Garden Floor are BOSE Acoustic Wave Cannons, and play low frequency sounds.)

╺╸ＢＯＳＥ ®
Sound System® Software

Direct Field on Walls

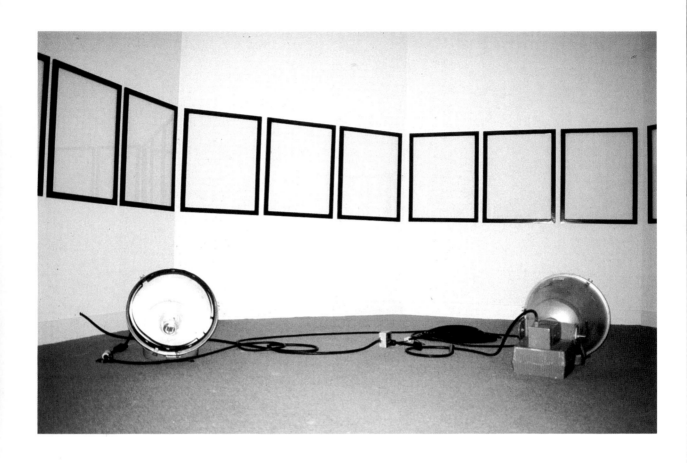

DAWN FRYLING   *No Title*   1990

Born in Pasadena, California, 1960; studied at the University of California, Santa Cruz (1982), University of Arizona, Tucson (BFA, 1985), San Francisco Art Institute (MFA, 1988); lives in San Francisco.

ONE-ARTIST EXHIBITIONS

1985

Zgany Gallery
Tucson

1989

The Lab
San Francisco

1990

San Francisco Museum of Modern Art

Southern Exposure Gallery
San Francisco

GROUP EXHIBITIONS

1986

Joseph Gross Gallery,
University of Arizona
Tucson
"Performance Exhibition"

Mandeville Gallery,
University of California,
San Diego
La Jolla
"Exchange"

181 Club
San Francisco
"Post Studio"

1987

Diego Rivera Gallery,
San Francisco Art Institute
"Sculpture: Dawn Fryling
and Charles Gute"

Emanuel Walter/Atholl
McBean Galleries, San
Francisco Art Institute
"Spring Show"

1988

New Langton Arts
San Francisco
"Contention"

Pro Arts
Oakland
"3rd Annual Juried
Exhibition"

1989

Hallwalls
Buffalo
"Bay Area Conceptualism:
Two Generations"

Richmond Art Center
Richmond, California
"Bill Bury, Dawn Fryling,
Ivan Majdrakoff, Mathew
Matsuoka, Kent Roberts"

1990

Gallery Paule Anglim
San Francisco
"Introductions '90: Margo
Adams, Dawn Fryling,
Frank Jackson, and
Robert Ortbal"

BIBLIOGRAPHY

Baker, Kenneth
"Dawn Fryling: The Lab."
ARTFORUM, 28 (September
1989), pp. 152-53.

Baker, Kenneth
"Galleries: A Triple 'New'
Treat from Dawn Fryling."
SAN FRANCISCO CHRONICLE,
October 9, 1990.

Bonetti, David
"Fryling: 'Toast' of the
Town." SAN FRANCISCO
EXAMINER, September 21,
1990, p. C2.

Gregor, Katherine
"Ten for the '90s. San
Francisco: Dawn Fryling."
ART NEWS, 89 (April 1990),
p. 153.

Helfand, Glen
"The Beauty of Simplicity."
ARTWEEK, March 11, 1989,
p. 4.

Levy, Mark
"San Francisco: Images
of Power." ART
INTERNATIONAL, 6
(Spring 1989), p. 66.

Moser, Charlotte
"Identity from Two
Directions: Dawn Fryling
and Laurel Beckman at
Southern Exposure
Gallery." ARTWEEK,
April 19, 1990.

DAWN FRYLING

Toast (Units 3 and 4)   1990*

Flour Slots   1990*

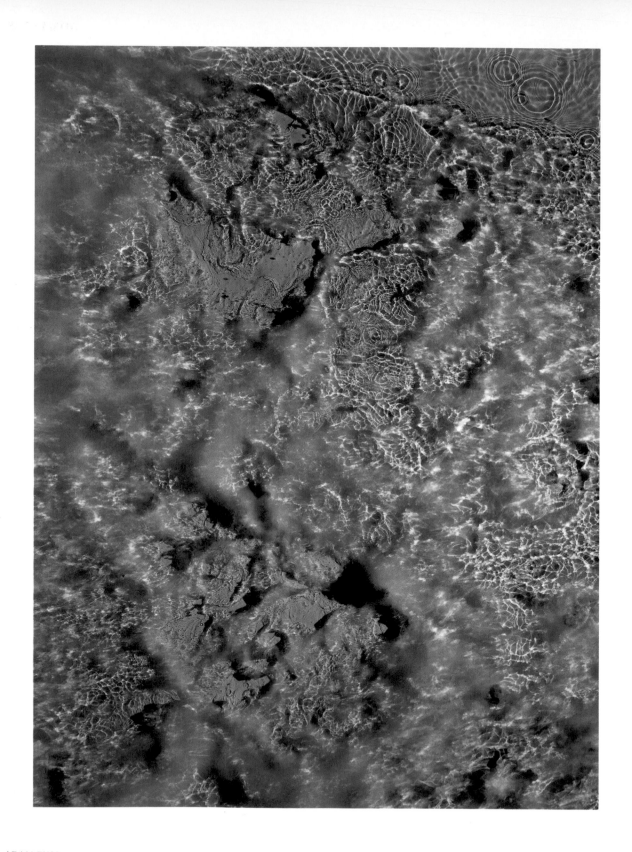

ADAM FUSS

Untitled 1991

Born in London, 1961; lives in New York.

ONE-ARTIST EXHIBITIONS

1985

Massimo Audiello Gallery
New York

1988

Massimo Audiello Gallery
New York

1989

Massimo Audiello Gallery
New York

1990

Robert Miller Gallery
New York

Thomas Solomon's Garage
Los Angeles

GROUP EXHIBITIONS

1985

Alternative Museum
New York
"Seeing Is Believing"

1986

Stux Gallery
Boston
"Fact, Fiction, Fragment,
Fetish-Photography Exhibit"

1987

Massimo Audiello Gallery
New York
"Adam Fuss, Mark Morrisroe,
The Starn Twins"

1988

Damon Brandt Gallery
New York
"Invitational"

Fine Arts Museum of
Long Island
Hempstead
"Through a Pinhole Darkly"
(traveled)

1989

Centre Saidye Bronfman
Montreal
"Pinhole Photography"

Emerson Gallery, Hamilton
College
Clinton, New York
"Abstraction in Contemporary
Photography" (traveled)

Frankfurter Kunstverein
Frankfurt
"Prospect Photographie"

Salama-Caro Gallery
London
"International Camera"

1990

Sala d'Exposicions,
Fundació Caixa de Pensions
Barcelona
"Javier Baldeón and Adam
Fuss"

BIBLIOGRAPHY

Aletti, Vince
"Choices." THE VILLAGE
VOICE, February 27, 1990,
p. 47.

Cotter, Holland
"Adam Fuss at Massimo
Audiello." ART IN AMERICA,
77 (June 1989), pp. 175-76.

Grundberg, Andy
"Abstraction Returns to
Haunt Photography." THE
NEW YORK TIMES, February
25, 1990, section 2, p. 35.

Grundberg, Andy
"Photography View: The
Pendulum Swings Away from
Cynicism." THE NEW YORK
TIMES, October 22, 1989.

Grundberg, Andy, and
Jerry Saltz
ABSTRACTION IN
CONTEMPORARY
PHOTOGRAPHY
(exhibition catalogue).
Clinton, New York:
Emerson Gallery, Hamilton
College, 1989.

Hagen, Charles
"Adam Fuss/Massimo
Audiello." ARTFORUM, 27
(May 1989), p. 154.

O'Brien, Glenn
"Adam Fuss/Massimo
Audiello Gallery."
ARTFORUM, 24 (March
1986), pp. 117-18.

"Photography." THE NEW
YORKER, February 19, 1990,
p. 19.

Weiermair, Peter
PROSPECT PHOTOGRAPHIE
(exhibition catalogue).
Frankfurt: Frankfurter
Kunstverein, 1989.

Untitled 1991

Untitled   1991

JOSEPH GLASCO

Born in Pauls Valley, Oklahoma, 1925; studied at the Art Center School, Los Angeles (1946), the School of Painting and Sculpture, San Miguel de Allende, Mexico (1948), the Art Students League, New York (1949); lives in Galveston, Texas.

ONE-ARTIST EXHIBITIONS

1950

Perls Gallery
New York

1953

Catherine Viviano Gallery
New York

1967

Rizzoli Gallery
New York

1979

Gimpel & Weitzenhoffer
Gallery
New York

1986

Contemporary Arts Museum
Houston

Gimpel & Weitzenhoffer
Gallery
New York

Meredith Long & Company
Houston

1989

Waddington Galleries
London

1990

University of Oklahoma
Museum of Art
Norman

GROUP EXHIBITIONS

1950

The Museum of Modern Art
New York
"Recent Acquisitions"

1951

The Art Institute of
Chicago
"60th Annual American
Exhibition: Paintings and
Sculpture"

1952

The Museum of Modern Art
New York
"15 Americans"

Whitney Museum of
American Art
New York
"1952 Annual Exhibition of
Contemporary American
Sculpture, Watercolors and
Drawings"

1954

The Solomon R.
Guggenheim Museum
New York
"Younger American Painters:
A Selection"

1955

The Corcoran Gallery of Art
Washington, D.C.
"The 24th Biennial
Exhibition of Contemporary
American Oil Paintings"

1956

Whitney Museum of
American Art
New York
"1956 Annual Exhibition of
Contemporary American
Sculpture, Watercolors and
Drawings"

1963

The Corcoran Gallery of Art
Washington, D.C.
"The 28th Biennial
Exhibition of Contemporary
American Painting"

1985

The Museum of Fine Arts
Houston
"Fresh Paint: The Houston
School"

1988

The Menil Collection
Houston
"Texas Art"

BIBLIOGRAPHY

Ashbery, John
"Reviews and Previews."
ART NEWS, 57 (April 1958),
p. 16.

Judd, Donald
"In the Galleries: Joseph
Glasco." ARTS, 35
(March 1961), p. 56.

Lieb, Vered
"Joseph Glasco: Painting
Under Construction."
ARTFORUM, 18 (November
1979), pp. 35-37.

Mayo, Marti, Michael
Berryhill, and
Julian Schnabel
JOSEPH GLASCO 1948-1986:
A SESQUICENTENNIAL
EXHIBITION (exhibition
catalogue). Houston:
Contemporary Arts
Museum, 1986.

McBride, Henry
"Joseph Glasco's Color." ART
NEWS, 50 (May 1951), p. 46.

Porter, Fairfield
"Reviews and Previews."
ART NEWS, 55 (March 1956),
pp. 52-53.

Rose, Barbara, and
Susie Kalil
FRESH PAINT: THE HOUSTON
SCHOOL (exhibition
catalogue). Houston: The
Museum of Fine Arts, 1985.

JOSEPH GLASCO

Big Green   1990

ROBERT GOBER

Untitled 1990

Born in Wallingford, Connecticut, 1954; studied at the Tyler School of Art, Temple University, Rome (1973-74), Middlebury College, Middlebury, Vermont (BA, 1976); lives in New York.

ONE-ARTIST EXHIBITIONS

1984

Paula Cooper Gallery
New York

1985

Paula Cooper Gallery
New York

Daniel Weinberg Gallery
Los Angeles

1986

Daniel Weinberg Gallery
Los Angeles

1987

Galerie Jean Bernier
Athens

Paula Cooper Gallery
New York

1988

The Art Institute of
Chicago

Galerie Gisela Capitain
Cologne

Galerie Max Hetzler
Cologne

Tyler Gallery, Tyler School
of Art, Temple University
Elkins Park, Pennsylvania

1989

Paula Cooper Gallery
New York

1990

Galeria Marga Paz
Madrid

Museum Boymans-
van Beuningen
Rotterdam

GROUP EXHIBITIONS

1979

112 Greene Street
New York

1984

P.S. 122 Gallery
New York

1986

The Renaissance Society at
The University of Chicago
"New Sculpture: Robert
Gober, Jeff Koons, Haim
Steinbach"

1988

The Institute of
Contemporary Art
Boston
"Utopia Post Utopia:
Configurations of Nature
and Culture in Recent
Sculpture and
Photography"

Venice
"XLIII Biennale di Venezia"

1989

Stedelijk Museum
Amsterdam
"Horn of Plenty: Sixteen
Artists from NYC"

Whitney Museum of
American Art
New York
"1989 Biennial Exhibition"

1990

Hirshhorn Museum
and Sculpture Garden,
Smithsonian Institution
Washington, D.C.
"Culture and Commentary:
An Eighties Perspective"

Newport Harbor Art Museum
Newport Beach, California
"Objectives: The New
Sculpture"

BIBLIOGRAPHY

Benezra, Neil
ROBERT GOBER (exhibition
brochure). Chicago: The
Art Institute of Chicago,
1988.

Caldwell, John
NEW WORK: A NEW
GENERATION (exhibition
catalogue). San Francisco:
San Francisco Museum of
Modern Art, 1990.

Halbreich, Kathy
CULTURE AND COMMENTARY:
AN EIGHTIES PERSPECTIVE
(exhibition catalogue).
Washington, D.C.:
Hirshhorn Museum and
Sculpture Garden,
Smithsonian Institution,
1990.

Indiana, Gary
A PROJECT: ROBERT GOBER/
CHRISTOPHER WOOL
(exhibition catalogue). New
York: 303 Gallery, 1988.

Jameson, Fredric, et al.
UTOPIA POST UTOPIA:
CONFIGURATIONS OF NATURE
AND CULTURE IN RECENT
SCULPTURE AND
PHOTOGRAPHY (exhibition
catalogue). Boston: The
Institute of Contemporary
Art, 1988.

Loock, Ulrich, Karel
Schampers, and Trevor
Fairbrother
ROBERT GOBER (exhibition
catalogue). Rotterdam:
Museum Boymans-
van Beuningen, 1990.

Schimmel, Paul, et al.
OBJECTIVES: THE NEW
SCULPTURE (exhibition
catalogue). Newport Beach,
California: Newport Harbor
Art Museum, 1990.

ROBERT GOBER

Untitled 1990*

FELIX GONZALEZ-TORRES   *Untitled (Somewhere Better Than This Place/Nowhere Better Than This Place)*   1990 *

Born in Güaimaro, Cuba, 1957; studied at the Independent Study Program, Whitney Museum of American Art, New York (1981), Pratt Institute, Brooklyn, New York (BFA, 1983), Independent Study Program, Whitney Museum of American Art, New York (1983), New York University/International Center of Photography (MA, 1987); lives in New York.

ONE-ARTIST EXHIBITIONS

1988

INTAR Gallery
New York

The New Museum of
Contemporary Art
New York

Rastovski Gallery
New York

1989

Billboard, Sheridan Square
New York

The Brooklyn Museum
New York

Lower Manhattan Cultural
Council
New York

1990

Andrea Rosen Gallery
New York

Fine Arts Gallery,
University of British
Columbia
Vancouver

Neue Gesellschaft für
Bildende Kunst
Berlin

GROUP EXHIBITIONS

1987

Artists Space
New York
"Selections from the Artists
File"

1988

White Columns
New York
"Real World"

1989

The Contemporary
Arts Center
Cincinnati
"Double Take: Advertising
Reconsidered"

Hallwalls
Buffalo
"Amerikarma"

Massimo Audiello Gallery
New York
"In the Center of Doubt"

Paula Allen Gallery
New York
"Tom Burr, Felix Gonzalez-
Torres, Michael Jenkins,
John Lindell"

Terrain Gallery
San Francisco
"Matter/Anti-Matter"

Wessel O'Connor Gallery
New York
"To Probe and to Push:
Artists of Provocation"

1990

Andrea Rosen Gallery
New York
"The Stendhal Syndrome:
The Cure"

Galerie Christine &
Isy Brachot
Brussels
"Red"

Jay Gorney Modern Art
New York
"Felix Gonzalez-Torres,
Michael Jenkins, and
Tim Rollins + K.O.S."

Musei di Spoleto
Italy
"Artedomani"

Neue Gesellschaft für
Bildende Kunst
Berlin
"Übers Sofa: auf die Strasse!"

The New Museum of
Contemporary Art
New York
"The Rhetorical Image"

Robbin Lockett Gallery
Chicago
"Get Well Soon"

Simon Watson Gallery
New York
"The Clinic"

BIBLIOGRAPHY

Atkins, Robert
"New This Week: Felix
Gonzalez-Torres." 7 DAYS,
February 21, 1990.

Faust, Gretchen
"New York in Review." ARTS
MAGAZINE, 64 (October
1989), pp. 102-03.

Heartney, Eleanor
"Felix Gonzalez-Torres at
Andrea Rosen." ART IN
AMERICA, 78 (May 1990),
pp. 235-36.

Liu, Catherine
"Felix Gonzalez-Torres:
Rastovski." FLASH ART,
no. 142 (October 1988),
pp. 130-31.

Mahoney, Robert
"Felix Gonzalez-Torres:
Andrea Rosen Gallery."
FLASH ART, no. 152 (May–
June 1990), p. 156.

Smith, Roberta
"Minimalism on the March:
More and More Less and
Less." THE NEW YORK
TIMES, January 26, 1990.

Watson, Scott
FELIX GONZALEZ-TORRES
AND DONALD MOFFETT:
STRANGE WAYS HERE WE
COME (exhibition catalogue).
Vancouver: Fine Arts
Gallery, University of
British Columbia, 1990.

FELIX GONZALEZ-TORRES   *Untitled (U.S.A. Today)*   1990*

GROUP MATERIAL

AIDS Timeline   1989–90

An artists' collaborative founded in New York in 1979 to organize exhibitions and public projects on social themes.

DOUG ASHFORD
Born in Rabat, Morocco, 1958; studied at Cooper Union, New York (BFA, 1981); lives in New York.

JULIE AULT
Born in Boston, 1957; studied at the University of Maine, Augusta (1973-75); lives in New York.

FELIX GONZALEZ-TORRES
Born in Güaimaro, Cuba, 1957; lives in New York.

KAREN RAMSPACHER
Born in Pennsylvania, 1965; studied at Wellesley College, Wellesley, Massachusetts (BA, 1987); lives in New York.

In 1981, the United States government began documenting cases of an immunosuppressive illness later called AIDS (Acquired Immune Deficiency Syndrome). HIV, the virus thought to cause AIDS, is transmitted through the exchange of blood or semen. Specific groups of Americans identified as "at risk" for HIV—gay men and intra-venous drug users—were allowed to die as a result of government inaction and an unresponsive medical system. The focus on "risk groups" rather than "risk behaviors" created a false sense of security, denying that everyone is at risk of contracting HIV.

AIDS is a sexually transmissible disease. Sexuality is a taboo subject in American public discourse. The inability of many to accept or even discuss the need for prevention programs, including sexually explicit education and clean needle exchange programs for I.V. drug-users, continues to contribute to the magnitude of the AIDS crisis. To date, approximately 102,802 deaths from AIDS have been documented in the U.S., and an estimated 1.5 million people are HIV infected. An estimated 8-10 million people are infected worldwide.

The AIDS Timeline project is an attempt to chronologically trace the AIDS crisis in the United States and reveal the social and political conditions in which it was allowed to develop. Like any representation of history, this project is subjective in that it includes certain information and excludes other information. AIDS Timeline juxtaposes responses to this health crisis from the

media, the Reagan and Bush administrations, national and local governments, the medical establishment, and the communities most directly affected by AIDS. This project encourages a reading of history as interconnected conditions and complex relations rather than a constructed series of isolated facts. Timeline documents the impact that homophobia, heterosexism, sexism, and racism have had on the formation of effective public policy. Virtually all the major social inequities that compromise democracy in the U.S. are reflected in the decade-long history of AIDS.

EXHIBITIONS AND PROJECTS

1980

Group Material
New York
"Alienation"

1981

Group Material
New York
"It's a Gender Show"

1982

Artists Space
New York
"Primer (for Raymond Williams)"

1984

P.S. 1, Institute for Art and Urban Resources
Long Island City, New York
"Timeline: The Chronicle of U.S. Intervention in Central and Latin America"

1985

Whitney Museum of American Art
New York
"1985 Biennial Exhibition"

1987

Kassel, West Germany
"Documenta 8"

1988

Dia Art Foundation
New York
"Democracy"

1989

Matrix Gallery, University Art Museum, University of California, Berkeley
"AIDS Timeline"

1990

Wadsworth Atheneum
Hartford
"AIDS Timeline (Hartford, 1990)"

BIBLIOGRAPHY

Berkson, Bill
"Group Material, AIDS Timeline." ARTFORUM, 28 (March 1990), pp. 168-69.

Miller, John
"Baudrillard and His Discontents." ARTSCRIBE INTERNATIONAL, no. 63 (May 1987), pp. 48-51.

Olander, William
"Material World." ART IN AMERICA, 77 (January 1989), pp. 123-28, 167.

Smith, Valerie
"Group Material. Consumption: Metaphor, Pastime, Necessity." FLASH ART, no. 103 (Summer 1981), pp. 53-54.

Wallis, Brian, ed.
DEMOCRACY: A PROJECT BY GROUP MATERIAL. New York: Dia Art Foundation, 1990.

The Centers for Disease Control (CDC) approaches Lyphomed drug company, the manufacturers of a drug called I.V. Pentamidine used to treat a rare type of pneumonia. The CDC asks Lyphomed to manufacture I.V. Pentamidine to treat AIDS-related pneumonia (PCP). PCP is the leading cause of death in People With AIDS. The company hesitates because there is no potential profit in so small a market.

Dr. Robert Gallo, head of the AIDS division of the National Institutes of Health, claims to have discovered the cause of AIDS by isolating a virus he terms HTLV3. This is almost a year after French researchers at the Pasteur Institute announced the discovery of a similar virus, LAV. Gallo's claim causes a controversy over the crediting of the discovery of the virus.

William F. Buckley Jr., editor of the *National Review,* publishes an article for his syndicated column in which he states, "Everyone detected with AIDS should be tatooed on the upper forearm, to protect common needle-users, and on the buttocks to prevent the victimization of other homosexuals."

The city government of Amsterdam, The Netherlands, starts an exemplary needle exchange program distributing clean needles to drug users from vans. The exchange of blood, through shared "works," (needle, syringe, etc.) can put I.V. drug users at risk of contracting HIV.

It is proven that there is HIV infection in vaginal secretions as well as menstrual blood. As early as 1984, there are documented cases of woman-to-woman transmission but the Centers for Disease Control (CDC) refuses to study cunnilingus (oral sex) as a mode of transmission. The CDC also ignores the specific diseases that affect women with HIV.

The National Cancer Institute states that the drug AZT (Azidothymidine) slows replication of HIV in laboratory experiments. AZT was originally developed as a cancer drug in 1964.

HIGH ENERGY

Untitled, from the Interment Camp series, 1942 Dorothea Lange; *Advertising Executive,* Mike Glier; video still: *Keep Your Laws Off My Body,* Catherine Saalfield and Zoe Leonard; *The Ruby Slippers,* Rudy Lemcke

With much fanfare, the Coca-Cola Company begins distributing its "New Coke." Within weeks, grassroots groups organize to bring back "old" Coke. The company responds to this nationwide campaign by introducing "Coke Classic."

Prostitutes are among the first groups to be tested for HIV. The results reveal that most prostitutes who are HIV antibody positive have contracted the virus through the use of shared I.V. drug "works." Most prostitutes use condoms to practice safer-sex. Despite these facts, the media and the public continue to scapegoat sexworkers as vectors of illness.

1985

Rock Hudson discloses that he has AIDS. The American media quadruples its coverage of the syndrome and President Reagan, who has never said the word AIDS in any public address, calls to wish Hudson well.

Assistant Secretary of Defense, William E. Mayer, announces that the Department will screen all prospective military recruits for possible HIV infection. Three months later, he decides to initiate screening of all 2.1 million military personnel.

The PWA coalition is formed in New York City. It is created by and for People With AIDS and People With AIDS Related Complex (ARC) to promote self-empowerment. In June, the first issue of the PWA Coalition Newsline is published. The Newsline provides a forum for diverse opinions and includes treatment information, feature articles, memorials, and a resource list.

Two protesters chain themselves to the Federal Building in San Francisco demanding that more federal money be allocated for AIDS research and that ARC patients receive the same benefit as AIDS patients.

Publicity still of Rock Hudson; *US Magazine,* 1985; untitled photo, Evan Estern; *Selections from The Disco, Various BPM, 1979–1990,* Steven Evans

PETER HALLEY   *Double Elvis*   1990

Born in New York, 1953; studied at Yale University, New Haven (BA, 1975), University of New Orleans (MFA, 1978); lives in New York.

ONE-ARTIST EXHIBITIONS

1985

International With Monument Gallery
New York

1986

Galerie Daniel Templon
Paris

1987

Margo Leavin Gallery
Los Angeles

1988

Galerie Bruno Bischofberger
Zurich

1989

Institute of Contemporary Arts
London

Museum Haus Esters
Krefeld, West Germany
(traveled)

Sonnabend Gallery
New York

1990

Daniel Weinberg Gallery
Santa Monica

Jablonka Galerie
Cologne

Mario Diacono Gallery
Boston

GROUP EXHIBITIONS

1984

White Columns
New York
"The New Capital"

1987

Sala de Exposiciones,
Fundación Caja de Pensiones
Madrid
"Art and Its Double:
A New York Perspective"

Whitney Museum of
American Art
New York
"1987 Biennial Exhibition"

1988

The Carnegie Museum
of Art
Pittsburgh
"1988 Carnegie International"

Deste Foundation
Athens
"Cultural Geometry"

The Institute of
Contemporary Art and the
Museum of Fine Arts
Boston
"The BiNATIONAL:
American Art of the Late
80s" (traveled)

1989

Modern Art Museum of
Fort Worth
"Ten + Ten: Contemporary
Soviet and American
Painters" (traveled)

Stedelijk Museum
Amsterdam
"Horn of Plenty: Sixteen
Artists from NYC"

1990

Wiener Secession
Vienna
"Umweg Moderne/Modern
Detour: R.M. Fischer,
Peter Halley, Laurie
Simmons"

Tony Shafrazi Gallery
New York
"The Last Decade: American
Artists of the 80's"

BIBLIOGRAPHY

Adams, Brooks
"Peter Halley at
Sonnabend." ART IN
AMERICA, 78 (March 1990),
pp. 195-96.

Blazwick, Iwona, and
Peter Halley
PETER HALLEY: RECENT
PAINTINGS (exhibition
catalogue). London:
Institute of Contemporary
Arts, 1989.

Cameron, Dan
"In the Path of Peter
Halley." ARTS MAGAZINE,
60 (December 1987),
pp. 70-73.

Decter, Joshua
"Peter Halley."
CONTEMPORANEA, 3
(March 1990), p. 89.

Gilbert-Rolfe, Jeremy
"Nonrepresentation in 1988:
Meaning Production
Beyond the Scope of the
Pious." ARTS MAGAZINE, 62
(May, 1988), pp. 124-25.

Halley, Peter
PETER HALLEY: COLLECTED
ESSAYS 1981-1987. Zurich:
Galerie Bruno
Bischofberger, 1988.

Heynen, Julian
PETER HALLEY (exhibition
catalogue). Krefeld, West
Germany: Museum Haus
Esters, 1989.

Miller, John
"Lecture Theatre: Peter
Halley's 'Geometry and the
Social.'" ARTSCRIBE
INTERNATIONAL, no. 74
(March-April, 1989), p. 65.

Taylor, Paul
"Cumulus from America:
The Return of (Conceptual)
Art." PARKETT, no. 9
(June 1986), pp. 120-22.

PETER HALLEY   *The Moment Passed*   1989*

The Terminator 1990 *

KEITH HARING   *Brazil*   1989–90*

Born in Kutztown, Pennsylvania, 1958; studied at the School of Visual Arts, New York (1978-79); died in New York, 1990.

ONE-ARTIST EXHIBITIONS

1978

Pittsburgh Center for the Arts

1981

Club 57
New York

P.S. 122
New York

1982

Tony Shafrazi Gallery
New York

1983

Fun Gallery
New York

Galleria Lucio Amelio
Naples

Wadsworth Atheneum
Hartford

1985

CAPC Musée d'Art Contemporain
Bordeaux

Leo Castelli Gallery
New York

1986

Galerie Daniel Templon
Paris

Stedelijk Museum
Amsterdam

1988

Hans Mayer Gallery
Düsseldorf

1990

The Queens Museum
New York (traveled)

Tony Shafrazi Gallery
New York

GROUP EXHIBITIONS

1980

New York
"Times Square Show"

1981

P.S. 1, Institute for Art and Urban Resources
Long Island City, New York
"New York/New Wave"

1982

Kassel, West Germany
"Documenta 7"

1983

Whitney Museum of American Art
New York
"1983 Biennial Exhibition"

Whitney Museum of American Art,
Downtown Branch
New York
"The Comic Art Show"

1984

Venice
"XLI Biennale di Venezia"

1986

Whitney Museum of American Art
New York
"Sacred Images in Secular Art"

1987

Institute of Contemporary Arts
London
"Comic Iconoclasm"

Los Angeles County Museum of Art
"Avant-Garde in the Eighties"

1988

The Museum of Modern Art
New York
"Committed to Print"

BIBLIOGRAPHY

Blinderman, Barry
KEITH HARING: FUTURE PRIMEVAL (exhibition catalogue). Normal: University Galleries, Illinois State University, 1990.

Deitch, Jeffrey
KEITH HARING: PAINTINGS, DRAWINGS, AND A VELUM (exhibition catalogue). Amsterdam: Stedelijk Museum, 1986.

Fox, Howard N.
AVANT-GARDE IN THE EIGHTIES (exhibition catalogue). Los Angeles: Los Angeles County Museum of Art, 1987.

Froment, Jean-Louis, Brion Gysin, and Sylvie Couderc
KEITH HARING: PEINTURES, SCULPTURES ET DESSINS (exhibition catalogue). Bordeaux: CAPC Musée d'Art Contemporain, 1985.

Hager, Steven
ART AFTER MIDNIGHT: THE EAST VILLAGE SCENE. New York: St. Martin's Press, 1986.

Haring, Keith, and Henry Geldzahler
ART IN TRANSIT: SUBWAY DRAWINGS BY KEITH HARING. New York: Harmony Books, 1984.

Pincus-Witten, Robert, Jeffrey Deitch, and David Shapiro
KEITH HARING (exhibition catalogue). New York: Tony Shafrazi Gallery, 1982.

KEITH HARING   *Untitled*   1989

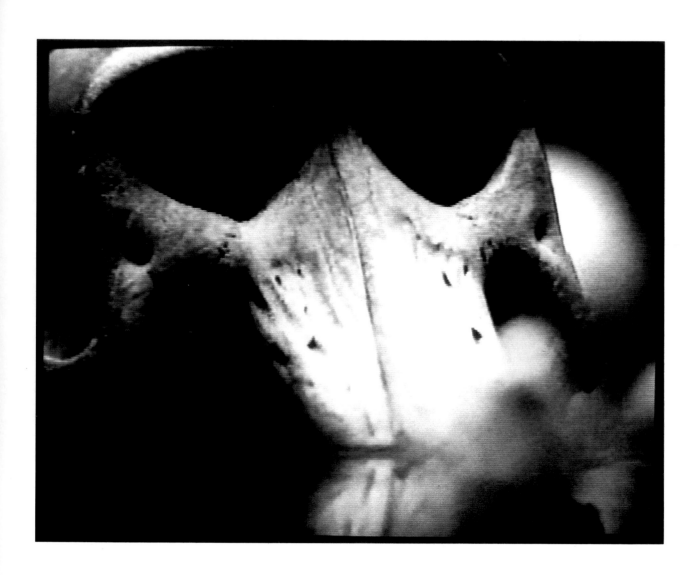

GARY HILL

Site/Recite (A Prologue) 1989

Born in Santa Monica, 1951; studied at the Art Students League, Woodstock, New York (1969); lives in Seattle.

ONE-ARTIST EXHIBITIONS

1976

Anthology Film Archives
New York

1979

Everson Museum of Art
Syracuse, New York

The Kitchen
New York

1980

The Museum of Modern Art
New York

1983

American Center
Paris

1986

Whitney Museum of
American Art
New York

1987

The Museum of
Contemporary Art
Los Angeles

1989

Musée d'Art Moderne
Villeneuve d'Ascq, France

1990

Galerie des Archives
Paris

The Museum of Modern Art
New York

GROUP EXHIBITIONS

1975

The Museum of Modern Art
New York
"Projects Video V"

1979

Everson Museum of Art
Syracuse, New York
"Video Revue" (traveled)

1983

Walter Phillips Gallery
Banff, Alberta
"The Second Link:
Viewpoints on Video in the
Eighties" (traveled)

1984

Venice
"XLI Biennale di Venezia"

1985

Whitney Museum of
American Art
New York
"1985 Biennial Exhibition"
(traveled)

1987

Kassel, West Germany
"Documenta 8"

Whitney Museum of
American Art,
Fairfield County
Stamford, Connecticut
"Contemporary Diptychs:
Divided Visions"

1988

Long Beach Museum of Art
Long Beach, California
"Degrees of Reality"

1989

Whitney Museum of
American Art
New York
"1989 Biennial Exhibition"
(traveled)

1990

Centro de Arte Reina Sofía
Madrid
"Bienal de la imagen en
movimiento '90"

Musée National d'Art
Moderne, Centre
Georges Pompidou
Paris
"Passages de l'image"
(traveled)

Stedelijk Museum
Amsterdam
"Energieen"

BIBLIOGRAPHY

Bellour, Raymond
"Le dernier homme en
croix." In CINQ PIÈCES AVEC
VUE (exhibition catalogue).
Geneva: Centre Genevois de
Gravure Contemporaine,
1987.

Derrida, Jacques
"Videor." In PASSAGES DE
L'IMAGE (exhibition
catalogue). Paris: Musée
National d'Art Moderne,
Centre Georges Pompidou,
1990, pp. 158-61.

Furlong, Lucinda
"A Manner of Speaking: An
Interview with Gary Hill."
AFTERIMAGE, 10 (March
1983), pp. 9-16.

Hanhardt, John G.
GARY HILL (Program notes:
The New American
Filmmakers Series, 30).
New York: Whitney
Museum of American Art
1986.

Kolpan, Steven
"Bateson Through the
Looking Glass." VIDEO AND
THE ARTS, no. 11 (Winter
1986), pp. 20-22, 35, 56.

Lageira, Jacinto, and
Christine van Assche
"Gary Hill: The Imager of
Disaster." GALERIES
MAGAZINE, no. 40
(December 1990-January
1991), pp. 74-77, 140-41.

GARY HILL

Beacon 1990 *

RONI HORN

Asphere VII   1989*

Born in New York, 1955; studied at the Rhode Island School of Design, Providence (BFA, 1975), Yale University School of Art, New Haven (MFA, 1978); lives in New York.

ONE-ARTIST EXHIBITIONS

1980

The Clocktower, Institute for Art and Urban Resources
New York

1983

Kunstraum München
Munich

1986

Galerie Maeght Lelong
New York

Neuberger Museum, State University of New York, College at Purchase

1987

Galerie Maeght Lelong
Paris

1988

Chinati Foundation
Marfa, Texas

The Detroit Institute of Arts

Galerie Lelong
New York

1989

Jay Gorney Modern Art
New York

Paula Cooper Gallery
New York

1990

Leo Castelli Gallery
New York

Margo Leavin Gallery
Los Angeles

The Museum of Contemporary Art
Los Angeles

GROUP EXHIBITIONS

1980

Hayden Gallery, Massachusetts Institute of Technology
Cambridge
"The Material Object"

1984

Barbara Braathen Gallery
New York
"Large Works"

1985

Alfred Kren Gallery
New York
"Group Show"

Burnett Miller Gallery
Los Angeles
"Recent Drawings"

Lorence Monk Gallery
New York
"Drawings"

1986

Barbara Krakow Gallery
Boston
"Drawings"

Chris Middendorf Gallery
Washington, D.C.
"The Hidden Surface"

1987

Städtische Kunsthalle
Düsseldorf
"Similia/Dissimilia: Modes of Abstractions in Painting, Sculpture, and Photography Today" (traveled)

1990

Whitney Museum of American Art
New York
"Recent Drawing: Roni Horn, Charles Ray, Jim Shaw, Michael Tetherow"

Stephen Wirtz Gallery
San Francisco
"Lead & Wax"

BIBLIOGRAPHY

Gilbert-Rolfe, Jeremy
RONI HORN: PAIR OBJECTS I, II, III (exhibition catalogue). New York: Galerie Lelong, 1988.

Halbreich, Kathy
THE MATERIAL OBJECT (exhibition catalogue). Cambridge: Hayden Gallery, Massachusetts Institute of Technology, 1980.

Hammann, Barbara, Helmut Friedel, and Luise Horn
RONI HORN (exhibition catalogue). Munich: Kunstraum München, 1983.

Horn, Roni
BLUFF LIFE (vol. 1 of TO PLACE). New York: Peter Blum, 1990.

Kern, Hermann
RONI HORN (exhibition catalogue). Munich: Kunstraum München, 1980.

Kertess, Klaus
LEAD. New York: Hirschl & Adler Modern, 1987.

Kertess, Klaus
RONI HORN (exhibition catalogue). Los Angeles: The Museum of Contemporary Art, 1990.

Norden, Linda
"Roni Horn." In SIMILIA/ DISSIMILIA: MODES OF ABSTRACTIONS IN PAINTING, SCULPTURE, AND PHOTOGRAPHY TODAY (exhibition catalogue), Rainer Crone, ed. Düsseldorf: Städtische Kunsthalle Düsseldorf, 1987, pp. 118-23.

Saunders, Wade
"Talking Objects: Interviews with Ten Younger Sculptors." ART IN AMERICA, 73 (November 1985), pp. 110-37.

RONI HORN

Thicket No. 2   1990

WENDY JACOB

Untitled 1990*

Born in Rochester, New York, 1958; studied at Mount Holyoke College, South Hadley, Massachusetts (1976-78), Williams College, Williamstown, Massachusetts (BA, 1980), School of The Art Institute of Chicago (MFA, 1989); lives in Chicago.

ONE-ARTIST EXHIBITIONS

1986

Lake Placid Center for
the Arts
New York

1988

Goodrich Gallery, Williams
College
Williamstown,
Massachusetts

1990

Andrea Rosen Gallery
New York

GROUP EXHIBITIONS

1989

School of The Art Institute
of Chicago
"Bookchin-Hogan-Jacob-
Koenen"

Robbin Lockett Gallery
Chicago
"Plus"

University Galleries, Illinois
State University
Normal
"Biokinetic: Poetry Through
Motion" (traveled)

1990

Kansas City Art Institute
Missouri
"Plenty"

Robbin Lockett Gallery
Chicago
"Get Well Soon"

BIBLIOGRAPHY

Dahlberg, Laurie
OUR CORNER OF THE WORLD:
SEVENTEEN ILLINOIS ARTISTS
(exhibition catalogue).
Normal: University
Galleries, Illinois State
University, 1989.

Gamble, Allison
"The Myths That Work."
NEW ART EXAMINER, 16
(May 1989), pp. 22-25.

Golden, Deven
"In the Dark Open House."
NEW ART EXAMINER, 16
(September 1989), pp. 47-48.

Golden, Deven
"'Murmur' Raises a Din."
NEW ART EXAMINER, 17
(June 1990), pp. 30-32.

Schwabsky, Barry
"Wendy Jacob/Zoe Leonard."
ARTS MAGAZINE, 65 (October
1990), p. 95.

Spooner, Peter
BIOKINETIC: POETRY
THROUGH MOTION
(exhibition catalogue).
Normal: University
Galleries, Illinois State
University, 1989.

WENDY JACOB

Untitled 1990*

Untitled   1990*

LUIS JIMENEZ

Steelworker—Hunky 1990

Born in El Paso, 1940; studied at the University of Texas at El Paso (BS, 1964), Cuidad Universitaria, Mexico City (1964); lives in Hondo, New Mexico.

ONE-ARTIST EXHIBITIONS

1973

Long Beach Museum of Art
Long Beach, California

1975

Contemporary Arts Museum
Houston

1980

Joslyn Art Museum
Omaha

1983

Laguna Gloria Art Museum
Austin

1985

University of Arizona
Museum of Art
Tucson

1986

Adair Margo Gallery
El Paso

University of Texas
El Paso

1990

Moody Gallery
Houston

GROUP EXHIBITIONS

1969

Whitney Museum of
American Art
New York
"Human Concern/Personal
Torment" (traveled)

1973

Whitney Museum of
American Art
New York
"1973 Biennial Exhibition"

1979

Contemporary Arts Museum
Houston
"Fire!"

1983

Alternative Museum and
The Sculpture Center
New York
"Showdown"

1984

The Museum of
Contemporary Art
Los Angeles
"Automobile and Culture"

1985

Albright-Knox Art Gallery
Buffalo
"Awards in the Visual Arts 4"
(traveled)

1987

The Museum of Fine Arts
Houston
"Hispanic Art in the
United States: Thirty
Contemporary Painters and
Sculptors" (traveled)

1988

The Hirshhorn Museum
and Sculpture Garden,
Smithsonian Institution
Washington, D.C.
"Different Drummers"

1989

Archer M. Huntington Art
Gallery, University of
Texas at Austin
"A Century of Sculpture in
Texas: 1889-1989" (traveled)

1990

Museum of Contemporary
Hispanic Art, The New
Museum of Contemporary
Art, and The Studio
Museum in Harlem
New York
"The Decade Show:
Frameworks of Identity
in the 1980s"

BIBLIOGRAPHY

Beardsley, John
"Personal Sensibilities in
Public Places." ARTFORUM,
19 (June 1981), pp. 43-45.

Carlozzi, Annette DiMéo
and Laurel H. Jones
50 TEXAS ARTISTS. San
Francisco: Chronicle
Books, 1986.

Gambrell, Jamey
"Texas: State of the Art."
ART IN AMERICA, 75 (March
1987), pp. 114-30, 151.

Harithas, James
PROGRESS I (exhibition
catalogue). Houston:
Contemporary Arts
Museum, 1975.

Hickey, Dave, and Annette
DiMéo Carlozzi
LUIS JIMENEZ (exhibition
catalogue). Austin: Laguna
Gloria Art Museum, 1983.

Holmes, Jon
TEXAS: A SELF-PORTRAIT.
New York: Harry N.
Abrams, 1983.

Peterson, William
"Luis Jimenez, Jr.: Southwest
Pieta." ARTSPACE, 12
(Summer 1988), pp. 62-64.

Ratcliff, Carter
"New York Letter."
ART INTERNATIONAL, 14
(Summer 1970), p. 140.

Sandback, Amy Baker
"Signs: A Conversation
with Luis Jimenez."
ARTFORUM, 23 (September
1984), pp. 84-87.

Smith, Roberta
"Twelve Days of Texas."
ART IN AMERICA, 64 (July-
August 1976), p. 42.

Stevens, Mark
"Devotees of the Fantastic."
NEWSWEEK, September 7,
1987, pp. 66-68.

LUIS JIMENEZ   *Fiesta—Jarabe* (in progress)   1989–91*

Border Crossing—Cruzando El Rio Bravo   1989

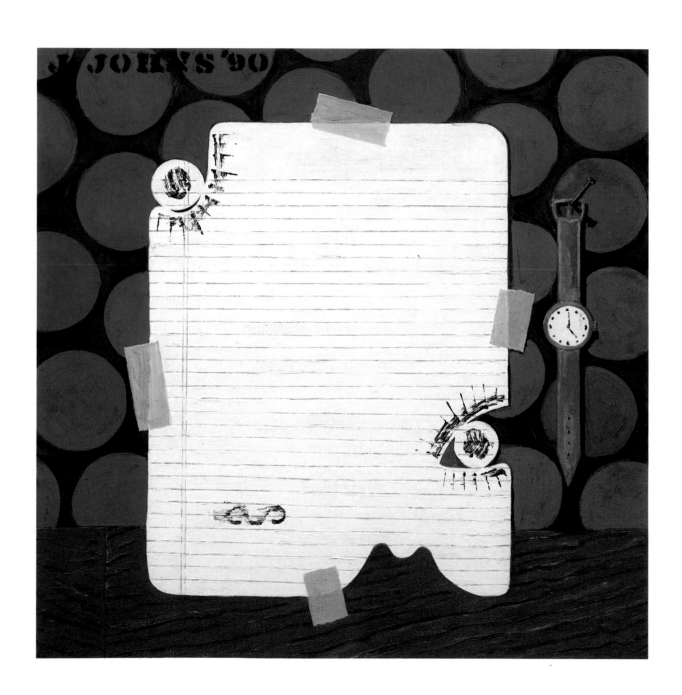

JASPER JOHNS   *Untitled*   1990 *

Born in Augusta, Georgia, 1930; studied at the University of South Carolina, Columbia (1947-48); lives in New York.

ONE-ARTIST EXHIBITIONS

1958

Leo Castelli Gallery
New York

1962

Galerie Ileana Sonnabend
Paris

1964

The Jewish Museum
New York

1977

Whitney Museum of
American Art
New York (traveled)

1978

Museum of Fine Arts
Boston

Center for the Arts,
Wesleyan University
Middletown, Connecticut
(traveled)

1979

Kunstmuseum Basel
(traveled)

1982

Whitney Museum of
American Art
New York (traveled)

1986

The Museum of Modern Art
New York (traveled)

1987

Leo Castelli Gallery
New York

The Grunewald Center for
the Graphic Arts, Wight
Art Gallery, University of
California
Los Angeles (traveled)

1988

Philadelphia Museum
of Art

1990

National Gallery of Art
Washington, D.C.
(traveled)

GROUP EXHIBITIONS

1957

The Jewish Museum
New York
"Second Generation"

1959

The Museum of Modern Art
New York
"Sixteen Americans"

Whitney Museum of
American Art
New York
"1959 Annual Exhibition:
Contemporary American
Painting"

1969

The Metropolitan Museum
of Art
New York
"New York Painting and
Sculpture: 1940-1970"

1976

The Museum of Modern Art
New York
"Drawing Now" (traveled)

1977

Kassel, West Germany
"Documenta 6"

1984

Museum of Fine Arts
Boston
"10 Painters and
Sculptors Draw"

Whitney Museum of
American Art
New York
"BLAM! The Explosion of
Pop, Minimalism, and
Performance, 1958-1964"

1988

Venice
"XLIII Biennale di Venezia"

1989

Anthony d'Offay Gallery
London
"Dancers on a Plane:
Cage, Cunningham,
Johns" (traveled)

BIBLIOGRAPHY

Cage, John, and
Alan R. Solomon
JASPER JOHNS (exhibition
catalogue). New York:
The Jewish Museum, 1964.

Crichton, Michael
JASPER JOHNS (exhibition
catalogue). New York:
Whitney Museum of
American Art, 1977.

Field, Richard S.
JASPER JOHNS: PRINTS
1960-1970 (exhibition
catalogue). Philadelphia:
Philadelphia Museum of Art,
1970.

Geelhaar, Christian
JASPER JOHNS WORKING
PROOFS (exhibition
catalogue). Basel:
Kunstmuseum Basel, 1979.

Goldman, Judith
JASPER JOHNS: 17 MONOTYPES
(exhibition catalogue). New
York: Whitney Museum of
American Art, 1982.

Rosenthal, Mark
JASPER JOHNS: WORK SINCE
1974 (exhibition catalogue).
Philadelphia: Philadelphia
Museum of Art, 1988.

Rosenthal, Nan, and
Ruth E. Fine
THE DRAWINGS OF JASPER
JOHNS (exhibition
catalogue). Washington,
D.C.: National Gallery of
Art, 1990.

JASPER JOHNS   *Untitled*   1990

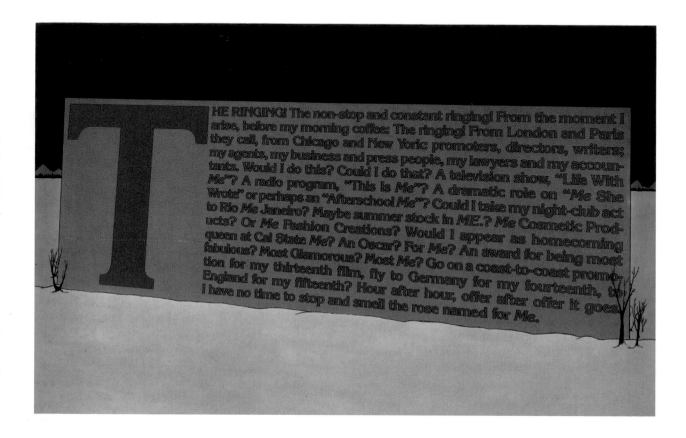

THE RINGING! The non-stop and constant ringing! From the moment I arise, before my morning coffee: The ringing! From London and Paris they call, from Chicago and New York: promoters, directors, writers; my agents, my business and press people, my lawyers and my accountants. Would I do this? Could I do that? A television show, "Life With *Me*"? A radio program, "This is *Me*"? A dramatic role on "*Me* She Wrote" or perhaps an "Afterschool *Me*"? Could I take my night-club act to Rio *Me* Janeiro? Maybe summer stock in *ME.*? *Me* Cosmetic Products? Or *Me* Fashion Creations? Would I appear as homecoming queen at Cal State *Me*? An Oscar? For *Me*? An award for being most fabulous? Most Glamorous? Most *Me*? Go on a coast-to-coast promotion for my thirteenth film, fly to Germany for my fourteenth, to England for my fifteenth? Hour after hour, offer after offer it goes. I have no time to stop and smell the rose named for *Me*.

LARRY JOHNSON

Untitled (Winter Me) 1990

Born in Long Beach, California, 1959; studied at the California Institute of the Arts, Valencia (BFA, 1982; MFA, 1984); lives in Los Angeles.

ONE-ARTIST EXHIBITIONS

1986

303 Gallery
New York

1987

Galerie Isabella Kacprzak
Stuttgart

Kuhlenschmidt/Simon
Gallery
Los Angeles

303 Gallery
New York

1989

Le Case d'Arte
Milan

303 Gallery
New York

1990

Galerie Isabella Kacprzak
Cologne

Stuart Regen Gallery
Los Angeles

303 Gallery
New York

GROUP EXHIBITIONS

1984

Artists Space
New York
"Three Artists Select
Three Artists"

1987

Hoffman/Borman Gallery
Santa Monica
"The New Who's Who"

The Renaissance Society at
The University of Chicago
and the Newport Harbor
Art Museum, Newport
Beach, California
"CalArts: Skeptical Belief(s)"

1988

The Institute of
Contemporary Art
Boston
"Utopia Post Utopia:
Configurations of Nature
and Culture in Recent
Sculpture and
Photography"

Venice
"XLIII Biennale di Venezia"

1989

The Museum of
Contemporary Art
Los Angeles
"A Forest of Signs: Art in
the Crisis of Representation"

The Museum of Modern Art
New York
"California Photography:
Remaking Make-Believe"

National Museum of
American Art,
Smithsonian Institution
Washington, D.C.
"The Photography of
Invention: American
Pictures of the 1980s"

Whitney Museum of
American Art
New York
"Image World: Art and
Media Culture"

1990

Galeries Daniel Buchholz,
Gisela Capitain, Tanja
Grunert, Max Hetzler,
Jablonka, Isabella
Kacprzak, Esther Schipper,
Monika Sprüth, Sophia
Ungers
Cologne
"Nachschub/Supply:
The Köln Show"

Milwaukee Art Museum
"Word as Image: American
Art 1960-1990" (traveled)

BIBLIOGRAPHY

Decter, Joshua
"Review." ARTS MAGAZINE,
63 (April 1989), pp. 102-03.

Goldstein, Ann,
Mary Jane Jacob, and
Howard Singerman
A FOREST OF SIGNS:
ART IN THE CRISIS OF
REPRESENTATION (exhibition
catalogue). Los Angeles:
The Museum of
Contemporary Art, 1989.

Grundberg, Andy
"Hybrids by Larry Johnson
Stretch Language to Its
Limits." THE NEW YORK
TIMES, March 30, 1990,
p. C22.

Liu, Catherine
"Larry Johnson: 303
Gallery." ARTFORUM, 29
(September 1990),
pp. 160-161.

Lord, Catherine, et al.
CALARTS: SKEPTICAL
BELIEF(S) (exhibition
catalogue). Chicago: The
Renaissance Society at
The University of Chicago;
Newport Beach, California:
Newport Harbor Art
Museum, 1987.

Rimanelli, David
"Interview." FLASH ART, no.
155 (November-December
1990), pp. 121-23.

Welchman, John
"Cal-Aesthetics." FLASH ART,
no. 141 (Summer 1988),
pp. 106-08.

THERE WERE two neighbors. One had three lop-eared rabbits, the other, three greyhound dogs. The spoiled dogs had free rein of the neighborhood, rummaging through trash by day and digging up gardens by night, which prompted the first neighbor to deliver this stern warning: Keep your greyhound dogs away from my lop-eared rabbits. Though heedful of this request, the second neighbor became careless and it was three bad dogs who greeted their dismayed owner early one morning, each with a dead and dirty lop-eared rabbit. Inhaling fast, the guilty neighbor grabbed the rabbits and, after a quick shampoo and blowdry, crept next door and placed the dead creatures back in their cage. To this day the first neighbor has never understood how three dead and buried lop-eared rabbits got back in their hutch.

LARRY JOHNSON

Untitled (Dead + Buried) 1990 *

JESUS AND I now face December with a smile. As Capricorns and think alikes, we both have birthdays within the last 10 days of the month. I know too much of birthdays and mirrors. Better to look inward than at externals, although I must admit to amusing myself one recent Sunday afternoon by spending a few hours in the bathroom with a slew of Dorian Grey, Ltd. products that had been sent for my sampling. I tried the Aloe Aid Tightening Creme, the Silicone Plus Hand and Body Lotion, the Deep Penetrating Collagen Creme, Vita-Pac Creme and Aloe Creme with Vitamin E. I cleansed myself with the Super Aloe Lemon Cleanser, used the Honey and Almond Scrub, and finished with a Face and Body Beamer and a little Eye Disguise Shading Creme. Exhausted but happy after all the work, I was greeted at dinner by a friend who commented smartly on my glistening tan.

Untitled (Jesus + I)   1990

ALEX KATZ

Black Brook 11　　1990 *

Born in New York, 1927; studied at the Cooper Union Art School, New York (1946-49), Skowhegan School of Painting and Sculpture (1949-50); lives in New York.

ONE-ARTIST EXHIBITIONS

1954

Roko Gallery
New York

1959

Tanager Gallery
New York

1960

Stable Gallery
New York

1964

Fischbach Gallery
New York

1971

Utah Museum of Fine Arts,
University of Utah
Salt Lake City (traveled)

1973

Marlborough Gallery
New York

1978

Rose Art Museum,
Brandeis University
Waltham, Massachusetts

1979

Robert Miller Gallery
New York

1986

Whitney Museum of
American Art
New York (traveled)

1988

The Brooklyn Museum
New York

The Seibu Museum of Art
Tokyo (traveled)

GROUP EXHIBITIONS

1960

Whitney Museum of
American Art
New York
"Young America 1960:
Thirty American Painters
under Thirty-six" (traveled)

1961

The Art Institute of
Chicago
"64th American Exhibition:
Paintings and Sculpture"

1967

Whitney Museum of
American Art
New York
"1967 Annual Exhibition of
Contemporary American
Painting"

1970

Colby College Art Museum
Waterville, Maine
"Landscape in Maine:
1820-1970" (traveled)

1980

The Museum of Modern Art
New York
"Printed Art: A View
of Two Decades"

Whitney Museum of
American Art
New York
"The Figurative Tradition
and the Whitney Museum
of American Art: Paintings
and Sculpture from the
Permanent Collection"

1981

Pennsylvania Academy of
the Fine Arts
Philadelphia
"Contemporary American
Realism since 1960"
(traveled)

1986

Whitechapel Art Gallery
London
"In Tandem: The Painter-
Sculptor in the Twentieth
Century"

1988

Newport Harbor Art Museum
Newport Beach, California
"The Figurative Fifties:
New York Figurative
Expressionism (traveled)

BIBLIOGRAPHY

Marshall, Richard, and
Robert Rosenblum
ALEX KATZ (exhibition
catalogue). New York:
Whitney Museum of
American Art, 1986.

Ratcliff, Carter
ALEX KATZ (exhibition
catalogue). New York:
Marlborough Gallery, 1973.

Sandler, Irving
ALEX KATZ. New York:
Harry N. Abrams, 1979.

Sandler, Irving
ALEX KATZ: 1957-1959
(exhibition catalogue).
New York: Robert Miller
Gallery, 1981.

Scholnick, Michael
ALEX KATZ: FROM THE
EARLY 60s (exhibition
catalogue). New York:
Robert Miller Gallery, 1987.

Smith, Roberta
ALEX KATZ IN THE SEVENTIES
(exhibition catalogue).
Waltham, Massachusetts:
Rose Art Museum, Brandeis
University, 1978.

Walker, Barry
ALEX KATZ: A PRINT
RETROSPECTIVE (exhibition
catalogue). New York: The
Brooklyn Museum, 1987.

ALEX KATZ

Black Brook 4 1989

Black Brook 10   1990

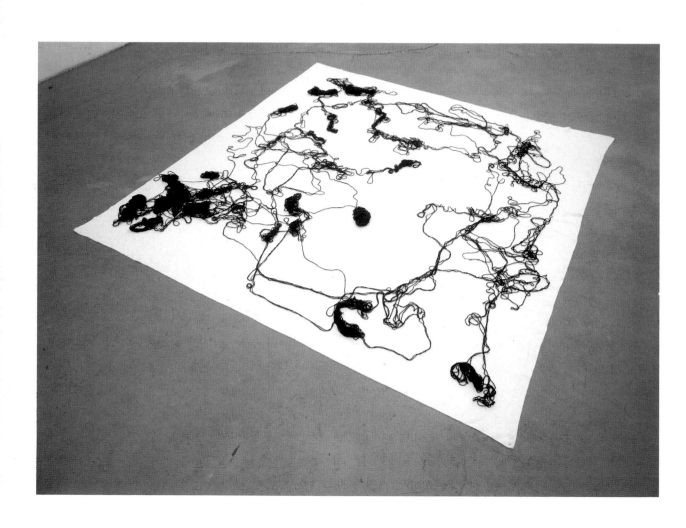

MIKE KELLEY

Untitled   1990

Born in Dearborn, Michigan, 1954; studied at the University of Michigan, Ann Arbor (BFA, 1976), California Institute of the Arts, Valencia (MFA, 1978); lives in Los Angeles.

ONE-ARTIST EXHIBITIONS

1978

LACE
Los Angeles (performance)

La Jolla Museum of Contemporary Art
(performance)

1979

Foundation for Art Resources
Los Angeles (performance)

1981

Riko Mizuno Gallery
Los Angeles

1982

Metro Pictures
New York

1983

Rosamund Felsen Gallery
Los Angeles

1988

Metro Pictures
New York

The Renaissance Society at The University of Chicago

1989

Galerie Peter Pakesch
Vienna

Metro Pictures
New York

Rosamund Felsen Gallery
Los Angeles

1990

Galerie Ghislaine Hussenot
Paris

Metro Pictures
New York

Rosamund Felsen Gallery
Los Angeles

GROUP EXHIBITIONS

1983

The Museum of Contemporary Art
Los Angeles
"The First Show: Painting and Sculpture from Eight Collections, 1940-1980"

1987

MIT List Visual Arts Center
Cambridge, Massachusetts
"LA: Hot and Cool: The Eighties"

The Renaissance Society at The University of Chicago and the Newport Harbor Art Museum, Newport Beach, California
"CalArts: Skeptical Belief(s)"

1988

The Institute of Contemporary Art and the Museum of Fine Arts
Boston
"The BiNATIONAL: American Art of the Late 80s" (traveled)

Venice
"XLIII Biennale di Venezia"

Whitney Museum of American Art
New York
"Recent Drawings: George Condo, Mike Kelley, Ellen Phelan, Janis Provisor"

1989

The Museum of Contemporary Art
Los Angeles
"A Forest of Signs: Art in the Crisis of Representation"

Whitney Museum of American Art
New York
"1989 Biennial Exhibition"

1990

Museum of Fine Arts
Boston
"Figuring the Body"

BIBLIOGRAPHY

Armstrong, Richard
RECENT DRAWINGS: GEORGE CONDO, MIKE KELLEY, ELLEN PHELAN, JANIS PROVISOR (exhibition brochure). New York: Whitney Museum of American Art, 1988.

Friis-Hansen, Dana, Dennis Cooper, Rita Valencia, et al.
LA: HOT AND COOL: THE EIGHTIES (exhibition catalogue). Cambridge, Massachusetts: MIT List Visual Arts Center, 1987.

Goldstein, Ann, Mary Jane Jacob, and Howard Singerman
A FOREST OF SIGNS: ART IN THE CRISIS OF REPRESENTATION (exhibition catalogue). Los Angeles: The Museum of Contemporary Art, 1989.

Knight, Christopher
MIKE KELLEY (exhibition catalogue). Cologne: Jablonka Galerie, 1989.

Lord, Catherine, et al.
CALARTS: SKEPTICAL BELIEF(S) (exhibition catalogue). Chicago: The Renaissance Society at The University of Chicago; Newport Beach, California: Newport Harbor Art Museum, 1987.

Miller, John, and Howard Singerman
MIKE KELLEY: THREE PROJECTS (exhibition catalogue). Chicago: The Renaissance Society at The University of Chicago, 1988.

MIKE KELLEY   *Empathy Displacement: Humanoid Morphology (2nd and 3rd Remove) #7*   1990

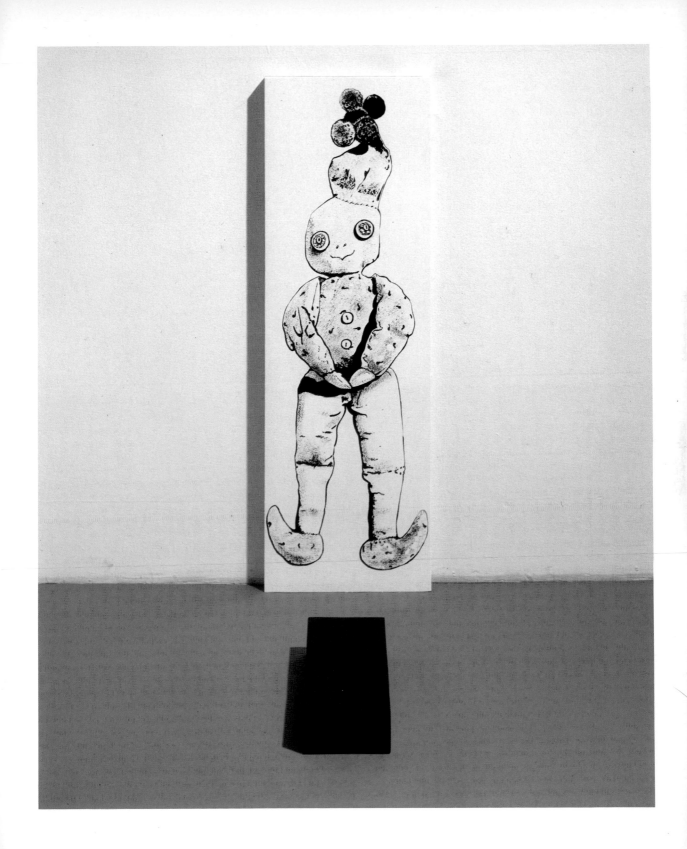

Empathy Displacement: Humanoid Morphology (2nd and 3rd Remove) #9   1990

ELLSWORTH KELLY

Green Curve with White Panel 1989

Born in Newburgh, New York, 1923; studied at Pratt Institute, Brooklyn, New York (1941-42), School of the Museum of Fine Arts, Boston (1946-47); lives in New York.

ONE-ARTIST EXHIBITIONS

1982

Whitney Museum of American Art
New York (traveled)

1986

Blum Helman Warehouse
New York

1987

Blum Helman Gallery
New York

The Detroit Institute of Arts (traveled)

Museum of Fine Arts
Boston

1988

Blum Helman Gallery
New York

1990

Leo Castelli Graphics
New York

65 Thompson Street
New York

Susan Sheehan Gallery
New York

GROUP EXHIBITIONS

1982

The Aspen Center for the Visual Arts
"Castelli and His Artists: Twenty-Five Years" (traveled)

1984

Stedelijk Museum
Amsterdam
"La grande parade"

1985

The Aldrich Museum of Contemporary Art
Ridgefield, Connecticut
"A Second Talent: Painters and Sculptors Who Are Also Photographers"

The Solomon R. Guggenheim Museum
New York
"Transformations in Sculpture: Four Decades of American and European Art"

Whitney Museum of American Art
New York
"Drawing Acquisitions 1981-1985"

1986

MIT List Visual Arts Center
Cambridge, Massachusetts
"Natural Forms and Forces: Abstract Images in American Sculpture" (traveled)

1987

The Museum of Modern Art
New York
"Philip Johnson: Selected Gifts"

The Phillips Collection
Washington, D.C.
"After Matisse"

1990

Richard Green Gallery
Santa Monica
"Five Artists from Coenties Slip, 1956-1965: Paintings by Robert Indiana, Ellsworth Kelly, Agnes Martin, James Rosenquist and Jack Youngerman"

The Museum of Modern Art
New York
"Artist's Choice: Fragmentation and the Single Form" (curated by Ellsworth Kelly)

BIBLIOGRAPHY

Axsom, Richard H. THE PRINTS OF ELLSWORTH KELLY: A CATALOGUE RAISONNÉ, 1949-1985. New York: Hudson Hills Press and The American Federation of Arts, 1987.

Fairbrother, Trevor J. ELLSWORTH KELLY: SEVEN PAINTINGS (1952-55/1987) (exhibition catalogue). Boston: Museum of Fine Arts, 1987.

Kelly, Ellsworth ELLSWORTH KELLY: FRAGMENTATION AND THE SINGLE FORM (exhibition brochure). New York: The Museum of Modern Art, 1990.

Kelly, Ellsworth 256 FARBEN & BASICS OF FORM (exhibition catalogue). Zurich: Stiftung für Konstruktive und Konkrete Kunst, 1989.

Kline, Katy ELLSWORTH KELLY: SMALL SCULPTURE 1958-1987 (exhibition catalogue). Cambridge, Massachusetts: MIT List Visual Arts Center, 1988.

Rose, Barbara THE BARCELONA EXPERIENCE: THE ROLE OF SCULPTURE IN CONTEMPORARY URBAN ENVIRONMENTS (exhibition catalogue). New York: Spanish Institute, 1987.

Sandler, Irving THE NEW YORK SCHOOL: THE PAINTERS AND SCULPTORS OF THE FIFTIES. New York: Harper & Row, 1978.

Sims, Patterson, and Emily Rauh Pulitzer ELLSWORTH KELLY: SCULPTURE (exhibition catalogue). New York: Whitney Museum of American Art, 1982.

ELLSWORTH KELLY

Blue Panel with Green Curve   1989 *

Orange Red Relief (for Delphine Seyrig)   1991

WHAT'S THE FASTEST WAY TO MAKE A MILLION?

Invent something....something useful like inflatable soles for orthopedic shoes, or a soundproof tent to cover the TV <u>and</u> the kids. Maybe you should target a specific group ... that's it, essence of Irish stew, made in Dublin and exported to New Jersey. Say, what about a white trash restaurant ... you could serve opossum ... no? Okay, something for the masses then ... a square football?

PECUNIA N&N OLET

Born in Fort Dodge, Iowa, 1941; studied at the College of St. Theresa, Winona, Minnesota (BA, 1963), Instituto Pius XII, Florence (MA, 1965), St. Martin's School of Art, London (Post-Graduate Diploma, 1970); lives in New York.

ONE-ARTIST EXHIBITIONS

1976

Institute of Contemporary Arts
London

1977

Museum of Modern Art
Oxford, England

1981

Anna Leonowens Gallery
Halifax, England

1982

George Paton Gallery
Melbourne

1985

Fruitmarket Gallery
Edinburgh (traveled)

1986

A Space
Toronto

1988

Galerie Powerhouse
Montreal

LACE
Los Angeles

1989

CEPA
Buffalo

Postmasters Gallery
New York

1990

The New Museum of
Contemporary Art
New York (traveled)

GROUP EXHIBITIONS

1979

Musée d'Art Moderne de
la Ville de Paris
"Un certain art anglais"

1980

Institute of Contemporary
Arts
London
"Issue: Social Strategies by
Women Artists"

1982

Art Gallery of
New South Wales
Sydney
"The 4th Biennale of Sydney"

1983

Protetch-McNeil Gallery
New York
"The Revolutionary Power
of Woman's Laughter"
(traveled)

1984

Yale Center for British Art
New Haven
"The Critical Eye/I"

1985

The New Museum of
Contemporary Art
New York
"Difference: On
Representation and
Sexuality" (traveled)

1986

Artists Space
New York
"The Fairy Tale: Politics,
Desire, and Everyday Life"

Collins Gallery, University
of Strathclyde
Glasgow
"Identity/Desire:
Representing the Body"

1987

Ikon Gallery
Birmingham, England
"Conceptual Clothing"
(traveled)

The Institute of
Contemporary Art
Boston
"The British Edge"

Institute of Contemporary
Arts
London
"State of the Art" (traveled)

BIBLIOGRAPHY

Bryson, Norman, Hal
Foster, Griselda Pollock,
and Marcia Tucker
MARY KELLY (exhibition
catalogue). New York:
The New Museum of
Contemporary Art, 1990.

Foster, Hal
"The Future of an Illusion
(or the Contemporary Artist
as Cargo Cultist)." In
ENDGAME: REFERENCE AND
SIMULATION IN RECENT
PAINTING AND SCULPTURE
(exhibition catalogue).
Boston: The Institute of
Contemporary Art, 1986.

Iversen, Margaret
"Fashioning Feminine
Identity." ART
INTERNATIONAL, no. 2
(Spring 1988), pp. 52-57.

Kelly, Mary
"From Corpus." In TAKING
OUR TIME, ed. Frieda
Forman. Oxford: Pergamon
Press, 1989.

Kelly, Mary
"Re-Presenting the Body."
In PSYCHOANALYSIS AND
CULTURAL THEORY:
THRESHOLDS, James
Donald, ed. London:
Macmillan, 1990.

Marnicola, Paula
"Mary Kelly." ARTFORUM, 26
(Summer 1988), pp. 142-43.

Watney, Simon
"Mary Kelly." ARTSCRIBE
INTERNATIONAL, no. 62
(March–April 1987),
pp. 71-72.

MARY KELLY

Conju from *Interim Part II: Pecunia*   1989

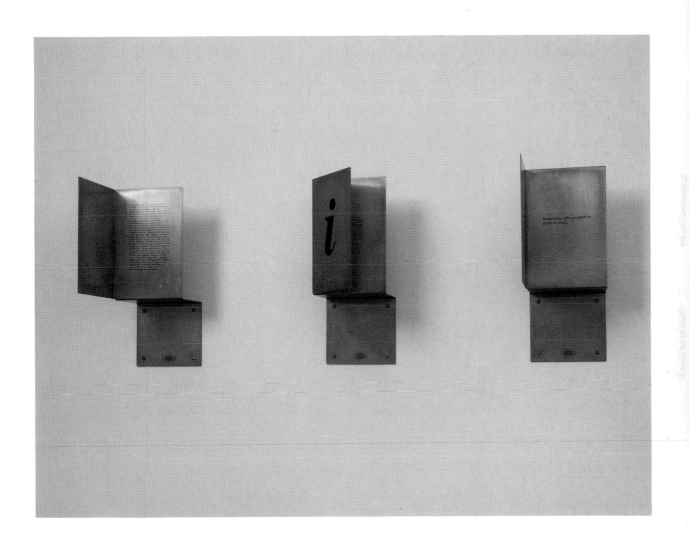

Filia from *Interim Part II: Pecunia* (detail)   1989

LOUISE LAWLER

Glass and Local Storms 1990*

Born in Bronxville, New York, 1947; studied at Cornell University, Ithaca, New York (BFA, 1969); lives in New York.

ONE-ARTIST EXHIBITIONS

1981

Jancar/Kuhlenschmidt
Gallery
Los Angeles

1984

Wadsworth Atheneum
Hartford

1985

Nature Morte Gallery
New York

1987

Galerie Isabella Kacprzak
Stuttgart

Kuhlenschmidt/Simon
Gallery
Los Angeles

Metro Pictures
New York

The Museum of Modern Art
New York

1988

Galerie Yvon Lambert
Paris

1989

Metro Pictures
New York

1990

Museum of Fine Arts
Boston

Galerie Yvon Lambert
Paris

GROUP EXHIBITIONS

1972

Protetch-Rivkin Gallery
Washington, D.C.

1978

Artists Space
New York
"Group Exhibition"

1981

Castelli Graphics
New York
"Love Is Blind"

1984

Diane Brown Gallery
New York
"Ideal Settings"

1986

The New Museum of
Contemporary Art
New York
"The Art of Memory/The
Loss of History"

Sala de Exposiciones,
Fundación Caja de Pensiones
Madrid
"Art and Its Double:
A New York Perspective"

1987

Moderna Museet
Stockholm
"Implosion: A Postmodern
Perspective"

1989

The Museum of
Contemporary Art
Los Angeles
"A Forest of Signs: Art in
the Crisis of Representation"

National Museum of
American Art,
Smithsonian Institution
Washington, D.C.
"The Photography of
Invention: American
Pictures of the 1980s"

Whitney Museum of
American Art, Downtown
at Federal Reserve Plaza
New York
"The Desire of the Museum"

1990

Museum of Contemporary
Hispanic Art, The New
Museum of Contemporary
Art, and The Studio
Museum in Harlem
New York
"The Decade Show:
Frameworks of Identity
in the 1980s"

BIBLIOGRAPHY

Altaló, Vicenç, Dan
Cameron, José Carlos
Cataño, Régis Durand,
and Chantal Grande
TO BE AND NOT TO BE
(exhibition catalogue).
Barcelona: Centre d'Art
Santa Mònica, 1990.

Bankowsky, Jack
"Spotlight: Louise Lawler."
FLASH ART, no. 133 (April
1987), p. 86.

Gilbert-Rolfe, Jeremy
"The Price of Goodness."
ARTSCRIBE INTERNATIONAL,
no. 78 (November-
December 1989), pp. 48-53.

Gintz, Claude
THE SAME AND THE OTHER
IN THE WORK OF LOUISE
LAWLER (exhibition
catalogue). Saint-Étienne,
France: Maison de la
Culture et de la
Communication de Saint-
Étienne, 1986.

Joselit, David
"Investigating the Real." ART
IN AMERICA, 76 (May 1988),
pp. 148-55.

Linker, Kate
"Rites of Exchange."
ARTFORUM, 25 (November
1986), pp. 99-101.

Storr, Robert
"Louise Lawler: Unpacking
the White Cube." PARKETT,
no. 22 (December 1989),
pp. 105-08.

LOUISE LAWLER

(Bought from Leo Castelli in 1963 and Bought from Martha Jackson around 1960)
Bought from Count Panza di Biumo in 1985 1989

Detail 1990*

ROY LICHTENSTEIN

Interior with Built-in Bar   1991*

Born in New York, 1923; studied at the Art Students League (1940), Ohio State University, Columbus (BFA, 1946, MFA, 1949); lives in New York.

ONE-ARTIST EXHIBITIONS

1951
Carlebach Gallery
New York

1952
John Heller Gallery
New York

1962
Leo Castelli Gallery
New York

1967
Pasadena Art Museum
(traveled)

1969
The Solomon R.
Guggenheim Museum
New York (traveled)

1975
Centre National d'Art
Contemporain
Paris (traveled)

1978
The Institute of
Contemporary Art
Boston

1981
The Saint Louis Art Museum
(traveled)

1983
Leo Castelli Gallery
New York

1987
The Museum of Modern Art
New York (traveled)

1989
Leo Castelli Gallery
New York

GROUP EXHIBITIONS

1951
The Brooklyn Museum
New York
"5th National Print Annual
Exhibition"

1963
The Art Institute of
Chicago
"66th Annual American
Exhibition"

The Oakland Museum
"Pop Art USA"

The Solomon R.
Guggenheim Museum
New York
"Six Painters and the Object"

1966
Venice
"XXXIII Biennale di Venezia"

1967
Whitney Museum of
American Art
New York
"1967 Annual Exhibition of
Contemporary American
Painting"

The Metropolitan Museum
of Art
New York
"New York Painting and
Sculpture: 1940-1970"

1984
Whitney Museum of
American Art
New York
"Blam! The Explosion of
Pop, Minimalism, and
Performance 1958-1964"

1986
Whitechapel Art Gallery
London
"In Tandem: The Painter-
Sculptor in the Twentieth
Century"

1987
University Art Museum,
University of California,
Berkeley
"Made in USA: An
Americanization in Modern
Art, the '50s and '60s"
(traveled)

1990
Milwaukee Art Museum
"Word As Image: American
Art 1960-1990" (traveled)

The Museum of Modern Art
New York
"High and Low: Modern Art
and Popular Culture"
(traveled)

BIBLIOGRAPHY

Alloway, Lawrence
ROY LICHTENSTEIN
(exhibition catalogue).
Houston: Contemporary
Arts Museum, 1972.

Alloway, Lawrence
ROY LICHTENSTEIN. New
York: Abbeville Press, 1983.

Coplans, John
ROY LICHTENSTEIN
(exhibition catalogue).
Pasadena: Pasadena Art
Museum, 1967.

Cowart, Jack
ROY LICHTENSTEIN, 1970-
1980 (exhibition catalogue).
New York and Saint Louis:
The Saint Louis Art Museum,
1981.

Rose, Bernice
THE DRAWINGS OF ROY
LICHTENSTEIN (exhibition
catalogue). New York: The
Museum of Modern Art,
1987.

Waldman, Diane
ROY LICHTENSTEIN
(exhibition catalogue).
New York: The Solomon
R. Guggenheim Museum, 1969.

ROY LICHTENSTEIN

Interior with African Mask   1991

Interior with Mirrored Wall   1991

GLENN LIGON

Untitled (I Remember the Very Day That I Became Colored) 1990

Born in New York, 1960; studied at the Rhode Island School of Design, Providence (1980), Wesleyan University, Middletown, Connecticut (BA, 1982), Independent Study Program, Whitney Museum of American Art, New York (1985), National Studio Program, The Clocktower Gallery, The Institute for Contemporary Art, New York (1989-90); lives in New York.

ONE-ARTIST EXHIBITIONS

1982

Davison Art Center,
Wesleyan University
Middletown, Connecticut

1990

BACA Downtown
Brooklyn, New York
"How It Feels to Be
Colored Me"

P.S. 1 Museum,
The Institute for
Contemporary Art
Long Island City, New York

GROUP EXHIBITIONS

1984

The Bronx Museum of
the Arts
New York
"Artist in the Marketplace:
The Fourth Annual
Exhibition"

1989

The Drawing Center
New York
"Selections 46"

1990

The Clocktower Gallery,
The Institute for
Contemporary Art
New York
"Open Studio"

The New Museum of
Contemporary Art at
Marine Midland Bank
New York
"Spent: Currency, Security,
and Art on Deposit"

Stedman Art Gallery,
Rutgers, The State
University of New Jersey
Camden
"Rutgers National '90:
Works on Paper"

BIBLIOGRAPHY

Faust, Gretchen
"New York in Review: Glenn
Ligon." ARTS MAGAZINE, 65
(December 1990), p. 104.

Wilde, Betty
ARTIST IN THE
MARKETPLACE: THE FOURTH
ANNUAL EXHIBITION
(exhibition catalogue). New
York: The Bronx Museum
of the Arts, 1984.

GLENN LIGON

Untitled (I Do Not Always Feel Colored) 1990

I FEEL MOST COLORED WHEN I AM THROWN
AGAINST A SHARP WHITE BACKGROUND. I
FEEL MOST COLORED WHEN I AM THROWN
AGAINST A SHARP WHITE BACKGROUND.
I FEEL MOST COLORED WHEN I AM THROWN
AGAINST A SHARP WHITE BACKGROUND. I
FEEL MOST COLORED WHEN I AM THROWN
AGAINST A SHARP WHITE BACKGROUND. I
FEEL MOST COLORED WHEN I AM THROWN A
GAINST A SHARP WHITE BACKGROUND. I
FEEL MOST COLORED WHEN I AM THROWN A
GAINST A SHARP WHITE BACKGROUND. I FEEL
MOST COLORED WHEN I AM THROWN AGAINST
A SHARP WHITE BACKGROUND. I FEEL MOST
COLORED WHEN I AM THROWN AGAINST A
SHARP WHITE BACKGROUND. I FEEL MOST
COLORED WHEN I AM THROWN AGAINST A
SHARP WHITE BACKGROUND. I FEEL MOST CO
LORED WHEN I AM THROWN AGAINST A SHARP
WHITE BACKGROUND. I FEEL MOST COLORED
WHEN I AM THROWN AGAINST A SHARP WHITE
BACKGROUND. I FEEL MOST COLORED WHEN
I AM THROWN AGAINST A SHARP WHITE BACK
GROUND. I FEEL MOST COLORED WHEN I
AM THROWN AGAINST A SHARP WHITE BACK
GROUND. I FEEL MOST COLORED WHEN I AM
THROWN AGAINST A SHARP WHITE BACKGRO
UND. I FEEL MOST COLORED WHEN I AM
THROWN AGAINST A SHARP WHITE BACKGROU
ND. I FEEL MOST COLORED WHEN I AM THROW
N AGAINST A SHARP WHITE BACKGROUND. I
FEEL MOST COLORED WHEN I AM THROWN
AGAINST A SHARP WHITE BACKGROUND. I AM
FEEL MOST COLORED WHEN I AM THROWN
AGAINST A SHARP WHITE BACKGROUND. I
FEEL MOST COLORED WHEN I AM THROWN A
GAINST A SHARP WHITE BACKGROUND. I
FEEL MOST COLORED WHEN I AM THROWN
AGAINST A SHARP WHITE BACKGROUND. I
FEEL MOST COLORED WHEN I AM THROWN A
GAINST A SHARP WHITE BACKGROUND. I FEEL
MOST COLORED WHEN I AM THROWN AGAINST
A SHARP WHITE BACKGROUND. I FEEL MOST
COLORED WHEN I AM THROWN AGAINST A
SHARP WHITE BACKGROUND. I FEEL MOST
COLORED WHEN I AM THROWN AGAINST A
SHARP WHITE BACKGROUND. I FEEL MOST CO
LORED WHEN I AM THROWN AGAINST A SHARP
WHITE BACKGROUND. I FEEL MOST COLORED
WHEN I AM THROWN AGAINST A SHARP WHITE
BACKGROUND. I FEEL MOST COLORED WHEN
I AM THROWN AGAINST A SHARP WHITE BACK
GROUND. I FEEL MOST COLORED WHEN I
AM THROWN AGAINST A SHARP WHITE BACK
GROUND. I FEEL MOST COLORED WHEN I
THROWN AGAINST A SHARP WHITE BACKGR
UND I FEEL MOST COLORED WHEN I AM THROW
AGAINST A SHARP WHITE BACKGROUND I
FEEL MOST COLORED WHEN I AM THROWN A
GAINST A SHARP WHITE BACKGROUND I FEEL
MOST COLORED WHEN I AM THROWN AGAINST
A SHARP WHITE BACKGROUND I FEEL
MOST COLORED WHEN I AM THROWN AGAINST
A SHARP WHITE BACKGROUND I FEEL MOST
COLORED WHEN I AM THROWN AGAINST A
SHARP WHITE BACKGROUND I FEEL MOST
COLORED WHEN I AM THROWN AGAINST A
SHARP WHITE BACKGROUND I FEEL MOST
COLORED WHEN I AM THROWN AGAINST A
SHARP WHITE BACKGROUND I FEEL MOST
COLORED WHEN I AM THROWN AGAINST A SH
SHARP WHITE BACKGROUND I FEEL MOST
COLORED WHEN I AM THROWN AGAINST A SH
ARP WHITE BACKGROUND I FEEL MOST
THROWN AGAINST A SHARP
WHITE BACKGROUND I FEEL MOST COLORED
WHEN I AM THROWN AGAINST A SHARP WHITE
BACKGROUND I FEEL MOST COLORED WHEN

Untitled (I Feel Most Colored When I Am Thrown Against a Sharp White Background)   1990

DONALD LIPSKI

White, No Tracer 1990*

Born in Chicago, 1947; studied at the University of Wisconsin, Madison (BA, 1970), Cranbrook Academy of Art, Bloomfield Hills, Michigan (MFA, 1973); lives in New York.

ONE-ARTIST EXHIBITIONS

1975

Everson Museum of Art
Syracuse, New York

O.K. Harris Gallery
New York

1978

Artists Space
New York

1979

The Museum of Modern Art
New York

1980

Fort Worth Art Museum

Pittsburgh Center for
the Arts

1983

Germans van Eck Gallery
New York

1984

Margo Leavin Gallery
Los Angeles

Rhona Hoffman Gallery
Chicago

1989

Danforth Museum of Art
Framingham, Massachusetts

1990

The Fabric Workshop
Philadelphia (traveled)

Freedman Gallery,
Albright College
Reading, Pennsylvania
(traveled)

Lennon Weinberg Gallery
New York

GROUP EXHIBITIONS

1979

Hunter College Art Gallery
New York
"Sculptors' Photographs"

1981

Neuberger Museum, State
University of New York,
College at Purchase
"Seven Artists"

The New Museum of
Contemporary Art
New York
"Stay Tuned"

1983

The New Museum of
Contemporary Art
New York
"Language, Drama, Source,
and Vision"

1985

The Brooklyn Museum
New York
"Working in Brooklyn/
Sculpture"

1986

The Clocktower, Institute
for Art and Urban Resources
New York
"Donald Lipski, Matt
Mullican, Kiki Smith"

1988

The Arts Club of Chicago
"The Objects of Sculpture"

University Art Galleries,
Wright State University
Dayton, Ohio
"Redefining the Object"

Walker Art Center
Minneapolis
"Sculpture Inside Outside"
(traveled)

1990

The Morris Museum
Morristown, New Jersey
"Diverse Representations
1990"

BIBLIOGRAPHY

Benezra, Neal
THE OBJECTS OF SCULPTURE
(exhibition catalogue).
Chicago: The Arts Club of
Chicago, 1988.

Cameron, Dan
REDEFINING THE OBJECT
(exhibition catalogue).
Dayton, Ohio: University
Art Galleries, Wright State
University, 1988.

Goldwater, Marge
DONALD LIPSKI (exhibition
catalogue). Fort Worth: Fort
Worth Art Museum, 1980.

Kotik, Charlotta
WORKING IN BROOKLYN/
SCULPTURE (exhibition
catalogue). New York: The
Brooklyn Museum, 1985.

Kuspit, Donald
DONALD LIPSKI (exhibition
catalogue). New York:
Germans van Eck Gallery,
1985.

Rubin, David S.
DONALD LIPSKI: POETIC
SCULPTURE (exhibition
catalogue). Reading,
Pennsylvania: Freedman
Gallery, Albright College,
1990.

Wylie, Elizabeth
DONALD LIPSKI: RECENT
WORK (exhibition
catalogue). Framingham,
Massachusetts: Danforth
Museum of Art, 1989.

DONALD LIPSKI

Untitled #91–8   1991

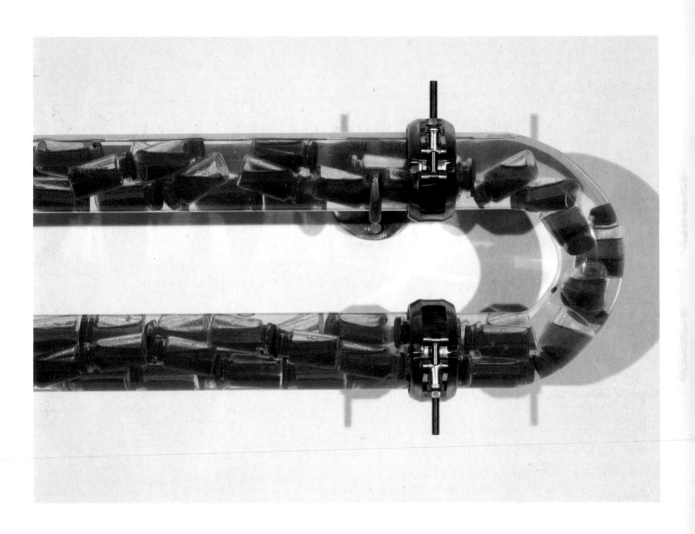

Blood #1 (detail)　1991

SALLY MANN

The 42-Pound Squash   1989

Born in Lexington, Virginia, 1951; studied at Bennington College, Bennington, Vermont (1969-71), Hollins College, Roanoke, Virginia (BA, 1974; MA, 1975); lives in Lexington, Virginia.

ONE-ARTIST EXHIBITIONS

1977

The Corcoran Gallery of Art
Washington, D.C.

1979

Greenville County Museum
of Art
South Carolina

1984

Focus Gallery
San Francisco

1986

Marcuse Pfeifer Gallery
New York

1988

Marcuse Pfeifer Gallery
New York

The Southeastern Center
for Contemporary Art
Winston-Salem,
North Carolina

1989

Museum of Photographic Art
San Diego

1990

The Cleveland Center for
Contemporary Art

Firehouse Gallery
Houston

Houk Gallery
Chicago

GROUP EXHIBITIONS

1980

The Chrysler Museum
Norfolk, Virginia
"Not Fade Away: Four
Contemporary Virginia
Photographers"

1982

Daniel Wolff Gallery
New York
"The New Pictorialism"

Friends of Photography
Carmel, California
"The Ferguson Grant
Winners Show"

1985

Visual Arts Gallery,
University of Alabama
in Birmingham
"Big Shots: 20 × 24 Polaroid
Photographs" (traveled)

1988

Virginia Museum of
Fine Arts
Richmond
"Un/Common Ground:
Virginia Artists 1988"

1990

Hallwalls
Buffalo
"Insect Politics"

International Center of
Photography Midtown
New York
"The Indomitable Spirit:
Photographers & Friends
United Against AIDS"
(traveled)

New Orleans Museum
of Art
"Awards in the Visual Arts
19" (traveled)

Robert Klein Gallery
Boston
"Provocations: Challenging
Contemporary Photographs"

St. Olaf's College
Northfield, Minnesota
"Her Family"

BIBLIOGRAPHY

Ballou, Bari
STILL TIME: THE
PHOTOGRAPHS OF SALLY
MANN (exhibition
catalogue). Clifton Forge,
Virginia: Allegheny
Highlands Arts and Crafts
Center, Inc., 1988.

Brandt, Frederick R.,
Julia W. Boyd, Margo
A. Crutchfield, and
H. Ashley Kistler
UN/COMMON GROUND:
VIRGINIA ARTISTS 1988
(exhibition catalogue).
Richmond: Virginia
Museum of Fine Arts, 1988.

Carothers, Steven, and
Gail Roberts
PHOTOGRAPHER'S
DIALOGUE: POPULAR AND
PREFERRED IMAGERY IN
AMERICAN PHOTOGRAPHY
(exhibition catalogue). Boca
Raton, Florida: Boca Raton
Museum of Art, 1990.

Cottingham, Laura
"Sally Mann/Marcuse
Pfeifer." FLASH ART, no. 137
(December 1987), p. 107.

Risatti, Howard
BIG SHOTS: 20 × 24
POLAROID PHOTOGRAPHS
(exhibition catalogue).
Birmingham: Visual Arts
Gallery, University of
Alabama, 1985.

Sullivan, Constance, ed.
WOMEN PHOTOGRAPHERS.
New York: Harry N.
Abrams, 1990.

Vetrocq, Marcia E.
"AVA 9." ARTS MAGAZINE, 65
(September 1990), p. 80.

Weiermair, Peter
PROSPECT PHOTOGRAPHIE
(exhibition catalogue).
Frankfurt: Frankfurter
Kunstverein, 1989.

SALLY MANN

Gorjus 1989

Sorry Game 1989

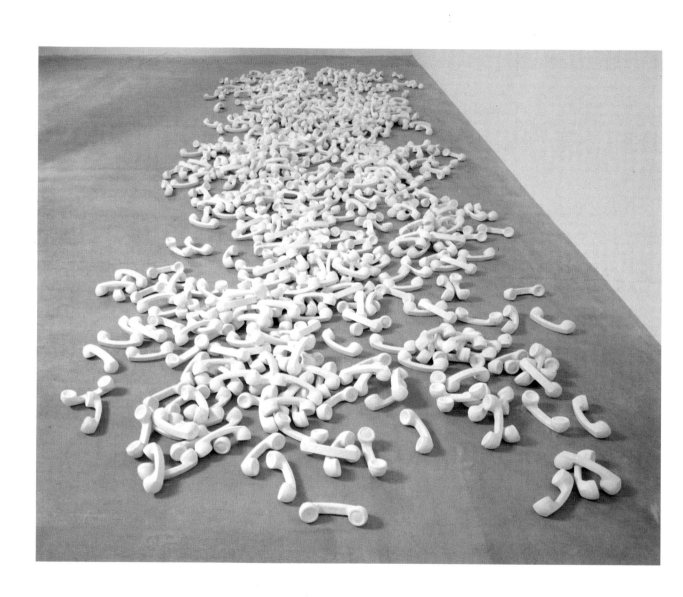

CHRISTIAN MARCLAY

Bone Yard 1990

Born in San Rafael, California, 1955; studied at the École Supérieure d'Art Visuel, Geneva (1975-77), Massachusetts College of Art, Boston (BFA, 1980); lives in New York.

ONE-ARTIST EXHIBITIONS

1987

The Clocktower, Institute for Art and Urban Resources
New York

1988

Tom Cugliani Gallery
New York

1989

Shedhalle Zürich

Tom Cugliani Gallery
New York

1990

Hirshhorn Museum and Sculpture Garden, Smithsonian Institution
Washington, D.C.

Tom Cugliani Gallery
New York

GROUP EXHIBITIONS

1983

Washington Project for the Arts
Washington, D.C.
"Sound Seen"

1985

Hayden Gallery, Massachusetts Institute of Technology
Cambridge
"On the Wall/On the Air: Artists Make Noise"

1988

Dia Art Foundation
New York
"Group Material: 'Politics and Election'"

Emily Harvey Gallery
New York
"Extended Play"

1989

The New Museum of Contemporary Art
New York
"Strange Attractors: Signs of Chaos"

1990

Andrea Rosen Gallery
New York
"The Stendhal Syndrome: The Cure"

L'Espace Lyonnais d'Art Contemporain, Centre d'Échanges de Perrache
Lyons
"Le statut de la sculpture" (traveled)

Massimo Audiello Gallery
New York
"Loving Correspondences"

University Art Galleries, Wright State University
Dayton, Ohio
"Assembled"

Wexner Center for the Visual Arts, Ohio State University
Columbus
"New Work For New Spaces: Into the 90s"

BIBLIOGRAPHY

Cameron, Dan
"Pop 'n' Rock." ART ISSUES, no. 7 (November 1989), pp. 9-12.

Cruz, Amada
DIRECTIONS: CHRISTIAN MARCLAY (exhibition brochure). Washington, D.C.: Hirshhorn Museum and Sculpture Garden, Smithsonian Institution, 1990.

Marclay, Christian
EXTENDED PLAY (exhibition catalogue). New York: Emily Harvey Gallery, 1988.

McCormick, Carlo
"Poptometry." ARTFORUM, 24 (November 1985), pp. 87-91.

Reust, Hans Rudolf
"Christian Marclay." ARTSCRIBE INTERNATIONAL, no. 79 (January-February 1990), p. 87.

Rockwell, John
"Marclay, Hoberman, Sound and Fury." THE NEW YORK TIMES, October 22, 1989, section 2, p. 64.

Rubinstein, Meyer Raphael, and Daniel Wiener
"Christian Marclay/Tom Cugliani." FLASH ART, no. 147 (Summer 1989), p. 149.

Saltz, Jerry
"Beautiful Dreamer: Christian Marclay's 'The Beatles.'" ARTS MAGAZINE, 64 (December 1989), pp. 21-22.

Schwendenwien, Jude
"Christian Marclay/The Hirshhorn Museum." CONTEMPORANEA, no. 22 (November 1990), p. 95.

Smith, Roberta
"Christian Marclay." THE NEW YORK TIMES, May 20, 1988.

CHRISTIAN MARCLAY

Sound Sheet 1990

Tape Fall   1989–90*

DAVID McDERMOTT AND PETER McGOUGH   *Pail in Equilibrium on a Stick, 1884* from *Les Recréations Scientifiques, 1884*   1990

DAVID McDERMOTT
Born in Hollywood, California, 1952; studied at Syracuse University, New York (1970-74); lives in New York.

PETER McGOUGH
Born in Syracuse, New York, 1958; studied at Syracuse University, New York (1976), Fashion Institute of Technology, New York (1977); lives in New York.

TWO-ARTIST EXHIBITIONS

1985

Massimo Audiello Gallery
New York

1986

Frankfurter Kunstverein
Frankfurt

Galleria Lucio Amelio
Naples

Massimo Audiello Gallery
New York

Pat Hearn Gallery
New York

1987

Mario Diacono Gallery
Boston

1988

Massimo Audiello Gallery
New York

1989

Robert Miller Gallery
New York

1990

Fraenkel Gallery
San Francisco

Sperone Westwater Gallery
New York

GROUP EXHIBITIONS

1983

Monique Knowlton Gallery
New York
"Intoxication"

1984

Holly Solomon Gallery
New York
"Group Show"

1985

Galerie Rudolf Zwirner
Cologne
"Group Show"

Massimo Audiello Gallery
New York
"The Chi-Chi Show"

1986

Hallwalls
Buffalo
"Poetic Mediations"

Tony Shafrazi Gallery
New York
"What It Is"

1987

Whitney Museum of
American Art
New York
"1987 Biennial Exhibition"

1988

The Institute of
Contemporary Art and the
Museum of Fine Arts
Boston
"The BiNATIONAL:
American Art of the Late
80s" (traveled)

1989

Frankfurter Kunstverein
Frankfurt
"Prospect Photographie"

Musée National d'Art
Moderne, Centre
Georges Pompidou
Paris
"L'invention d'un art"

1990

Independent Curators
Incorporated
New York
"Team Spirit" (traveled)

Whitney Museum of
American Art, Downtown
at Federal Reserve Plaza
New York
"The Charade of Mastery:
Deciphering Modernism in
Contemporary Art"

BIBLIOGRAPHY

Black, Carl John, and
Diego Cortez
FINE ART PICTORIAL GUIDE
OF THE HUDSON RIVER
VALLEY (exhibition
catalogue). Naples:
Lucio Amelio, 1986.

Cortez, Diego
"AIDS: The Advent of the
Infinite Divine Spirit."
FLASH ART, no. 129
(Summer 1986), pp. 58-61.

deAk, Edit
SOME MODERN ARTISTS AND
THEIR WORK (exhibition
catalogue). New York:
Massimo Audiello Gallery
and Pat Hearn Gallery,
1986.

Diacono, Mario
DAVID McDERMOTT/PETER
McGOUGH (exhibition
catalogue). Boston: Mario
Diacono Gallery, 1987.

Dickhoff, Wilfried, ed.
WHAT IT IS (exhibition
catalogue). New York: Tony
Shafrazi Gallery, 1986.

Heartney, Eleanor
"Combined Operations."
ART IN AMERICA, 77 (June
1989), pp. 140-47.

Martin, Richard
"McDermott & McGough."
ARTS MAGAZINE, 62 (April
1988), p. 90.

Ratcliff, Carter
"Modern Life." ARTFORUM,
24 (May 1986), p. 12.

DAVID McDERMOTT AND PETER McGOUGH

A Siphon Formed with a Small Band of Cloth, 1884 from
Les Recréations Scientifiques, 1884   1990

Spiral of Cardboard Put in Rotation by the Ascending Movement of a Current of Warm Air, 1884 from *Les Recréations Scientifiques, 1884*   1990

JOHN MILLER

Untitled   1990*

Born in Cleveland, 1954; studied at the Rhode Island School of Design, Providence (BFA, 1977), Independent Study Program, Whitney Museum of American Art, New York (1978), California Institute of the Arts, Valencia (MFA, 1979); lives in New York.

ONE-ARTIST EXHIBITIONS

1984

Metro Pictures
New York

1985

Metro Pictures
New York

Rosamund Felsen Gallery
Los Angeles

1986

Metro Pictures
New York

1987

American Fine Arts
New York

1988

Metro Pictures
New York

Galerie Sophia Ungers
Cologne

1990

Galerie Isabella Kacprzak
Cologne

Metro Pictures
New York

Standard Graphik
Cologne

GROUP EXHIBITIONS

1982

Lisson Gallery
London
"London/New York"

White Columns
New York
"Real Life Magazine Presents"

1987

The Renaissance Society at The University of Chicago and the Newport Harbor Art Museum, Newport Beach, California
"CalArts: Skeptical Belief(s)"

1989

Massimo Audiello Gallery
New York
"In the Center of Doubt"

Terrain Gallery
San Francisco
"Information"

Villa Gillet-Frac Rhones-Alpes
Lyons
"Avant 1989"

1990

Galeries Daniel Buchholz, Gisela Capitain, Tanja Grunert, Max Hetzler, Jablonka, Isabella Kacprzak, Esther Schipper, Monika Sprüth, Sophia Ungers
Cologne
"Nachschub/Supply: The Köln Show"

Rosamund Felsen Gallery
Los Angeles
"Just Pathetic"

BIBLIOGRAPHY

Bankowsky, Jack
"John Miller at Metro Pictures." EAST VILLAGE EYE (June 1984), p. 21.

Bankowsky, Jack
"Summer Show at Metro Pictures." EAST VILLAGE EYE (September 1984).

Cooper, Denis
"John Miller Metro Pictures." ARTFORUM, 26 (Summer 1988), p. 139.

Evans, Steven, and Michael Jenkins
"John Miller, Gary Mirabelle, Lawrence Weiner: American Fine Arts, Co." ARTSCRIBE INTERNATIONAL, 79 (January-February 1990), p. 81.

Gould, Claudia
NINE PAINTERS (exhibition catalogue). Buffalo: Hallwalls, 1982.

Lord, Catherine, et al.
CALARTS: SKEPTICAL BELIEF(S) (exhibition catalogue). Chicago: The Renaissance Society at The University of Chicago; Newport Beach, California: Newport Harbor Art Museum, 1987.

McCoy, Pat
"Of Ever-Ever Land I Speak." ARTSCRIBE INTERNATIONAL, no. 67 (January-February 1988), pp. 73-74.

Miller, John
"The Greenberg Effect." ARTS MAGAZINE, 64 (December 1989), p. 61.

Miller, John
"In the Beginning There was Formica . . ." ARTSCRIBE INTERNATIONAL, 62 (March-April 1987), pp. 36-42.

Russell, John
"Sculpture." THE NEW YORK TIMES, October 29, 1982.

JOHN MILLER

Echo and Narcissus 1990

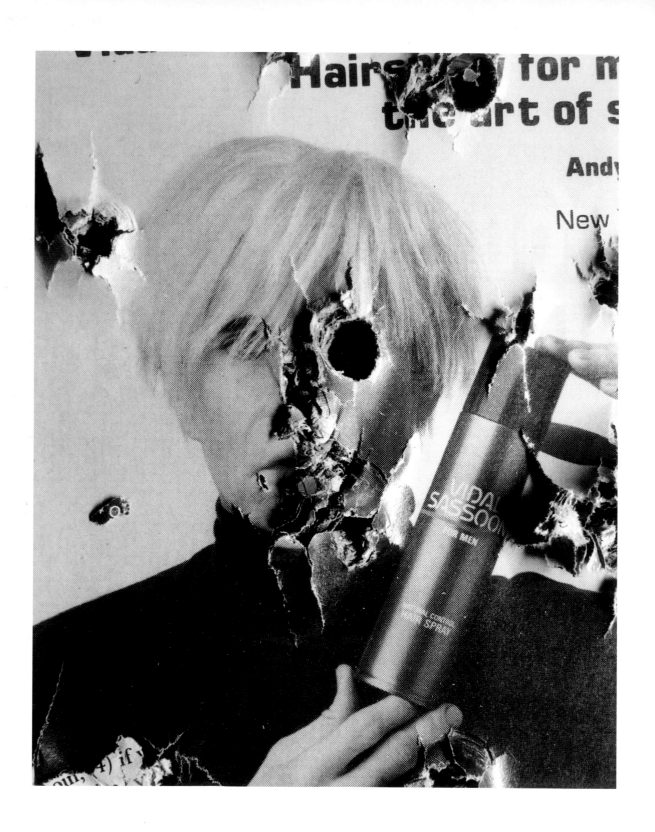

RICHARD MISRACH

Born in Los Angeles, 1949; studied at the University of California, Berkeley (BA, 1971); lives in Emeryville, California.

Desert Canto VI: The Pit.
On March 24, 1953, the Bulloch brothers were trailing 2,000 head of sheep across the Sand Springs Valley when they were exposed to extensive fallout from a dirty atomic test. Within a week the first ewes began dropping their lambs prematurely—stunted, woolless, legless, potbellied. Soon full-grown sheep started dying in large numbers with running sores, large pustules, and hardened hooves. Horses and cattle were found dead with beta burns. At final count, 4,390 animals were killed.

Initial investigations by government experts indicated that radiation was the cause. However, when the Atomic Energy Commission recognized the potential economic and political liability, all reports and findings were immediately classified. The AEC did provide a public explanation: a dry year and malnutrition were blamed.

Today, county-designated dead animal pits can be found throughout the West. They function much like trash dumps in which locals are encouraged to deposit livestock that die suddenly. The causes of the animals' deaths are often unknown.

Desert Canto XI: The Playboys.
Two Playboy magazines used for target practice by persons unknown were found at the northwest corner of the nuclear test site in Nevada. Although the women on the covers were the intended targets, all aspects of American culture, as reflected inside the magazines, were riddled with violence.

ONE-ARTIST EXHIBITIONS

1975
International Center of Photography
New York

1979
Musée National d'Art Moderne, Centre Georges Pompidou
Paris

1983
Los Angeles County Museum of Art

1986
Houston Center for Photography

1987
The Oakland Museum (traveled)

1988
The Art Institute of Chicago

The Cleveland Museum of Art

National Gallery of Art Wellington, New Zealand (traveled)

1989
University Art Museum, University of California, Berkeley

University Art Museum, University of New Mexico Albuquerque

1990
Donna Beam Fine Art Gallery, University of Nevada, Las Vegas (traveled)

Fraenkel Gallery San Francisco

Parco Gallery Tokyo (traveled)

GROUP EXHIBITIONS

1973
San Francisco Art Institute "Places"

1976
Fogg Art Museum, Harvard University
Cambridge, Massachusetts "Contemporary Photography"

1978
The Museum of Modern Art
New York
"Mirrors and Windows: American Photography since 1960" (traveled)

1979
The Corcoran Gallery of Art
Washington, D.C.
"American Images: New Work by Twenty American Photographers"

1984
San Francisco Museum of Modern Art
"Photography in California: 1945-1980" (traveled)

1985
University Art Museum, University of New Mexico
Albuquerque
"Mark Klett/Richard Misrach"

1989
The Oakland Museum "Picturing California: A Century of Photographic Genius"

1990
Whitney Museum of American Art at Equitable Center
New York
"The New American Pastoral: Landscape Photography in the Age of Questioning"

BIBLIOGRAPHY

Barich, Bill, and Therese Heyman
PICTURING CALIFORNIA: A CENTURY OF PHOTOGRAPHIC GENIUS (exhibition catalogue). Oakland: The Oakland Museum, 1989.

Misrach, Richard
DESERT CANTOS. Albuquerque: University of New Mexico Press, 1987.

Misrach, Richard
(a photographic book). San Francisco: Grapestake Gallery, 1979.

Misrach, Richard
RICHARD MISRACH: 1975-1987. Tokyo: Gallery Min, 1988.

Misrach, Richard
TELEGRAPH 3 A.M.: THE STREET PEOPLE OF TELEGRAPH AVENUE, BERKELEY. Berkeley: Cornucopia Press, 1974.

Misrach, Richard, and Myriam Weisang Misrach
BRAVO 20: THE BOMBING OF THE AMERICAN WEST. Baltimore and London: The Johns Hopkins University Press, 1990.

Sobieszek, Robert A.
THE NEW AMERICAN PASTORAL: LANDSCAPE PHOTOGRAPHY IN THE AGE OF QUESTIONING (exhibition catalogue). New York: Whitney Museum of American Art at Equitable Center, 1990.

Szarkowski, John
MIRRORS AND WINDOWS: AMERICAN PHOTOGRAPHY SINCE 1960 (exhibition catalogue). New York: The Museum of Modern Art, 1978.

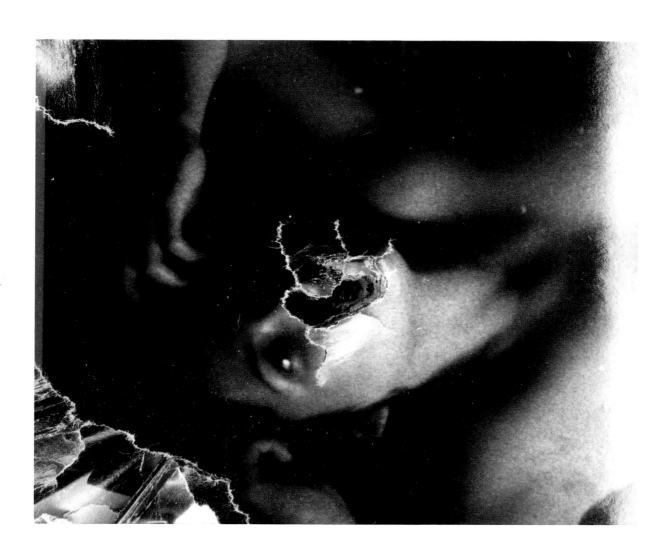

RICHARD MISRACH

Dead Animals #327   1989

JOAN MITCHELL

Champs 1990*

Born in Chicago, 1926; studied at Smith College, Northampton, Massachusetts (1942-44), The Art Institute of Chicago (BFA, 1947), Columbia University, New York (1950), The Art Institute of Chicago (MFA, 1950); lives in Vetheuil, France.

ONE-ARTIST EXHIBITIONS

1952
New Gallery
New York

1953
Stable Gallery
New York

1961
Dwan Gallery
Los Angeles

1968
Martha Jackson Gallery
New York

1974
Whitney Museum of
American Art
New York

1976
Xavier Fourcade Gallery
New York

1980
Xavier Fourcade Gallery
New York

1982
Musée d'Art Moderne de la
Ville de Paris

1988
Herbert F. Johnson
Museum of Art,
Cornell University
Ithaca, New York (traveled)

1989
Robert Miller Gallery
New York

1990
Galerie Jean Fournier
Paris

GROUP EXHIBITIONS

1951
Whitney Museum of
American Art
New York
"1951 Annual Exhibition of
Contemporary American
Painting"

1957
The Art Institute of
Chicago
"62nd Annual Exhibition of
American Painting and
Sculpture"

1958
Museum of Art,
Carnegie Institute
Pittsburgh
"1958 International
Exhibition of Contemporary
Painting and Sculpture"

Venice
"XXIX Biennale di Venezia"

Whitney Museum of
American Art
New York
"Nature in Abstraction:
The Relation of Abstract
Painting and Sculpture to
Nature in Twentieth-
Century American Art"
(traveled)

1959
Kassel, West Germany
"Documenta 2"

1983
Whitney Museum of
American Art
New York
"1983 Biennial Exhibition"

1984
Newport Harbor Art Museum
Newport Beach, California
"Action/Precision: The New
Direction in New York,
1955-60" (traveled)

1990
Museum Wiesbaden
"Künstlerinnen des 20.
Jahrhunderts"

BIBLIOGRAPHY

Bernstock, Judith E.
JOAN MITCHELL (exhibition catalogue). Ithaca, New York: Herbert F. Johnson Museum of Art, Cornell University, 1988.

Michaud, Yves
JOAN MITCHELL: NEW PAINTINGS (exhibition catalogue). New York: Xavier Fourcade Gallery, 1986.

Pleynet, Marcelin, and Barbara Rose
JOAN MITCHELL: CHOIX DES PEINTURES, 1970-1982 (exhibition catalogue). Paris: Musée d'Art Moderne de la Ville de Paris, 1982.

Sandler, Irving
THE NEW YORK SCHOOL: THE PAINTERS AND SCULPTORS OF THE FIFTIES. New York: Harper and Row, 1978.

Schimmel, Paul, B.H. Friedman, John Bernard Meyers, and Robert Rosenblum
ACTION/PRECISION: THE NEW DIRECTION IN NEW YORK, 1955-60 (exhibition catalogue). Newport Beach, California: Newport Harbor Art Museum, 1984.

Tucker, Marcia
JOAN MITCHELL (exhibition catalogue). New York: Whitney Museum of American Art, 1974.

JOAN MITCHELL

River 1989*

ED MOSES

Spectra Tres Ojos   1989

Born in Long Beach, California, 1926; studied at University of California, Los Angeles (BA, 1955; MFA, 1958); lives in Los Angeles.

ONE-ARTIST EXHIBITIONS

1979

Sidney Janis Gallery
New York

Texas Gallery
Houston

1981

James Corcoran Gallery
Los Angeles

1983

Dorothy Rosenthal Gallery
Chicago

1984

Larry Gagosian Gallery
Los Angeles

1985

L.A. Louver Gallery
Venice, California

1988

Iannetti Lanzone Gallery
San Francisco

1989

Galerie Georges Lavrov
Paris

Louver Gallery
New York

1990

L.A. Louver Gallery
Venice, California

GROUP EXHIBITIONS

1971

The Corcoran Gallery of Art
Washington, D.C.
"32nd Biennial Exhibition of
Contemporary American
Painting"

1972

Kunstverein Hamburg
"West Coast USA" (traveled)

1981

Fine Arts Gallery,
University of California,
Irvine
"Abstraction in L.A.,
1950-1980"

San Francisco Art Institute
"Abstraction"

1983

The Museum of
Contemporary Art
Los Angeles
"The First Show: Painting
and Sculpture from Eight
Collections, 1940-1980"

1984

Newport Harbor Art Museum
Newport Beach, California
"First Newport Biennial
1984: Los Angeles Today"

1985

Fisher Gallery, University
of Southern California
Los Angeles
"Sunshine and Shadow:
Recent Paintings in
Southern California"

1988

Wight Art Gallery,
University of California
Los Angeles
"Visions of Inner Space"
(traveled)

1990

Nagoya City Art Museum
Japan
"Abstraction: John Altoon,
Sam Francis, Craig
Kauffman, John McLaughlin,
and Ed Moses"

BIBLIOGRAPHY

Colpitt, Frances
"Ed Moses at L.A. Louver."
ART IN AMERICA, 73
(December 1985), p. 134.

Larsen, Susan C.
"First Newport Biennial."
ART NEWS, 85 (February
1985), pp. 111-13.

Masheck, Joseph
"Ed Moses and the Problem
of 'Western' Tradition."
ARTS MAGAZINE, 50
(December 1975), pp. 56-61.

Plagens, Peter
"Ed Moses: The Problem of
Regionalism." ARTFORUM,
10 (March 1972), pp. 83-85.

Selz, Peter, and Jane
Livingston
"Two Generations in L.A."
ART IN AMERICA, 57
(January-February 1969),
pp. 92-97.

Wilson, William
"The Art Galleries: Venice."
LOS ANGELES TIMES, May
29, 1987, part 6, p. 12.

Wilson, William
"The Galleries." LOS
ANGELES TIMES, September
25, 1981.

ED MOSES

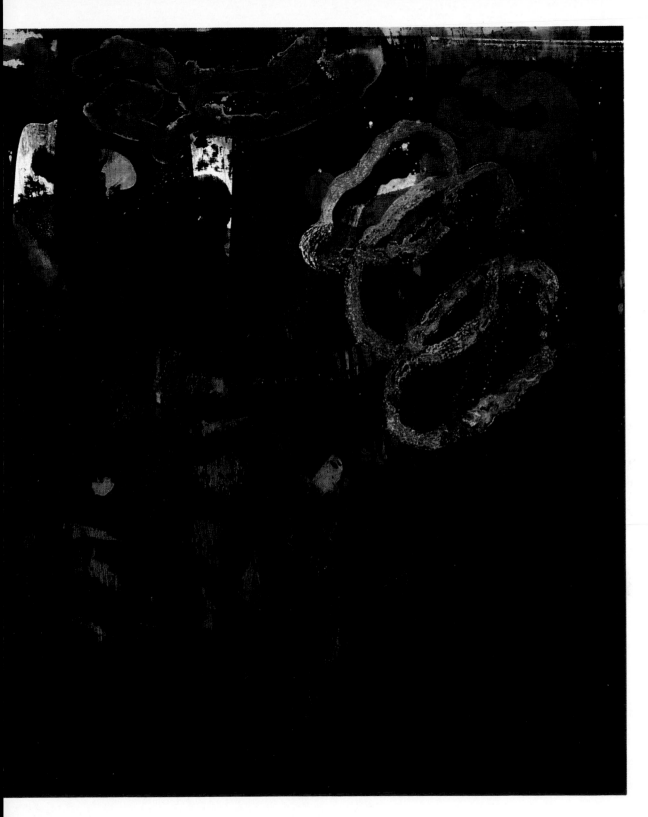

Kudjur   1990–91

CELIA ALVAREZ MUÑOZ   *Stories Your Mother Never Told You*   1990*

Born in El Paso, 1937; studied at the University of Texas at El Paso (BA, 1964), North Texas State University, Denton (MFA, 1982); lives in Arlington, Texas.

ONE-ARTIST EXHIBITIONS

1988

Lannan Museum
Lake Worth, Florida

Tyler Museum of Art
Tyler, Texas

1989

Bridge Center for
Contemporary Arts
El Paso

New Langton Arts
San Francisco

1990

Adair Margo Gallery
El Paso

Modern Dallas Art

University Museum,
University of Texas
at El Paso

GROUP EXHIBITIONS

1983

Long Beach Museum of Art
Long Beach, California
"At Home: A Decade of
Women's Art"

1984

Texas Christian University
Fort Worth
"New Talent in Texas"

1986

Midtown Art Center
Houston
"Chulas Fronteras"
(traveled)

1988

Contemporary Arts Museum
Houston
"The First Texas Triennial"

National Museum of
Women in the Arts
Washington, D.C.
"Texas Exhibition"

1989

Gallery of Contemporary
Art, University of Colorado
Colorado Springs
"Sin Fronteras: Crossing
Borders"

1990

Intar Gallery
New York
"Personal Odysseys: The
Photography of Celia
Alvarez Muñoz, Clarissa T.
Sligh, and María Martínez-
Cañas

Newhouse Center for
Contemporary Art, Snug
Harbor Cultural Center
Staten Island, New York
"Family Stories"

Wight Art Gallery,
University of California,
Los Angeles
"Chicano Art: Resistance
and Affirmation"

BIBLIOGRAPHY

Connor, Celeste
"Narrative in Question:
Murals by Celia Muñoz at
New Langton." ARTWEEK,
January 11, 1990, pp. 12-13.

Ennis, Michael
"The Ties That Bind."
TEXAS MONTHLY, 18
(September 1990),
pp. 30-33.

Gleason, Ron
POSTALES Y SIN REMEDIO: A
SERIES OF PAINTINGS AND AN
INSTALLATION BY CELIA
ALVAREZ MUÑOZ (exhibition
brochure). Tyler, Texas:
Tyler Museum of Art, 1988.

Huerta, Benito
CHULAS FRONTERAS
(exhibition catalogue).
Houston: Midtown Art
Center, 1986.

Jarmusch, Ann
"Celebrating the Art of
Hispanic Experience."
DALLAS TIMES HERALD,
May 1, 1989, pp. C1, 4.

Kutner, Janet
"Art with Roots."
DALLAS MORNING NEWS,
February 17, 1990, pp. C1-2.

Mesa-Bains, Amalia, Tomas
Ybarra-Frausto, and Victor
Zamudio-Taylor
CEREMONY OF MEMORY:
NEW EXPRESSION OF
SPIRITUALITY AMONG
CONTEMPORARY HISPANIC
ARTISTS (exhibition
catalogue). Santa Fe:
Amalia Mesa, Center for
Contemporary Arts of
Santa Fe, 1989.

Roth, Moira
PERSONAL ODYSSEYS: THE
PHOTOGRAPHY OF CELIA
ALVAREZ MUÑOZ, CLARISSA
T. SLIGH, AND MARÍA
MARTÍNEZ-CAÑAS
(exhibition catalogue). New
York: Intar Gallery, 1990.

CELIA ALVAREZ MUÑOZ

"ella"   "el"

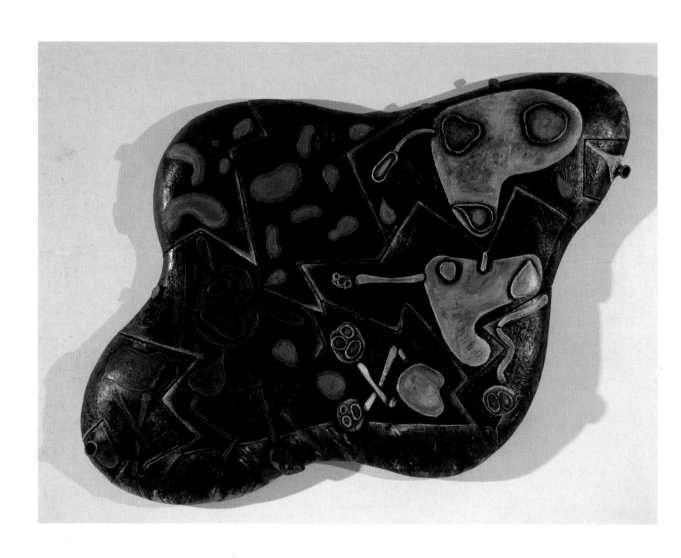

ELIZABETH MURRAY

Sorry Dogs   1990

*Born in Chicago, 1940; studied
at The Art Institute of Chicago
(BFA, 1962), Mills College,
Oakland (MFA, 1964); lives in
New York.*

ONE-ARTIST EXHIBITIONS

1975

Jared Sable Gallery
Toronto

1976

Paula Cooper Gallery
New York

1982

Hillyer Gallery,
Smith College
Northampton, Massachusetts

1983

Paula Cooper Gallery
New York

Portland Center for
the Visual Arts
Oregon

1984

The Institute of
Contemporary Art
Boston

Paula Cooper Gallery
New York

1987

Dallas Museum of Art
and MIT List Visual Arts
Center, Cambridge,
Massachusetts (traveled)

1988

Daniel Weinberg Gallery
Los Angeles

San Francisco Museum of
Modern Art

1989

Mayor Rowan Gallery
London

Paula Cooper Gallery
New York

1990

Barbara Krakow Gallery
Boston (traveled)

GROUP EXHIBITIONS

1973

Whitney Museum of
American Art
New York
"1973 Biennial Exhibition"

1977

The Solomon R.
Guggenheim Museum
New York
"Nine Artists: Theodoron
Awards"

1979

Hayward Gallery
London
"New Painting/New York"

1981

Whitney Museum of
American Art
New York
"1981 Biennial Exhibition"

1984

Whitney Museum of
American Art
New York
"Five Painters in New York"

1987

Institute of Contemporary
Arts
London
"Comic Iconoclasm"

1988

The Saatchi Collection
London
"Jennifer Bartlett, Elizabeth
Murray, Eric Fischl, Susan
Rothenberg"

1989

John and Mable Ringling
Museum of Art
Sarasota, Florida
"Abstraction in Question"

1990

The Museum of Modern Art
New York
"High and Low: Modern Art
and Popular Culture"
(traveled)

BIBLIOGRAPHY

Armstrong, Richard, and
Richard Marshall
FIVE PAINTERS IN NEW YORK
(exhibition catalogue). New
York: Whitney Museum of
American Art, 1984.

Becker, David P.
ELIZABETH MURRAY PRINTS
1979-1990 (exhibition
catalogue). Boston: Barbara
Krakow Gallery, 1990.

Gardner, Paul
"Elizabeth Murray Shapes
Up." ART NEWS, 83
(September 1984), pp. 46-55.

Graze, Sue, Kathy
Halbreich, Roberta Smith,
and Clifford S. Ackley
ELIZABETH MURRAY:
PAINTINGS AND DRAWINGS
(exhibition catalogue).
Dallas: Dallas Museum of
Art; Cambridge,
Massachusetts: MIT List
Visual Arts Center, 1987.

Larson, Kay
"One from the Heart." NEW
YORK MAGAZINE, February
10, 1986, pp. 40-45.

Madoff, Steven Henry
"A New Generation of
Abstract Painters." ART
NEWS, 82 (November 1983),
pp. 78-84.

ELIZABETH MURRAY

Hobo 1990

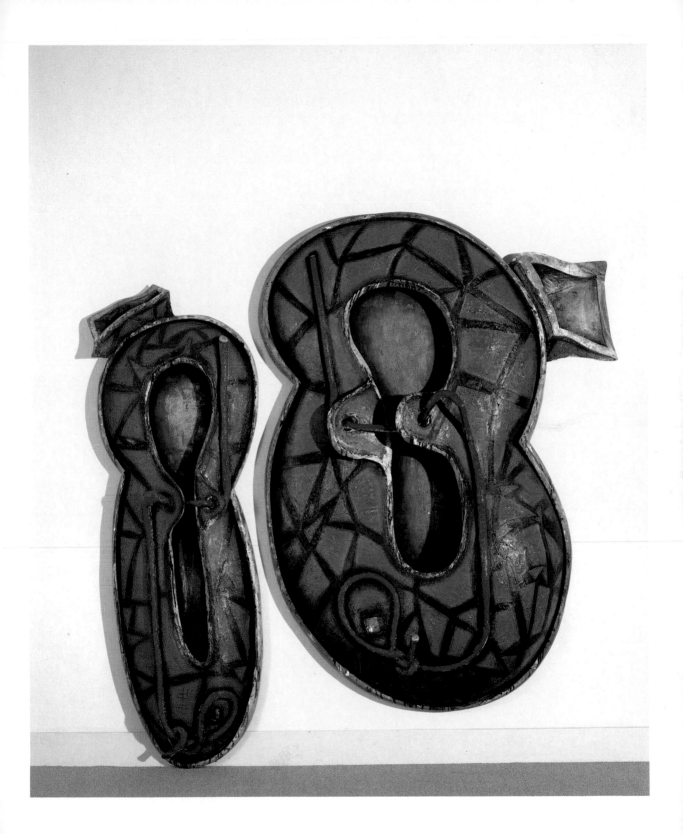

Lonely Rivers   1990*

BRUCE NAUMAN

Andrew Head/Andrew Head Stacked   1990

Born in Fort Wayne, Indiana, 1941; studied at the University of Wisconsin, Madison (BS, 1964), University of California, Davis (MA, 1966); lives in Pecos, New Mexico.

ONE-ARTIST EXHIBITIONS

1966

Nicholas Wilder Gallery
Los Angeles

1968

Galerie Konrad Fischer
Düsseldorf

Leo Castelli Gallery
New York

1970

Galleria Sperone
Turin

1972

Los Angeles County
Museum of Art (traveled)

1981

Rijksmuseum Kröller Müller
Otterlo, The Netherlands
(traveled)

1982

The Baltimore Museum
of Art

1983

Museum Haus Esters
Krefeld, West Germany

1986

Museum für Gegenwartskunst
Basel (traveled)

Whitechapel Art Gallery
London (traveled)

1989

Castelli Graphics
New York

1990

Anthony d'Offay Gallery
London

Museum für Gegenwartskunst
Basel (traveled)

GROUP EXHIBITIONS

1966

Fischbach Gallery
New York
"Eccentric Abstraction"

1968

Kassel, West Germany
"Documenta 4"

Leo Castelli Warehouse
New York
"Nine at Castelli"

1969

Kunsthalle Bern
"Live in Your Head/When
Attitude Becomes Form
Works-Concepts-Processes-
Situations-Information"

Whitney Museum of
American Art
New York
"Anti-Illusion: Procedures/
Materials"

1970

The Museum of Modern Art
New York
"Information"

1981

Neuberger Museum, State
University of New York,
College at Purchase
"Soundings"

1986

Palacio de Velázquez
Madrid
"Between Geometry and
Gesture: American
Sculpture, 1965-75"

1988

Los Angeles County
Museum of Art
"The Spiritual in Art:
Abstract Painting 1890-1985"
(traveled)

1989

Whitney Museum of
American Art
New York
"Image World: Art and
Media Culture"

1990

Whitney Museum of
American Art
New York
"The New Sculpture 1965-75"

BIBLIOGRAPHY

Bruggen, Coosje van
BRUCE NAUMAN. New York:
Rizzoli International
Publications, 1988.

Bruggen, Coosje van,
Dieter Koepplin, and
Franz Meyer
BRUCE NAUMAN: DRAWINGS/
ZEICHNUNGEN, 1965-1986

Livingston, Jane, and
Marcia Tucker
BRUCE NAUMAN: WORK FROM
1965 TO 1972 (exhibition
catalogue). Los Angeles:
Los Angeles County
Museum of Art, 1972.

Meyer, Franz, and
Jörg Zutter
BRUCE NAUMAN: SKULPTUREN
UND INSTALLATIONEN
1985-1990 (exhibition
catalogue). Basel: Museum
für Gegenwarstkunst, 1986.

Richardson, Brenda
BRUCE NAUMAN: NEONS
(exhibition catalogue).
Baltimore: The Baltimore
Museum of Art, 1982.

Serota, Nicholas, and
Joanna Skipwith, eds.
BRUCE NAUMAN (exhibition
catalogue). London:
Whitechapel Art Gallery,
1986.

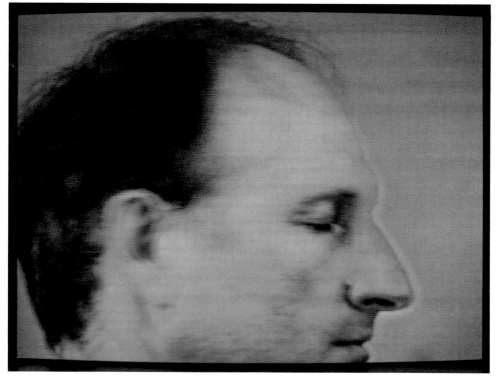

BRUCE NAUMAN

Raw Material—"MMMM"   1990

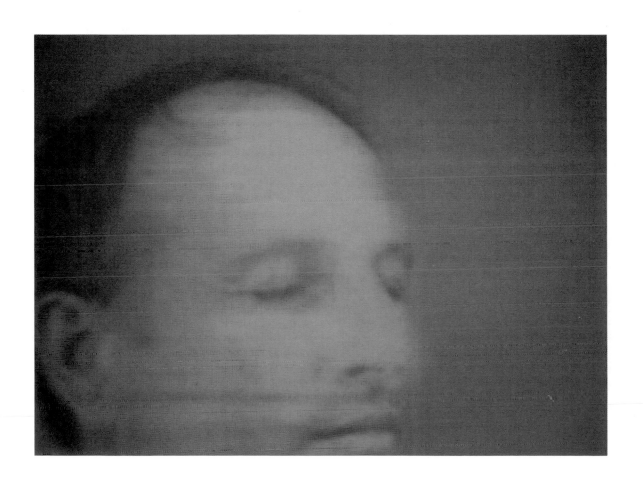

Raw Material—"MMMM"   1990

CADY NOLAND

This Piece Has No Title Yet   1989 *

Born in Washington, D.C., 1956; studied at Sarah Lawrence College, Bronxville, New York (BA, 1977); lives in New York.

ONE-ARTIST EXHIBITIONS

1988

Westersingel
Rotterdam

White Columns
New York

1989

American Fine Arts
New York

Anthony Reynolds Gallery
London

Massimo de Carlo Gallery
Milan

1990

Luhring Augustine Hetzler
Gallery
Santa Monica

GROUP EXHIBITIONS

1988

Galerie Hans Mayer
Düsseldorf
"Works, Concepts,
Processes, Situations,
Information"

1989

Galerie Barbara Farber
Amsterdam
"A Climate of Site"

Hallwalls
Buffalo
"Amerikarma"

The Mattress Factory
Pittsburgh

1990

L'Espace Lyonnais d'Art
Contemporain, Centre
d'Échanges de Perrache
Lyons
"Le statut de la sculpture"
(traveled)

Galerie Max Hetzler
Cologne
"Cady Noland, Sam Samore,
Karen Sylvester"

Neue Gesellschaft für
Bildende Kunst
Berlin
"Cady Noland und Felix
Gonzalez-Torres"

Rosamund Felsen Gallery
Los Angeles
"Just Pathetic"

San Francisco Museum of
Modern Art
"New Work: A New
Generation"

Venice
"XLIV Biennale di Venezia"

BIBLIOGRAPHY

Avgikos, Jan
"Degraded World."
ARTSCRIBE INTERNATIONAL,
no. 78 (November-
December 1989), pp. 54-57.

Cameron, Dan
"Changing Priorities in
American Art." ART
INTERNATIONAL, 10 (Spring
1990), pp. 86-90.

Cone, Michèle
"Interview with Cady Noland."
JOURNAL OF CONTEMPORARY
ART, 3 (Fall-Winter 1990),
pp. 20-25.

Liebmann, Lisa
"Cady Noland at American
Fine Arts." ART IN
AMERICA, 77 (November
1989), pp. 200-01.

Noland, Cady
"Towards a Metalanguage of
Evil." BALCON, 4 (1989),
pp. 71-85.

Rubinstein, Meyer Raphael
"Cady Noland/Massimo de
Carlo." FLASH ART, no. 151
(March-April 1990), p. 160.

Salvioni, Daniela
"Spotlight: Cady Noland,
The Homespun Violence of
the Hearth." FLASH ART,
no. 148 (October 1989),
p. 129.

Smith, Roberta
"Old, New, Traditional,
and Alternate Spaces."
THE NEW YORK TIMES,
May 5, 1989, p. C30.

CADY NOLAND

Frame Device (left) and *Oozwald* (right)   1989*

Corral Gates (foreground)　1989*

PHILIP PEARLSTEIN

Model Posing with Unfinished Painting   1990

Born in Pittsburgh, 1924; studied at the Carnegie Institute of Technology, Pittsburgh (BFA, 1949), New York University (MA, 1955); lives in New York.

ONE-ARTIST EXHIBITIONS

1955

Tanager Gallery
New York

1960

Allan Frumkin Gallery
Chicago

1972

Donald Morris Gallery
Detroit (traveled)

1976

Allan Frumkin Gallery
New York

1981

John and Mable Ringling
Museum of Art
Sarasota, Florida
(traveled)

1983

Milwaukee Art Museum
(traveled)

1985

Hirschl & Adler Modern
New York

1988

Hirschl & Adler Modern
New York

1989

Galerie Rudolf Zwirner
Cologne

The Brooklyn Museum
New York

GROUP EXHIBITIONS

1954

Kootz Gallery
New York
"Emerging Talent"

1955

Whitney Museum of
American Art
New York
"1955 Annual Exhibition of
Contemporary American
Painting"

1965

The Art Institute of
Chicago
"25th Annual Society for
Contemporary American
Art Exhibition"

1967

The Corcoran Gallery of Art
Washington, D.C.
"30th Biennial Exhibition of
Contemporary American
Painting"

1970

Whitney Museum of
American Art
New York
"22 Realists"

1979

Whitney Museum of
American Art
New York
"1979 Biennial Exhibition"

1981

San Antonio Museum of
Art
"Real, Really Real,
Superreal: Directions in
Contemporary Realism"
(traveled)

1982

Pennsylvania Academy of
the Fine Arts
Philadelphia
"Contemporary American
Realism Since 1960"
(traveled)

1986

Fort Lauderdale Museum
of Art
"An American Renaissance
in Art: Painting and
Sculpture Since 1940"

1987

Institute of Contemporary
Arts
London
"Comic Iconoclasm"
(traveled)

BIBLIOGRAPHY

Alloway, Lawrence
Review of "Philip
Pearlstein: The Complete
Paintings." ART IN AMERICA,
73 (February 1985), p. 19.

Glueck, Grace
"Artist and Model: Why the
Tradition Endures." THE
NEW YORK TIMES, June 8,
1986, section 2, pp. 1, 27.

Koether, Jutta
"Philip Pearlstein/Galerie
Zwirner." ARTFORUM, 28
(March 1990), p. 174.

Larson, Kay
"A Passion for the Flesh."
NEW YORK, August 1, 1983,
pp. 63-64.

Perreault, John
PHILIP PEARLSTEIN:
DRAWINGS AND
WATERCOLORS. New York:
Harry N. Abrams, 1988.

Russell, John
"Trials of the Sphinx, by
Philip Pearlstein." THE NEW
YORK TIMES, September 22,
1989.

Schjeldahl, Peter
"Philip Pearlstein: A
Retrospective." VANITY FAIR,
46 (September 1983), p. 145.

Shaman, Sanford Sivitz
"Philip Pearlstein: Painting
to Watercolors." ARTS
MAGAZINE, 59 (October
1984), pp. 134-36.

PHILIP PEARLSTEIN

Fox, Fish, Models, and Wooden Lady   1991

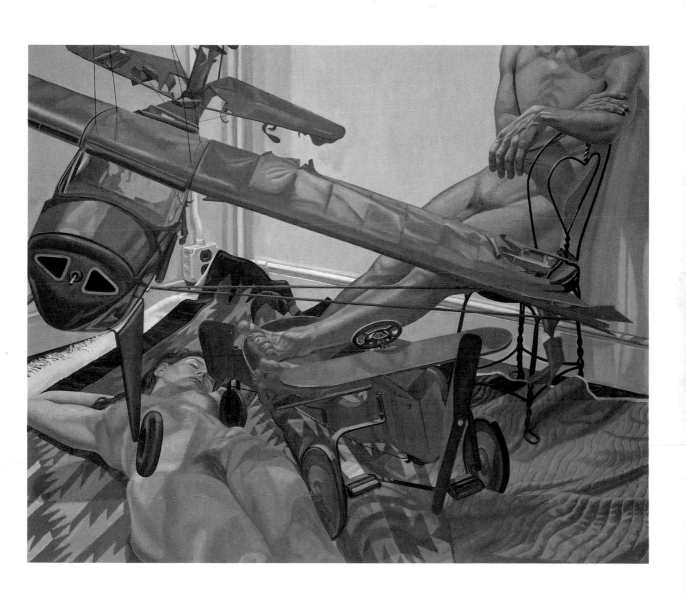

Kiddie Car-Plane, Airplane, and Models   1990 *

ELLEN PHELAN   *Meadow Hampshire—Lifting Clouds*   1989

Born in Detroit, 1943; studied at Wayne State University, Detroit (BFA, 1969; MFA 1971); lives in New York and Westport, New York.

ONE-ARTIST EXHIBITIONS

1980

The Clocktower, Institute for Art and Urban Resources
New York

1981

Dart Gallery
Chicago

1982

Hansen-Fuller-Goldeen Gallery
San Francisco

1986

Barbara Toll Fine Arts
New York

1988

Susanne Hilberry Gallery
Birmingham, Michigan

1989

Asher/Faure Gallery
Los Angeles

Barbara Toll Fine Arts
New York

1990

The Baltimore Museum of Art

Barbara Toll Fine Arts
New York

Susanne Hilberry Gallery
Birmingham, Michigan

GROUP EXHIBITIONS

1980

The Detroit Institute of Arts
"Kick Out the Jams"

1982

The Drawing Center
New York
"New Drawing in America"

1984

Artists Space
New York
"A Decade of Artists Space"

Cranbrook Academy of Art Museum
Bloomfield Hills, Michigan
"Viewpoint 84: Out of Square"

The Hudson River Museum
Yonkers
"New American Vistas: Contemporary American Landscapes" (traveled)

1987

Whitney Museum of American Art,
Fairfield County
Stamford, Connecticut
"The New Romantic Landscape"

1988

Curt Marcus Gallery
New York
"Works on Paper"

Whitney Museum of American Art
New York
"Recent Drawings: George Condo, Mike Kelley, Ellen Phelan, Janis Provisor"

1989

Edward Thorp Gallery
New York
"Epiphanies"

The Museum of Modern Art
New York
"Drawings of the '80's from the Collection: Part I"

BIBLIOGRAPHY

Adams, Brooks
"Ellen Phelan at Barbara Toll." ART IN AMERICA, 77 (November 1989), p. 192.

Armstrong, Richard
RECENT DRAWINGS: GEORGE CONDO, MIKE KELLEY, ELLEN PHELAN, JANIS PROVISOR (exhibition brochure). New York: Whitney Museum of American Art, 1988.

Belloli, Jay, and Mary Jane Jacob
KICK OUT THE JAMS (exhibition catalogue). Detroit: The Detroit Institute of Arts, 1980.

Gill, Susan
"Ellen Phelan/Barbara Toll." ART NEWS, 86 (February 1987), p. 137.

Henry, Gerrit
"Ellen Phelan: The Interpretation of Dolls." THE PRINT COLLECTOR'S NEWSLETTER, 19 (May-June 1988), pp. 51-53.

Johnson, Ken
"Ellen Phelan at Barbara Toll." ART IN AMERICA, 76 (March 1988), p. 151.

Loughery, John
"Ellen Phelan/Barbara Toll." ARTS MAGAZINE, 61 (January 1987), pp. 125-26.

Loughery, John
"Landscape Painting in the Eighties: April Gornik, Ellen Phelan, and Joan Nelson." ARTS MAGAZINE, 62 (May 1988), pp. 44-48.

Russell, John
"Reviews: Ellen Phelan at Barbara Toll." THE NEW YORK TIMES, November 21, 1986, p. C25.

Westfall, Stephen
"Ellen Phelan: Barbara Toll." FLASH ART, no. 139 (March-April 1988), pp. 114-15.

ELLEN PHELAN

Summer Light—Morning (Second Version)   1989

Island in the River—River Test   1989*

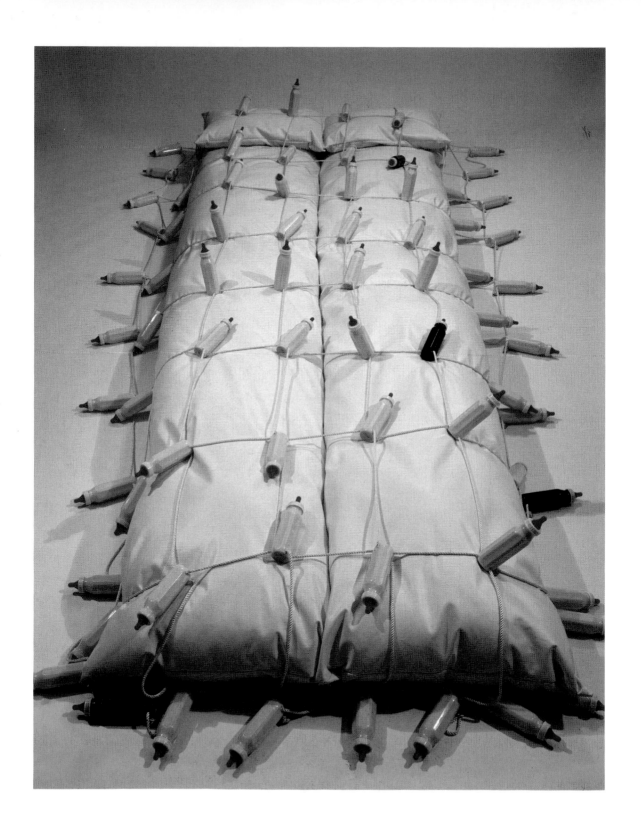

RONA PONDICK   *Double Bed*   1989

Born in New York, 1952; studied at Queens College, New York (BFA, 1974), Yale University, New Haven (MFA, 1977); lives in New York.

ONE-ARTIST EXHIBITIONS

1988

Fiction/Nonfiction Gallery
New York

Sculpture Center
New York

1989

Fiction/Nonfiction Gallery
New York

Hillman Holland Gallery
Atlanta

The Institute of
Contemporary Art
Boston

1990

Asher/Faure Gallery
Los Angeles

GROUP EXHIBITIONS

1987

Sculpture Center
New York
"Small Works"

1989

Simon Watson Gallery
New York
"Erotophobia: A Forum in
Contemporary Sexuality"

1990

Asher/Faure Gallery
Los Angeles
"The Home Show"

Emily Sorkin Gallery
New York
"Body, Once Removed"

Greenberg/Wilson Gallery
New York
"Collaborations"

Jack Tilton Gallery
New York
"Detritus: Transformation
and Re-Construction"

Marc Richards Gallery
Los Angeles
"Spellbound"

The Morris Museum
Morristown, New Jersey
"Diverse Representations"

Galerie Thaddäus Ropac
Salzburg
"Vertigo"

White Columns
New York
"Fragments, Parts, and
Wholes: The Body and
Culture"

BIBLIOGRAPHY

Altschuler, Bruce
RONA PONDICK (exhibition
brochure). New York:
Sculpture Center, 1988.

Brenson, Michael
"Rona Pondick: Fiction/
Nonfiction Gallery." THE
NEW YORK TIMES, May 20,
1988, p. C28.

Brenson, Michael
"Rona Pondick-'Beds.'"
THE NEW YORK TIMES,
September 9, 1988, p. C20.

Gookin, Kirby
RONA PONDICK: BED, MILK,
SHOE (exhibition catalogue).
New York: Fiction/
Nonfiction Gallery, 1989.

Joselit, David
CURRENTS: RONA PONDICK
(exhibition brochure).
Boston: The Institute of
Contemporary Art, 1989.

Liu, Catherine
"Let's Get Real." THE
VILLAGE VOICE, August 1,
1989, p. 90.

Myers, Terry R.
"Pressing Pleasures: The
Urgent Sculptures of Rona
Pondick." ARTS MAGAZINE, 65
(November 1990), pp. 90-95.

Pagel, David
"Rona Pondick: Asher/
Faure." ARTSCRIBE
INTERNATIONAL, no. 83
(September-October 1990),
pp. 91-92.

Princenthal, Nancy
"Rona Pondick at Fiction/
Nonfiction." ART IN
AMERICA, 78 (January
1990), p. 157.

RONA PONDICK

Chairman 1990

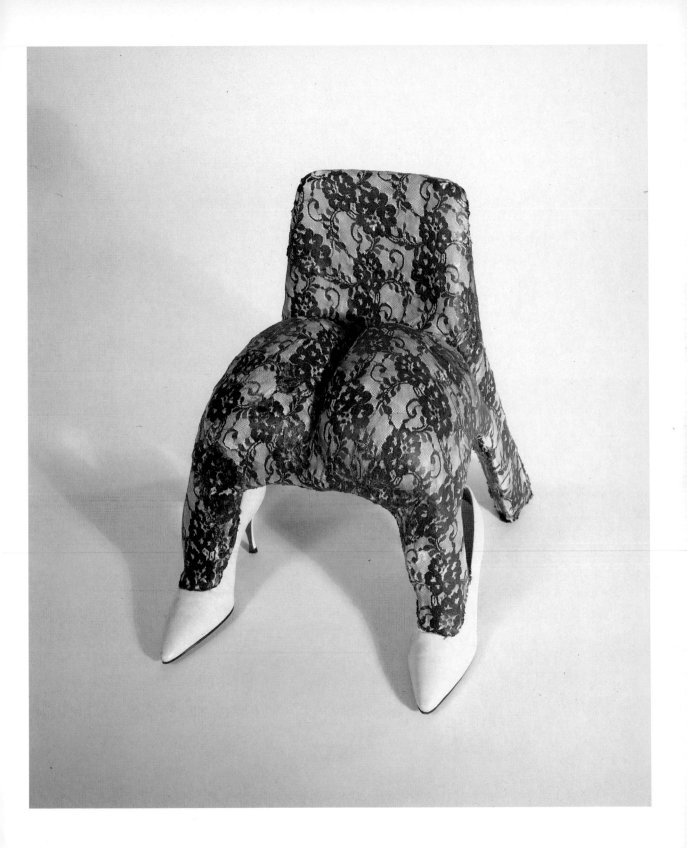

REBECCA PURDUM

Chin Up   1990 *

Born in Idaho Falls, Idaho, 1959; studied at Syracuse University, New York (BFA, 1981), Skowhegan School of Painting and Sculpture, Maine (summer 1981); lives in New York.

ONE-ARTIST EXHIBITIONS

1986

Jack Tilton Gallery
New York

1987

Jack Tilton Gallery
New York

1989

Jack Tilton Gallery
New York

1990

MIT List Visual Arts Center
Cambridge, Massachusetts

GROUP EXHIBITIONS

1981

Museum of Art, Munson-Williams-Proctor Institute
Utica, New York
"43rd Annual Artists of Central New York"

1985

Jack Tilton Gallery
New York
"Group Exhibition"

1986

Jack Tilton Gallery
New York
"Inspiration Comes from Nature"

1987

New York Studio School
"5 Abstract Artists"

1988

MIT List Visual Arts Center
Cambridge, Massachusetts
"Recent Acquisitions to the MIT Permanent Collection"

Robeson Center Art Gallery, Rutgers, The State University of New Jersey
New Brunswick
"Contemporary Syntax: Color & Saturation"

1989

Modern Art Museum of Fort Worth
"Ten + Ten: Contemporary Soviet and American Painters" (traveled)

BIBLIOGRAPHY

Beal, Graham J.W., John E. Bowlt, Viktor Misiano, et al. TEN+TEN: CONTEMPORARY SOVIET AND AMERICAN PAINTERS (exhibition catalogue). Fort Worth: Modern Art Museum of Fort Worth, 1989.

Friis-Hansen, Dana REBECCA PURDUM: PAINTINGS (exhibition catalogue). Cambridge, Massachusetts: MIT List Visual Arts Center, 1990.

Moorman, Margaret "Rebecca Purdum: In a Mysterious Light." ART NEWS, 87 (March 1988), pp. 105-06.

Russell, John "Bright Young Talents: Six Artists with a Future." THE NEW YORK TIMES, May 18, 1986, section 2, pp. 1, 31.

Seliger, Jonathan "The Effect That Paint Produces: New Paintings by Rececca Purdum." ARTS MAGAZINE, 61 (February 1987), pp. 78-79.

REBECCA PURDUM

Ribbon   1990

ALAN RATH

Voyeur II   1989

Born in Cincinnati, 1959; studied at the Massachusetts Institute of Technology, Cambridge, (BSEE, 1982); lives in Oakland.

ONE-ARTIST EXHIBITIONS

1984

Center for Advanced Visual Studies, Massachusetts Institute of Technology Cambridge

1986

Artist's Television Access Gallery San Francisco

Works/San Jose California

1987

Memorial Union Art Gallery, University of California, Davis

ProArts Oakland

1988

New Langton Arts San Francisco

1989

Katia Lacoste Gallery San Jose, California

1990

Contemporary Arts Center Cincinnati

Dorothy Goldeen Gallery Santa Monica

San Jose Museum of Art California

GROUP EXHIBITIONS

1986

San Francisco International Video Festival

1987

Everson Museum of Art Syracuse, New York "Computers and Art" (traveled)

1988

Badischer Kunstverein Karlsruhe, West Germany "Otto Piene und das CAVS"

1989

Brucknerhaus Linz, Austria "ARS Electronica"

Carl Solway Gallery Cincinnati "Sculpture"

Contemporary Arts Center Cincinnati "Singular Spaces, Phenomenal Places"

Intermedia Arts Minnesota Minneapolis "The Technological Imagination"

LACE Los Angeles "Self/Evidence"

Mary Porter Sesnon Art Gallery, University of California, Santa Cruz "Alternate Applications: Computer Technology in the Arts"

1990

San Francisco Museum of Modern Art "Bay Area Media"

BIBLIOGRAPHY

Baker, Kenneth "San Jose Exhibit Puzzles, Fascinates." SAN FRANCISCO CHRONICLE, March 11, 1990, pp. 14-15.

Berkson, Bill "San Francisco International Video Festival." ARTFORUM, 25 (January 1987), pp. 121-22.

Jan, Alfred "Alan Rath, Systems for Neo-Pagans." HIGH PERFORMANCE, no. 45 (Spring 1989), p. 54.

Seid, Steve "About Face: The Cybernetic Sculpture of Alan Rath." VIDEO NETWORKS, 12 (December 1988-January 1989), p. 23.

Stephens, Richard "Alan Rath." VISIONS, 4 (Spring 1990), pp. 22-25.

Tamblyn, Christine "The Eye of the Beholder." ARTWEEK, May 2, 1987, p. 9.

ALAN RATH

Magic Mushrooms 1990

ROBERT RAUSCHENBERG

Blue Gate Secret Spring Glut 1989*

Born in Port Arthur, Texas, 1925; studied at the Kansas City Art Institute (1947-48), Académie Julian, Paris (1948), Black Mountain College, North Carolina (1948-49), Art Students League, New York (1949-52); lives in Captiva, Florida, and New York.

ONE-ARTIST EXHIBITIONS

1951

Betty Parsons
New York

1953

Stable Gallery
New York

1958

Leo Castelli Gallery
New York

1962

Dwan Gallery
Los Angeles

1963

Galerie Ileana Sonnabend
Paris

The Jewish Museum
New York

1965

Walker Art Center
Minneapolis

1974

Los Angeles County
Museum of Art

Museum Haus Lange
Krefeld, West Germany

1976

National Collection of Fine
Arts, Smithsonian Institution
Washington, D.C. (traveled)

1981

Musée National d'Art
Moderne, Centre
Georges Pompidou
Paris (traveled)

1990

Whitney Museum of
American Art
New York

GROUP EXHIBITIONS

1958

Museum of Art,
Carnegie Institute
Pittsburgh
"The 1958 Carnegie
International"

1959

Kassel, West Germany
"Documenta 2"

The Museum of Modern Art
New York
"Sixteen Americans"

1963

The Solomon R.
Guggenheim Museum
New York
"Six Painters and the Object"

1964

Venice
"XXXII Biennale di Venezia"

1967

Los Angeles County
Museum of Art
"American Sculpture of
the Sixties" (traveled)

1974

Dallas Museum of Fine Arts
"Poets of the Cities: New
York and San Francisco,
1950-1965" (traveled)

Whitney Museum of
American Art
New York
"American Pop Art"
(traveled)

1984

Whitney Museum of
American Art
New York
"BLAM! The Explosion of
Pop, Minimalism, and
Performance 1958-1964"

1990

The Museum of Modern Art
New York
"High and Low: Modern Art
and Popular Culture"
(traveled)

BIBLIOGRAPHY

Ashton, Dore
RAUSCHENBERG: XXXIV
DRAWINGS FOR DANTE'S
INFERNO. New York: Harry
N. Abrams, 1964.

Feinstein, Roni
ROBERT RAUSCHENBERG:
THE SILKSCREEN PAINTINGS,
1962-64 (exhibition
catalogue). New York:
Whitney Museum of
American Art, 1990.

Forge, Andrew
ROBERT RAUSCHENBERG.
New York: Harry N.
Abrams, 1969.

Forge, Andrew
ROBERT RAUSCHENBERG.
New York: Harry N.
Abrams, 1972.

Geldzahler, Henry, John
Cage, and Max Kozloff
RAUSCHENBERG: PAINTINGS,
DRAWINGS AND COMBINES,
1949-1964 (exhibition
catalogue). London:
Whitechapel Art Gallery,
1964.

Kotz, Mary Lynn
RAUSCHENBERG: ART AND
LIFE. New York: Harry N.
Abrams, 1990.

Solomon, Alan R.
ROBERT RAUSCHENBERG
(exhibition catalogue). New
York: The Jewish Museum,
1963.

Tomkins, Calvin
OFF THE WALL: ROBERT
RAUSCHENBERG AND THE
ART WORLD OF OUR TIME.
Garden City, New York:
Doubleday and Company,
1980.

ROBERT RAUSCHENBERG

Yellow Visor   1989

Appalachian Double Latch Spring Glut   1989

The Temptation of Saint Antony: The Nicolaitans (detail) 1990

TIM ROLLINS
Born in Pittsfield, Maine, 1955;
studied at the School of Visual
Arts, New York (BFA, 1978),
New York University,
Department of Education (MA,
1980); lives in New York.

K.O.S. MEMBERS 1989-90
Angel Abreu (b. 1975)
George Garces (b. 1972)
Nelson Montes (b. 1972)
Jose Parissi (b. 1968)
Carlos Rivera (b. 1971)
Annette Rosado (b. 1972)
Nelson Savinon (b. 1972)

SOLO EXHIBITIONS

1987

Knight Gallery
Charlotte, North Carolina

1988

The Institute of
Contemporary Art
Boston

Walker Art Center
Minneapolis

1989

Galerie Johnen & Schöttle
Cologne

Interim Art
London

Jay Gorney Modern Art
New York

1990

Dia Art Foundation
New York (traveled)

Museum für
Gegenwartskunst
Basel

Wadsworth Atheneum
Hartford

GROUP EXHIBITIONS

1986

Sala de Exposiciones,
Fundación Caja de
Pensiones
Madrid
"Art and Its Double:
A New York Perspective"

1987

Städtische Kunsthalle
Düsseldorf
"Similia/Dissimilia: Modes of
Abstractions in Painting,
Sculpture, and Photography
Today" (traveled)

Josh Baer Gallery
New York
"The Beauty of
Circumstance"

P.S. 1, Institute for Art
and Urban Resources
Long Island City, New York
"Art Out of the Studio: Art
with Community"

The Saatchi Collection
London
"NY Art Now: The Saatchi
Collection"

1988

The Institute of
Contemporary Art and the
Museum of Fine Arts
Boston
"The BiNATIONAL:
American Art of the Late
80s" (traveled)

The Museum of Modern Art
New York
"Committed to Print"

Venice
"XLIII Biennale di Venezia"

1989

Stedelijk Museum
Amsterdam
"Horn of Plenty: Sixteen
Artists from NYC"

1990

Museum of Contemporary
Hispanic Art, The New
Museum of Contemporary
Art, and The Studio
Museum in Harlem
New York
"The Decade Show:
Frameworks of Identity
in the 1980s"

BIBLIOGRAPHY

Brooks, Rosetta
"Tim Rollins + K.O.S."
ARTSCRIBE INTERNATIONAL,
no. 63 (May 1987), pp. 40-47.

Decter, Joshua
"Tim Rollins + K.O.S.: The
workshop survived because
we love each other." FLASH
ART, no. 150 (January 1990),
pp. 89-93.

Garrels, Gary, Michele
Wallace, Arthur C. Danto,
and Tim Rollins
AMERIKA: TIM ROLLINS +
K.O.S. (exhibition catalogue).
New York: Dia Art
Foundation, 1989.

Koepplin, Dieter
TIM ROLLINS + K.O.S.:
THE TEMPTATION OF SAINT
ANTONY (exhibition
catalogue). Basel: Museum
für Gegenwartskunst, 1990.

Levin, Kim
"Tim Rollins + K.O.S. at
Jay Gorney Gallery." THE
VILLAGE VOICE, May 23,
1989, p. 94.

Lippard, Lucy
"Amerika: Art Against the
Odds." Z MAGAZINE,
2 (December 1989),
pp. 75-77.

Smith, Roberta
"Amerika by Tim Rollins
and K.O.S." THE NEW YORK
TIMES, November 3, 1989.

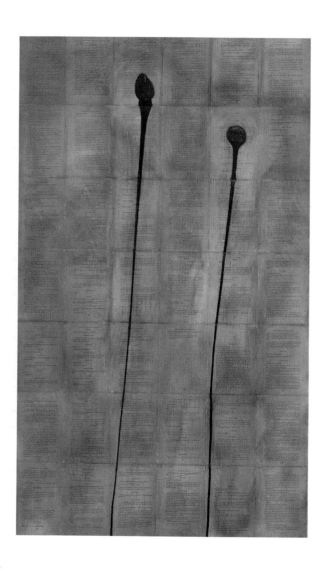

TIM ROLLINS + K.O.S.

The Temptation of Saint Antony: The Trinity 1990

ALLEN RUPPERSBERG   *How to Remember a Better Tomorrow, Sets and Props*   1989–90 *

Born in Cleveland, 1944; studied at the Chouinard Art Institute, Los Angeles (BFA, 1967); lives in New York.

ONE-ARTIST EXHIBITIONS

1970

Pasadena Art Museum

1971

Art and Project
Amsterdam

1973

Stedelijk Museum
Amsterdam

1974

Claire Copley Gallery
Los Angeles

1976

Texas Gallery
Houston

1979

Rosamund Felsen Gallery
Los Angeles

1980

The Clocktower, Institute
for Art and Urban Resources
New York

1985

The Museum of
Contemporary Art
Los Angeles

The New Museum of
Contemporary Art
New York

1988

Christine Burgin Gallery
New York

James Corcoran Gallery
Los Angeles

1990

John Weber Gallery
New York

GROUP EXHIBITIONS

1969

Kunsthalle Bern
"Live in Your Head/When
Attitudes Become Form:
Works-Concepts-Processes-
Situations-Information"

1970

Whitney Museum of
American Art
New York
"1970 Annual Exhibition:
Contemporary American
Sculpture"

1971

Los Angeles County
Museum of Art
"24 Young Los Angeles
Artists"

1972

Kassel, West Germany
"Documenta 5"

1975

Whitney Museum of
American Art
New York
"1975 Biennial Exhibition"

1976

San Francisco Museum of
Modern Art
"California Painting and
Sculpture: The Modern
Era" (traveled)

1977

The Solomon R.
Guggenheim Museum
New York
"Nine Artists: Theodoron
Awards"

1986

Newport Harbor Art Museum
Newport Beach, California
"Shift: LA/NY" (traveled)

1987

MIT List Visual Arts
Center
Cambridge, Massachusetts
"L.A.: Hot and Cool: The
Eighties"

1990

Massimo Audiello Gallery
New York
"The Last Laugh: Irony,
Humor, Self-Mockery, and
Derision"

BIBLIOGRAPHY

ALLEN RUPPERSBERG
(exhibition catalogue).
Amsterdam: Stedelijk
Museum, 1973.

Jones, Alan
"Where's Al? Allen
Ruppersberg Rewrites the
Rules of Hide and Seek."
ARTS MAGAZINE, 64 (May
1990), pp. 25-26.

McCormick, Carlo
"Allen Ruppersberg:
Christine Burgin."
ARTFORUM, 26 (April 1988),
pp. 142-43.

Morgan, Susan
"Allen Ruppersberg: 'The
Secret of Life and Death' at
The New Museum."
ARTSCRIBE INTERNATIONAL,
no. 55 (December 1985-
January 1986), p. 83.

Plagens, Peter
"Ruppersberg's
Encyclopedia." ART IN
AMERICA, 73 (December
1985), pp. 84-92.

Singerman, Howard
ALLEN RUPPERSBERG: THE
SECRET OF LIFE AND DEATH
(exhibition catalogue). Los
Angeles: The Museum of
Contemporary Art, 1985.

ALLEN RUPPERSBERG   *The Gift and the Inheritance (Looking Backward 2000-1887 by Edward Bellamy)*   1989*

The Gift and the Inheritance   1989 *   233

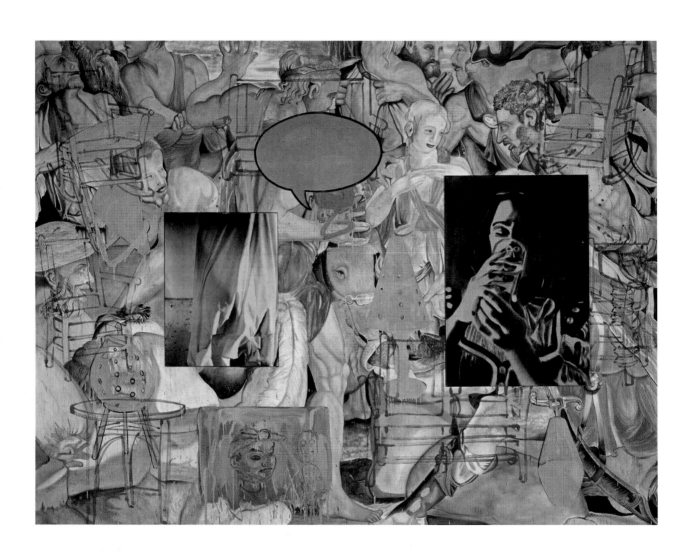

DAVID SALLE

Mingus in Mexico 1990

Born in Norman, Oklahoma, 1952; studied at the California Institute of the Arts, Valencia (BFA, 1973; MFA, 1975); lives in New York.

ONE-ARTIST EXHIBITIONS

1976

Artists Space
New York

1977

Fondation de Appel
Amsterdam

The Kitchen
New York

1980

Annina Nosei
New York

1981

Larry Gagosian Gallery
Los Angeles

Mary Boone Gallery
New York

1982

Anthony d'Offay Gallery
London

1984

Leo Castelli Gallery
New York

1986

Institute of Contemporary
Art, University of
Pennsylvania
Philadelphia (traveled)

1988

Fundación Caja de
Pensiones
Madrid

The Menil Collection
Houston

1990

Fred Hoffman Gallery
Los Angeles

GROUP EXHIBITIONS

1981

Museen der Stadt Köln
Cologne
"Westkunst: Heute"

1982

Kassel, West Germany
"Documenta 7"

Neuer Berliner Kunstverein
West Berlin
"Zeitgeist"

Venice
"XL Biennale di Venezia"

1983

The Tate Gallery
London
"New Art"

1985

Museum of Art,
Carnegie Institute
Pittsburgh
"1985 Carnegie International"

Whitney Museum of
American Art
New York
"1985 Biennial Exhibition"

1987

Los Angeles County
Museum of Art
"Avant-Garde in the
Eighties"

1989

Museum Ludwig
Cologne
"Bilderstreit: Widerspruch,
Einheit und Fragment in
der Kunst seit 1960"

1990

Tony Shafrazi Gallery
New York
"The Last Decade: American
Art of the 80's"

BIBLIOGRAPHY

Brooks, Rosetta
"From the Night of Consumerism to the Dawn of Simulation." ARTFORUM, 23 (February 1985), pp. 76-81.

Heartney, Eleanor
"David Salle: Impersonal Effects." ART IN AMERICA, 76 (June 1988), pp. 120-129, 175.

Kardon, Janet, and Lisa Phillips
DAVID SALLE (exhibition catalogue). Philadelphia: Institute of Contemporary Art, University of Pennsylvania, 1986.

Power, Kevin, and Carla Schulz-Hoffmann
DAVID SALLE (exhibition catalogue). Madrid: Fundación Caja de Pensiones, 1988.

Salle, David, and James Welling
"Images that Understand Us: A Conversation with David Salle and James Welling." JOURNAL: SOUTHERN CALIFORNIA ART MAGAZINE, 3 (June 1980), pp. 41-44.

Schjeldahl, Peter
DAVID SALLE: SIEBEN BILDER (exhibition catalogue). Cologne: Galerie Michael Werner, 1985.

Schjeldahl, Peter
"The Real Salle." ART IN AMERICA, 72 (September 1984), pp. 180-87.

Schjeldahl, Peter
SALLE. New York: Elizabeth Avedon Editions, Vintage Books, 1987.

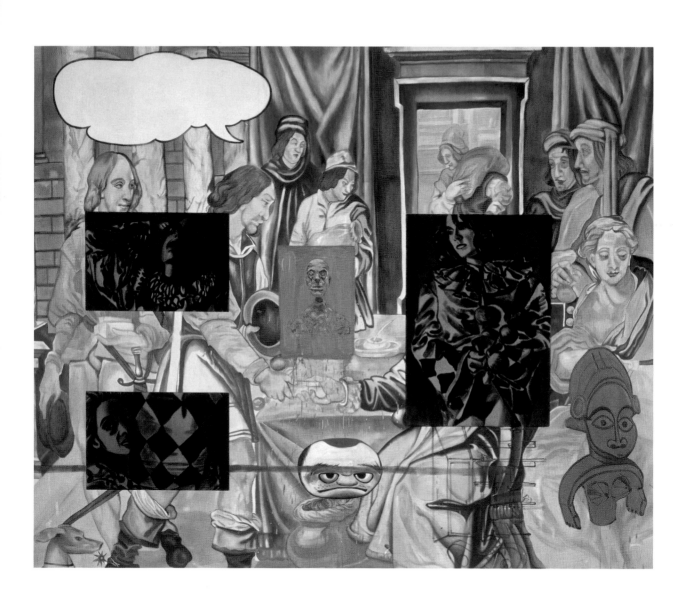

DAVID SALLE

E.A.J.A.   1990

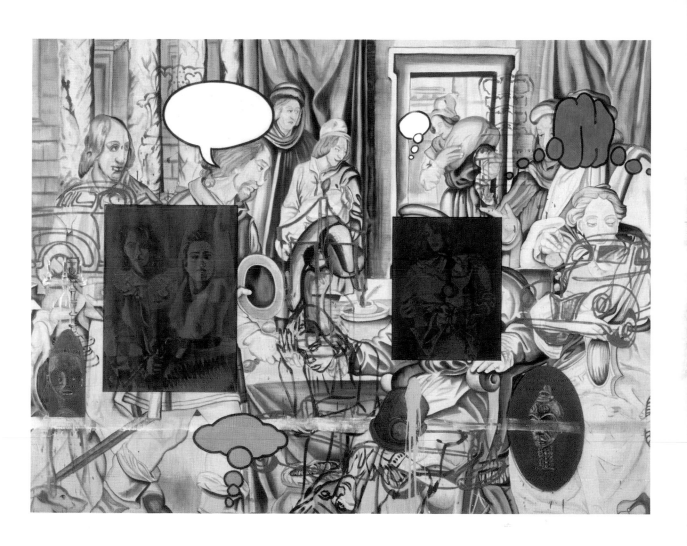

Ugolino's Room   1990–91*

JOSEPH SANTORE   *The Frayed Rope*   1988–89

*Born in Philadelphia, 1945;
studied at the Philadelphia
College of Art (BFA, 1969),
University of Arizona, (MFA
candidate, 1970-71), Yale
University, New Haven (MFA,
1973); lives in New York.*

ONE-ARTIST EXHIBITIONS

1973

Yale University Art Gallery
New Haven

1982

Edward Thorp Gallery
New York

1984

Edward Thorp Gallery
New York

1987

Edward Thorp Gallery
New York

1990

Edward Thorp Gallery
New York

GROUP EXHIBITIONS

1984

Edward Thorp Gallery
New York
"New Vistas: Contemporary
American Landscapes"
(traveled)

1985

Holly Solomon Gallery
New York
"Innovative Still Life"

Stephen Rosenberg Gallery
New York
"Exotica: Paintings and
Works on Paper"

1988

East Hampton Center for
Contemporary Art
East Hampton, New York
"Drawings from the Figure"

1989

American Academy and
Institute of Arts and Letters
New York
"Exhibition of Work by
Newly Elected Members
and Recipients of Awards"

Edward Thorp Gallery
New York
"Face Off"

1990

Edward Thorp Gallery
New York
"Summer"

Rosa Esman Gallery
New York
"Objects on the Edge:
Contemporary Still Life"

JOSEPH SANTORE

Peonies 1990 *

The Yellow Painting 1988–89

THOMAS LANIGAN SCHMIDT   *Olympio (The Naked Macho)*   1989–90

Born in Elizabeth, New Jersey, 1948; studied at Pratt Institute, Brooklyn, New York (1965-66), School of Visual Arts, New York (1967); lives in New York.

ONE-ARTIST EXHIBITIONS

1973

98 Greene Street Loft
New York

1974

Artists Space
New York

1978

Holly Solomon Gallery
New York

1980

Holly Solomon Gallery
New York

1983

Holly Solomon Gallery
New York

1985

Holly Solomon Gallery
New York

1986

The Walters Art Gallery
Baltimore

1988

Holly Solomon Gallery
New York (traveled)

GROUP EXHIBITIONS

1979

Hirshhorn Museum and
Sculpture Garden,
Smithsonian Institution
Washington, D.C.
"Directions"

1980

Neue Galerie, Sammlung
Ludwig
Aachen, West Germany
"Les Nouveaux Fauves/Die
Neuen Wilden"

San Francisco Art Institute
"Decoration"

1981

The New Museum
New York
"Alternatives in Retrospect:
An Historical Overview
1969–1975"

1982

Barbara Gladstone Gallery
New York
"The Crucifix Show"

Contemporary Arts Museum
Houston
"The Americans:
The Collage"

Kestner-Gesellschaft
Hannover, West Germany
"New York Now" (traveled)

1984

Hirshhorn Museum and
Sculpture Garden,
Smithsonian Institution
Washington, D.C.
"Content: A Contemporary
Focus, 1974–1984"

1985

Grey Art Gallery and Study
Center, New York University
"Precious: An American
Cottage Industry of the
Eighties"

1986

Whitney Museum of
American Art
New York
"Sacred Images in
Secular Art"

1989

The Hudson River Museum
Yonkers
"The Nature of the Beast"

1990

Nahan Contemporary
New York
"Concept Décoratif: Anti-
Formalist Art of the 70s"

BIBLIOGRAPHY

Atkins, Robert
"'The Center Show' Art on
Stone Walls." THE VILLAGE
VOICE, June 13, 1989,
pp. 90-91.

Boyce, Martin James
"Thomas Lanigan Schmidt:
Joy of Life, Predestination
and Class—Clash Realism."
FLASH ART, no. 114
(November 1983), pp. 60-61.

Brenson, Michael
"From Young Artists,
Defiance Behind a Smiling
Facade." THE NEW YORK
TIMES, September 29, 1985,
section 2, pp. 1, 35.

Fox, Howard N.
DIRECTIONS (exhibition
catalogue). Washington,
D.C.: Hirshhorn Museum
and Sculpture Garden,
Smithsonian Intitution,
1979.

Gambrell, Jamey
"Thomas Lanigan Schimdt at
Holly Solomon." ART IN
AMERICA, 71 (April 1983),
p. 180.

Glueck, Grace
"Religion Makes an Impact
As a Theme in Today's
Art." THE NEW YORK TIMES,
April 7, 1985, section 2,
pp. 1, 21.

Occhiogrosso, Peter
ONCE A CATHOLIC. Boston:
Houghton-Mifflin Company,
1987.

Putterman, Susan
"Thomas Lanigan Schmidt's
Testaments." ARTS
MAGAZINE, 57 (March 1983),
pp. 122-23.

Raynor, Vivien
"Art: Blue-Collar Lanigan
Schmidt." THE NEW YORK
TIMES, September 13, 1985.

THOMAS LANIGAN SCHMIDT   *Incomplete Caress*   1989–90

Platonic Love (Mozart and Candy Cubism)   1989–90

JULIAN SCHNABEL

Esso Ess   1990

Born in New York, 1951; studied at the University of Houston (BFA, 1972), Independent Study Program, Whitney Museum of American Art, New York (1973-74); lives in New York.

ONE-ARTIST EXHIBITIONS

1976

Contemporary Arts Museum
Houston

1979

Mary Boone Gallery
New York

Daniel Weinberg Gallery
San Francisco

1980

Galerie Bruno Bischofberger
Zurich

1981

Kunsthalle Basel

1982

Stedelijk Museum
Amsterdam

The Tate Gallery
London

1983

Leo Castelli Gallery
New York

1984

The Pace Gallery
New York

1986

Whitechapel Art Gallery
London (traveled)

1988

The Israel Museum
Jerusalem

1989

Museum für Gegenwartskunst
Basel (traveled)

1990

The Pace Gallery
New York

GROUP EXHIBITIONS

1971

University of Saint Thomas
Houston
"Hidden Houston"

1977

Holly Solomon Gallery
New York
"Surrogate Self-Portraits"

1979

The Renaissance Society at
The University of Chicago
"Visionary Images"

1980

Venice
"XXXIX Biennale di
Venezia"

1981

Kunsthalle Basel
"Schnabel, Rothenberg,
Moskowitz" (traveled)

Whitney Museum of
American Art
New York
"1981 Biennial Exhibition"

1982

The Art Institute of
Chicago
"74th American Exhibition"

Venice
"XL Biennale di Venezia"

1984

The Museum of Modern Art
New York
"An International Survey of
Recent Painting and
Sculpture"

1985

Museum of Art, Carnegie
Institute
Pittsburgh
"1985 Carnegie International"

1990

Hirshhorn Museum and
Sculpture Garden,
Smithsonian Institution
Washington, D.C.
"Culture and Commentary:
An Eighties Perspective"

BIBLIOGRAPHY

Ammann, Jean-Christophe,
and Julian Schnabel
JULIAN SCHNABEL
(exhibition catalogue).
Basel: Kunsthalle Basel,
1981.

Francis, Richard, and
Julian Schnabel
JULIAN SCHNABEL
(exhibition catalogue).
London: The Tate Gallery,
1982.

Ricard, René, and
Alexander van Grevenstein
JULIAN SCHNABEL
(exhibition catalogue).
Amsterdam: Stedelijk
Museum, 1982.

Schnabel, Julian
C.V.J.: NICKNAMES OF
MAITRE D'S & OTHER
EXCERPTS FROM LIFE. New
York: Random House, 1987.

Serota, Nicholas, Thomas
McEvilley, Lisa Phillips,
and Julian Schnabel
JULIAN SCHNABEL:
PAINTINGS 1975-1986
(exhibition catalogue).
London: Whitechapel Art
Gallery, 1986.

Zutter, Jörg, Brooks
Adams, and Donald Kuspit
JULIAN SCHNABEL: ARBEITEN
AUF PAPIER 1975-1988
(exhibition catalogue).
Basel: Museum für
Gegenwartskunst, 1989.

JULIAN SCHNABEL   *Golem*   1989

Self-Portrait with Champagne Glass   1987–90

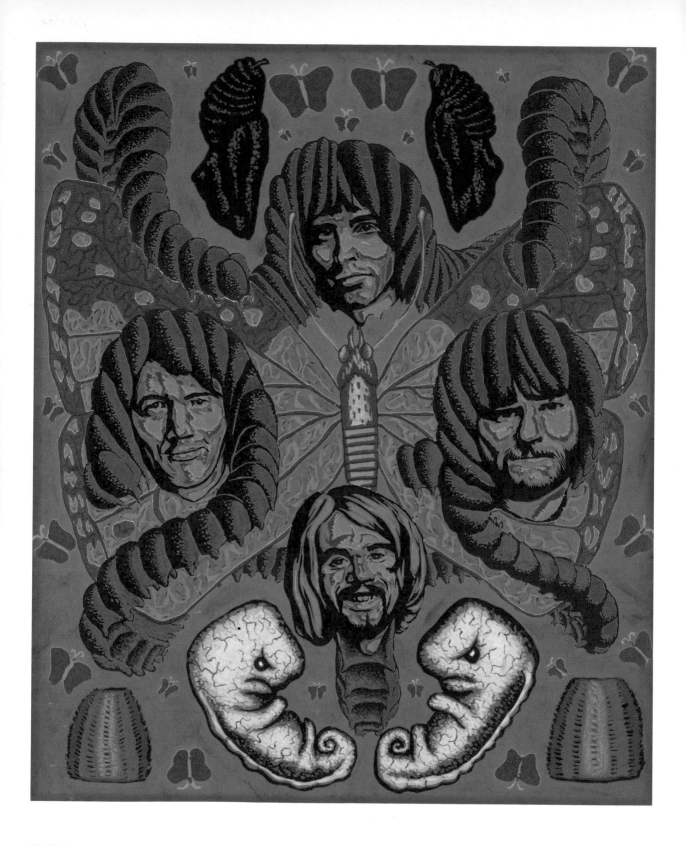

JIM SHAW

Devotional Art, 1987, from *My Mirage*   1986–90

Born in Midland, Michigan, 1952; studied at the University of Michigan, Ann Arbor (BFA, 1974), California Institute of the Arts, Valencia (MFA, 1978); lives in Los Angeles.

ONE-ARTIST EXHIBITIONS

1981

Zero Zero Club
Los Angeles

1989

Dennis Anderson Gallery
Los Angeles

1990

Feature Gallery
New York

Linda Cathcart Gallery
Santa Monica

Matrix Gallery, University Art Museum, University of California, Berkeley

GROUP EXHIBITIONS

1984

LACE
Los Angeles
"The Floor Show"

1985

LACE
Los Angeles
"TV Generations"

1986

LACE
Los Angeles
"Social Distortions"

1987

Long Beach Museum of Art
Long Beach, California
"New California Video, A Survey of Open Channels: Open Channels III"

MIT List Visual Arts Center
Cambridge, Massachusetts
"LA: Hot and Cool: The Eighties"

The Rennaissance Society at The University of Chicago and the Newport Harbor Art Museum, Newport Beach, California
"CalArts: Skeptical Belief(s)"

1988

Artists Space
New York
"Telling Tales"

1989

Feature Gallery
New York
"Buttinsky"

Hallwalls
Buffalo
"Amerikarma"

1990

The Museum of Modern Art
New York
"Video and Dream"

Simon Watson Gallery
New York
"Total Metal"

Whitney Museum of American Art
New York
"Recent Drawing: Roni Horn, Charles Ray, Jim Shaw, Michael Tetherow"

BIBLIOGRAPHY

Friis-Hansen, Dana
LA: HOT AND COOL: THE EIGHTIES (exhibition catalogue). Cambridge, Massachusetts: MIT List Visual Arts Center, 1987.

Gerstler, Amy
"Jim Shaw: Dennis Anderson Gallery." ARTFORUM, 28 (Summer 1989), p. 151.

Helfand, Glen
"Boy's Life." SAN FRANCISCO WEEKLY, November 14, 1990, p. 11.

Hickey, Dave
"Jim Shaw: Stopping the Image Wheel." VISIONS, 4 (Winter 1989), pp. 6-9.

Kertess, Klaus
RECENT DRAWING: RONI HORN, CHARLES RAY, JIM SHAW, MICHAEL TETHEROW (exhibition brochure). New York: Whitney Museum of American Art, 1990.

Knight, Christopher
"Recycling Art From a Heap of History." LOS ANGELES HERALD EXAMINER, March 31, 1989, p. 4.

Lord, Catherine, et al.
CALARTS: SKEPTICAL BELIEF(S) (exhibition catalogue). Chicago: The Renaissance Society at The University of Chicago; Newport Beach, California: Newport Harbor Art Museum, 1987.

Rinder, Lawrence
JIM SHAW: MY MIRAGE (exhibition catalogue). Berkeley: Matrix Gallery, University Art Museum, University of California, 1990.

Weissman, Benjamin
"Jim Shaw at Saxon-Lee." ART ISSUES, no. 1 (January 1989), p. 23.

My Mirage Logo #3, 1989, from *My Mirage*   1986–90

CINDY SHERMAN

Untitled 1989

Born in Glen Ridge, New Jersey, 1954; studied at State University of New York, College at Buffalo (BA, 1976); lives in New York.

ONE-ARTIST EXHIBITIONS

1979

Hallwalls
Buffalo

1980

Metro Pictures
New York

1982

Stedelijk Museum
Amsterdam (traveled)

1984

Akron Art Museum
Ohio (traveled)

The Seibu Museum of Art
Tokyo

1987

Whitney Museum of
American Art
New York (traveled)

1990

Galerie Monika Sprüth
Cologne

Linda Cathcart Gallery
Santa Monica

Metro Pictures
New York

GROUP EXHIBITIONS

1978

Artists Space
New York
"Four Artists"

1982

Institute of Contemporary
Art, University of
Pennsylvania
Philadelphia
"Image Scavengers:
Photography"

1983

The Tate Gallery
London
"New Art at The Tate
Gallery 1983"

Whitney Museum of
American Art
New York
"1983 Biennial Exhibition"

1984

Hirshhorn Museum and
Sculpture Garden,
Smithsonian Institution
Washington, D.C.
"Content: A Contemporary
Focus, 1974-1984"

1987

Sala de Exposiciones,
Fundación Caja de Pensiones
Madrid
"Art and Its Double:
A New York Perspective"

John and Mable Ringling
Museum of Art
Sarasota, Florida
"This Is Not a Photograph:
Twenty Years of Large-
Scale Photography
1966-1986" (traveled)

1989

The Museum of Fine Arts
Houston
"The Art of Photography:
1939-1989" (traveled)

The Museum of Modern Art
New York
"Photography Until Now"

Whitney Museum of
American Art
New York
"Image World: Art and
Media Culture"

1990

Hirshhorn Museum and
Sculpture Garden,
Smithsonian Institution
Washington, D.C.
"Culture and Commentary:
An Eighties Perspective"

BIBLIOGRAPHY

Danto, Arthur C.
CINDY SHERMAN: UNTITLED
FILM STILLS. New York:
Rizzoli International
Publications, 1990.

Grundberg, Andy
"Photography: Images of the
Past and Future." THE NEW
YORK TIMES, January 12,
1990, p. C29.

Jacobs, Joseph
THIS IS NOT A PHOTOGRAPH:
TWENTY YEARS OF LARGE-
SCALE PHOTOGRAPHY
1966-1986 (exhibition
catalogue). Sarasota,
Florida: John and Mable
Ringling Museum of Art,
1987.

Kuspit, Donald
"Inside Cindy Sherman."
ARTSCRIBE INTERNATIONAL,
no. 65 (September-October
1987), pp. 41-43.

Schjeldahl, Peter, and
Lisa Phillips
CINDY SHERMAN (exhibition
catalogue). New York:
Whitney Museum of
American Art, 1987.

Smith, Joshua P., and
Merry A. Forresta
THE PHOTOGRAPHY OF
INVENTION: AMERICAN
PICTURES OF THE 1980S
(exhibition catalogue).
Washington, D.C.: National
Museum of American Art,
Smithsonian Institution, 1989.

Smith, Roberta
"Art: Cindy Sherman at
Metro Pictures." THE NEW
YORK TIMES, May 8, 1987.

Weaver, Mike, and
Daniel Wolf
THE ART OF PHOTOGRAPHY:
1839-1989 (exhibition
catalogue). London: Royal
Academy of Arts, 1989.

CINDY SHERMAN

Untitled 1990

Untitled   1989*

LAURIE SIMMONS

Sitting Accordion 1990

Born in Far Rockaway, New York, 1949; studied at the Tyler School of Art, Philadelphia (BFA, 1971); lives in New York.

ONE-ARTIST EXHIBITIONS

1979

Artists Space
New York

1981

Metro Pictures
New York

1984

International with
Monument Gallery
New York

1985

Nature Morte Gallery
New York
(with Allan McCollum)
(traveled)

Weatherspoon Art Gallery,
University of North Carolina
at Greensboro

1989

Daniel Weinberg
New York

Jablonka Galerie
Cologne

1990

San Jose Museum of Art
California

GROUP EXHIBITIONS

1981

Hayden Gallery,
Massachusetts Institute
of Technology
Cambridge
"Body Language: Figurative
Aspects of Recent Art"
(traveled)

1985

Whitney Museum of
American Art
New York
"1985 Biennial Exhibition"

1987

John and Mable Ringling
Museum of Art
Sarasota, Florida
"This Is Not a Photograph:
Twenty Years of Large-
Scale Photography
1966-1986" (traveled)

Los Angeles County
Museum of Art
"Photography and Art:
Interactions Since 1946"
(traveled)

Walker Art Center
Minneapolis
"Past/Imperfect: Eric
Fischl, Vernon Fisher,
Laurie Simmons" (traveled)

1989

Cincinnati Art Museum
"Making Their Mark:
Women Artists Move into
the Mainstream, 1970-85"
(traveled)

The Museum of
Contemporary Art
Los Angeles
"A Forest of Signs: Art in
the Crisis of Representation"

National Museum of
American Art,
Smithsonian Institution
Washington, D.C.
"The Photography of
Invention: American
Pictures of the 1980s"

Whitney Museum of
American Art
New York
"Image World: Art and
Media Culture"

1990

Wiener Secession
Vienna
"Umweg Moderne/Modern
Detour: R. M. Fischer,
Peter Halley, Laurie
Simmons"

BIBLIOGRAPHY

Brooks, Rosetta
"Guys and Dolls." ZG
MAGAZINE, no. 11 (Summer
1984), pp. 7-8.

Cameron, Dan
"Recent Work by Laurie
Simmons." FLASH ART, no.
149 (November-December
1989), pp. 116-118.

Goldwater, Marge
PAST/IMPERFECT: ERIC
FISCHL, VERNON FISHER,
LAURIE SIMMONS (exhibition
catalogue). Minneapolis:
Walker Art Center, 1987.

Grundberg, Andy, and
Kathleen McCarthy Gauss
PHOTOGRAPHY AND ART:
INTERACTIONS SINCE 1946
(exhibition catalogue).
Los Angeles: Los Angeles
County Museum of Art,
1987.

Goldstein, Ann,
Mary Jane Jacob, and
Howard Singerman
A FOREST OF SIGNS:
ART IN THE CRISIS OF
REPRESENTATION (exhibition
catalogue). Los Angeles:
The Museum of
Contemporary Art, 1989.

Jones, Ronald
LAURIE SIMMONS (exhibition
catalogue). Cologne:
Galerie Jablonka, 1989.

Linker, Kate
"On Artificiality." FLASH
ART, no. 111 (March 1983),
pp. 33-35.

Sultan, Terry
SURROGATE SELVES: DAVID
LEVINTHAL, CINDY SHERMAN,
LAURIE SIMMONS (exhibition
catalogue). Washington,
D.C.: The Corcoran
Gallery of Art, 1989.

LAURIE SIMMONS

Bending Globe 1990

GUARDED CONDITIONS

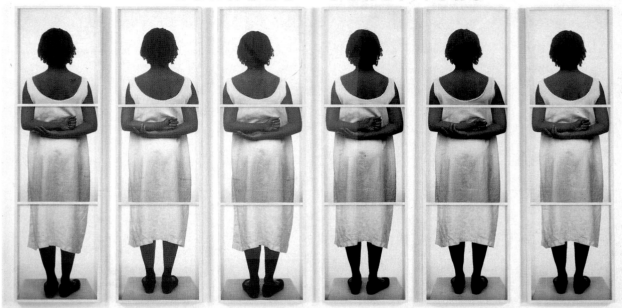

LORNA SIMPSON

Guarded Conditions   1989 *

Born in New York, 1960; studied at the School of Visual Arts, New York (BFA, 1982), University of California, San Diego (MFA, 1985); lives in New York.

ONE-ARTIST EXHIBITIONS

1989

Josh Baer Gallery
New York

Wadsworth Atheneum
Hartford

1990

Denver Art Museum

Portland Art Museum
Oregon

The Museum of Modern Art
New York

University Art Museum,
California State University,
Long Beach

University Art Museum,
University of California,
Berkeley

GROUP EXHIBITIONS

1986

The New Museum of
Contemporary Art
New York
"The Body"

1988

The Institute of
Contemporary Art
Boston
"Utopia Post Utopia:
Configurations of Nature
and Culture in Recent
Sculpture and
Photography"

The Institute of
Contemporary Art and the
Museum of Fine Arts
Boston
"The BiNATIONAL:
American Art of the Late
80s" (traveled)

White Columns
New York
"Real World"

1989

Alternative Museum
New York
"Prisoners of Image 1800-
1988: Ethnic and Gender
Stereotypes"

The Studio Museum
in Harlem
New York
"Constructed Images: New
Photography"

Whitney Museum of
American Art
New York
"Image World: Art and
Media Culture"

1990

Milwaukee Art Museum
"Word as Image: American
Art 1960-1990" (traveled)

New Jersey State Museum
Trenton
"A Force of Repetition"

Museum of Contemporary
Hispanic Art, The New
Museum of Contemporary
Art, and The Studio
Museum in Harlem
New York
"The Decade Show:
Frameworks of Identity in
the 1980s"

Venice
"XLIV Biennale di Venezia"

BIBLIOGRAPHY

Decter, Joshua
"Constructed Images:
New Photography." ARTS
MAGAZINE, 64 (December
1989), p. 97.

Hargrove, Yasmin
CENTRIC 38: LORNA SIMPSON
(exhibition brochure).
Long Beach: University Art
Museum, California State
University, 1989.

Heartney, Eleanor
"Lorna Simpson at Josh
Baer." ART IN AMERICA, 77
(November 1989), p. 185.

Jones, Kellie
LORNA SIMPSON (exhibition
catalogue). New York:
Josh Baer Gallery, 1989.

Joseph, Regina
"Interview with Lorna
Simpson." BALCON, nos. 5-6
(1990).

McKenna, Kristine
"Centric 38: High-Minded
World of New York's
Lorna Simpson." THE LOS
ANGELES TIMES, April
3, 1990.

Olander, William
"Material World." ART IN
AMERICA, 77 (January 1989),
pp. 123-28, 167.

Sims, Lowery Stokes
"The Mirror, The Other:
The Politics of Esthetics."
ARTFORUM, 7 (March 1990),
pp. 111-15.

Smith, Roberta
"Linking Words and Images
Explosively." THE NEW
YORK TIMES, July 20, 1990.

Weld, Alison
A FORCE OF REPETITION
(exhibition catalogue).
Trenton: New Jersey State
Museum, 1990.

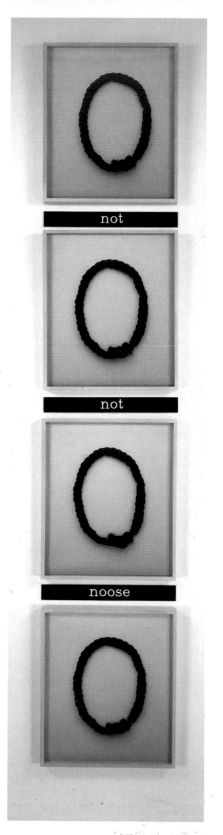

LORNA SIMPSON

Double Negative 1990

KIKI SMITH

Untitled 1990

Born in Nuremberg, 1954; lives in New York.

ONE-ARTIST EXHIBITIONS

1987

Piezo Electric Gallery
New York

1988

Fawbush Gallery
New York

1989

Dallas Museum of Art

Ezra and Cecile Zilkha
Gallery, Center for the Arts,
Wesleyan University
Middletown, Connecticut

Galerie René Blouin
Montreal

1990

Centre d'Art Contemporain
Geneva

The Clocktower Gallery,
The Institute for
Contemporary Art
New York

The Museum of Modern Art
New York

Tyler Gallery, Tyler School
of Art
Philadelphia

GROUP EXHIBITIONS

1980

New York
"Times Square Show"

1981

P.S.1, Institute for Art
and Urban Resources
Long Island City, New York
"New York, New Wave"

1982

Grace Borgenicht Gallery
New York
"Natural History"

Kassel, West Germany
"Documenta 7"

1986

The Clocktower, Institute
for Art and Urban Resources
New York
"Donald Lipski, Matt
Mullican and Kiki Smith"

1988

The Museum of Modern Art
New York
"Committed To Print"

1989

Artists Space
New York
"Witnesses: Against Our
Vanishing"

1990

Krieger Landau Gallery
Los Angeles
"Stained Sheets/Holy
Shrouds"

Museum of Fine Arts
Boston
"Figuring the Body"

White Columns
New York
"Fragments, Parts, and
Wholes: The Body and
Culture"

BIBLIOGRAPHY

Cook, Scott
NATURAL HISTORY
(exhibition catalogue). New
York: Grace Borgenicht
Gallery, 1982.

Decter, Joshua
"Kiki Smith." FLASH ART,
no. 148 (October 1989),
p. 134.

Lyon, Christopher
"Kiki Smith: Body and
Soul." ARTFORUM, 28
(February 1990),
pp. 102-06.

McCormick, Carlo
"Kiki Smith." ARTFORUM,
27 (October 1988), p. 145.

Smith, Roberta
"Kiki Smith." THE NEW
YORK TIMES, June 1, 1990.

Walker, Barry
PROJECTS & PORTFOLIOS:
THE 25TH NATIONAL PRINT
EXHIBITION (exhibition
catalogue). New York: The
Brooklyn Museum, 1989.

KIKI SMITH   *Untitled* 1989 *

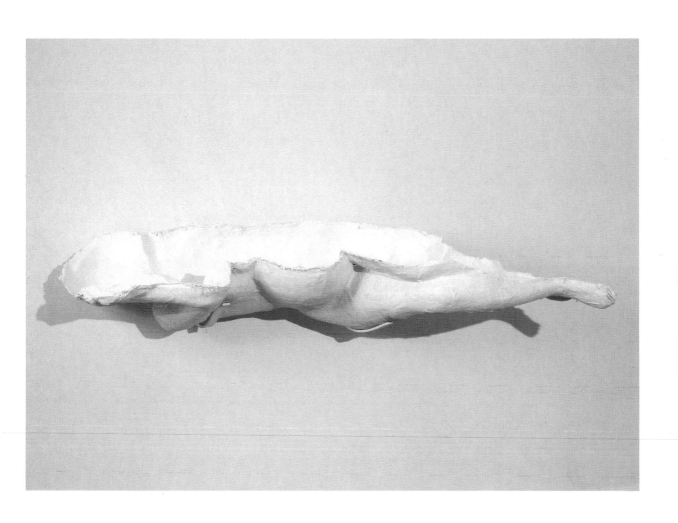

Trough   1990 *

PHILIP SMITH   *Epiphany II*   1990

Born in Miami, 1952; studied at Clark University, Worcester, Massachusetts (BA, 1974), Pratt Institute, Brooklyn, New York (1974-75); lives in New York and Miami.

ONE-ARTIST EXHIBITIONS

1979

South Campus Art Gallery, Miami-Dade Community College South
Miami

1982

Tony Shafrazi Gallery
New York

1983

Gabrielle Bryers Gallery
New York

1985

Art Palace
New York

1988

Jason McCoy Gallery
New York

1990

Jason McCoy Gallery
New York

GROUP EXHIBITIONS

1977

Artists Space
New York
"Pictures" (traveled)

1980

The Drawing Center
New York
"Illustration and Allegory"

1982

Contemporary Arts Museum
Houston
"The Americans:
The Collage"

The Drawing Center
New York
"New Drawing in America"

Tony Shafrazi Gallery
New York
"Young Americans"

1983

Monique Knowlton Gallery
New York
"Intoxication"

1984

Artists Space
New York
"A Decade of Art"

Charles Cowles Gallery
New York
"Totem"

1986

The Brooklyn Museum
New York
"Public and Private:
American Prints Today.
The 24th National Print
Exhibition" (traveled)

1988

Florida State University
Gallery and Museum
Tallahassee
"National Endowment for
the Arts Artists in Florida:
1987-1988 Awards"

1989

Vrej Baghoomian Gallery
New York
"Whatever It Is: Baechler,
Beckman, DiPalma,
Mosset, Rios, Schuyff,
Smith"

1990

The Artists' Museum
Lodz, Poland
"Construction in Process:
Back in Lodz 1990"

BIBLIOGRAPHY

Bishop, Joe
"Philip Smith." REAL LIFE
MAGAZINE (Winter 1980).

Borum, Jenifer
"Philip Smith." ARTFORUM,
19 (September 1990),
pp. 161-62.

Crimp, Douglas
PICTURES (exhibition
catalogue). New York:
Artists Space, 1977.

Martin, Richard
"Philip Smith's 'Gifts of the
Late Period.'" ARTS
MAGAZINE, 59 (February
1985), pp. 101-03.

Moufarrege, Nicolas A.
"The Mutant International,
II: The Still-Life Victims of
the Painter of a Thousand
Perils." ARTS MAGAZINE, 58
(October 1983), pp. 57-61.

Moufarrege, Nicolas A.
"Philip Smith." ARTS
MAGAZINE, 57 (September
1982), p. 31.

Palladino-Craig, Allys
NATIONAL ENDOWMENT FOR
THE ARTS ARTISTS IN
FLORIDA: 1987-1988 AWARDS
(exhibition catalogue).
Tallahassee: Florida State
University Gallery and
Museum, 1988.

Walker, Barry
PUBLIC AND PRIVATE:
AMERICAN PRINTS TODAY.
THE 24TH NATIONAL PRINT
EXHIBITION (exhibition
catalogue). New York: The
Brooklyn Museum, 1986.

Wallis, Brian, ed.
ART AFTER MODERNISM:
RETHINKING
REPRESENTATION. New
York: The New Museum of
Contemporary Art, 1984.

PHILIP SMITH   *Court of Law*   1989*

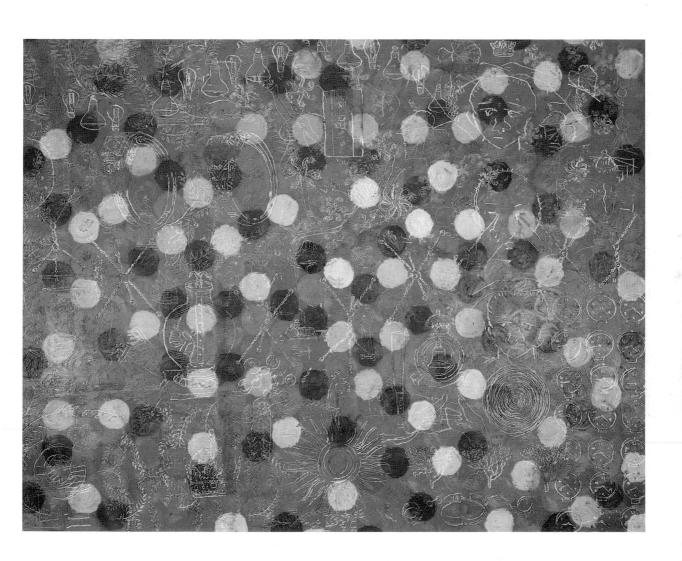

PAT STEIR   *Wolf Waterfall*   1990

Born in Newark, New Jersey, 1940; studied at Boston University (BA, 1960); Pratt Institute, Brooklyn, New York (BFA, 1962); lives in Amsterdam and New York.

ONE-ARTIST EXHIBITIONS

1964

Terry Dintenfass Gallery
New York

1973

The Corcoran Gallery of Art
Washington, D.C.

Max Protetch Gallery
Washington, D.C.

1975

Fourcade Droll Gallery
New York

1976

Xavier Fourcade Gallery
New York

1983

Contemporary Arts Museum
Houston

1984

The Brooklyn Museum
New York (traveled)

1986

Castelli Gallery
New York

Dallas Museum of Art

1987

Kunstmuseum Bern

M. Knoedler & Co.
New York

The New Museum of
Contemporary Art
New York

1989

Massimo Audiello Gallery
New York

1990

Musée d'Art Contemporain
Lyons

Robert Miller Gallery
New York

GROUP EXHIBITIONS

1972

Fine Arts Center,
University of Rhode Island
Kingston
"Three Painters"

Whitney Museum of
American Art
New York
"1972 Annual Exhibition of
Contemporary American
Painting"

1974

The Institute of
Contemporary Art
Boston
"Joan Snyder and Pat Steir"

1977

P.S. 1, Institute for Art
and Urban Resources
Long Island City, New York
"A Painting Show"

Whitney Museum of
American Art
"1977 Biennial Exhibition"

1983

Whitney Museum of
American Art
New York
"1983 Biennial Exhibition"

1984

Hirshhorn Museum and
Sculpture Garden,
Smithsonian Institution
Washington, D.C.
"Content: A Contemporary
Focus, 1974-1984"

1987

Los Angeles County
Museum of Art
"Avant-Garde in the Eighties"

São Paulo
"XIX Bienal de São Paulo"

BIBLIOGRAPHY

Broun, Elizabeth
FORM, ILLUSION, MYTH: PRINTS AND DRAWINGS OF PAT STEIR (exhibition catalogue). Lawrence: Helen Foresman Spencer Museum of Art, University of Kansas, 1983.

Chadwick, Whitney
WOMEN, ART AND SOCIETY. New York: Thames and Hudson, 1990.

Cotter, Holland
PAT STEIR (exhibition catalogue). New York: Robert Miller Gallery, 1990.

Graze, Sue
CONCENTRATIONS: PAT STEIR (exhibition catalogue). Dallas: Dallas Museum of Art, 1986.

Mayo, Marti
ARBITRARY ORDER: PAINTINGS BY PAT STEIR (exhibition catalogue). Houston: Contemporary Arts Museum, 1983.

Princenthal, Nancy
"The Self in Parts." ART IN AMERICA, 75 (November 1987), pp. 171-73.

Ratcliff, Carter
PAT STEIR PAINTINGS. New York: Harry N. Abrams, 1986.

Raven, Arlene
THE NEW CULTURE: WOMEN ARTISTS OF THE SEVENTIES (exhibition catalogue). Terre Haute, Indiana: Indiana State University, 1984.

Tucker, Marcia
PAT STEIR, SELF-PORTRAIT: AN INSTALLATION (exhibition catalogue). New York: The New Museum of Contemporary Art, 1987.

Zacharopoulos, Denys
PAT STEIR (exhibition catalogue). Lyons: Musée d'Art Contemporain, 1990.

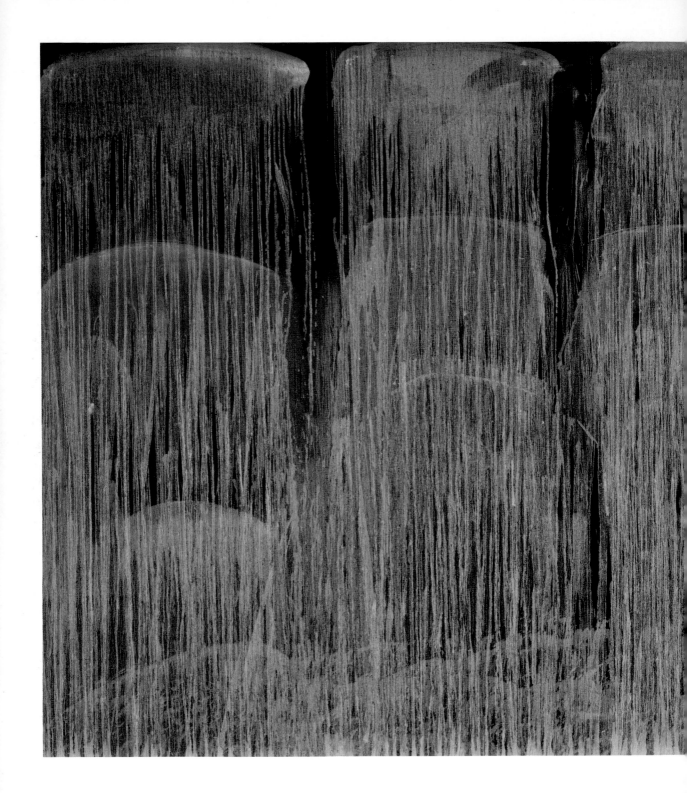

PAT STEIR

Sixteen Waterfalls of Dreams, Memories, and Sentiment   1990

FRANK STELLA

Born in Malden, Massachusetts, 1936; studied at Princeton University (BA, 1958); lives in New York.

ONE-ARTIST EXHIBITIONS

1960

Leo Castelli Gallery
New York

1963

Ferus Gallery
Los Angeles

1970

The Museum of Modern Art
New York

1978

Fort Worth Art Museum
Texas

1986

The Greenberg Gallery
Saint Louis

1987

Galerie Hans Strelow
Düsseldorf

Knoedler Gallery
London

The Museum of Modern Art
New York

1988

Akira Ikeda Gallery
Nagoya, Japan

1989

M. Knoedler & Co.
New York

GROUP EXHIBITIONS

1963

The Jewish Museum
New York
"Toward a New Abstraction"

1965

The Museum of Modern Art
New York
"The Responsive Eye"
(traveled)

Fogg Art Museum,
Harvard University
Cambridge, Massachusetts
"Three American Painters:
Kenneth Noland, Jules
Olitski, Frank Stella"
(traveled)

1966

The Solomon R.
Guggenheim Museum
New York
"Systemic Painting"

1971

The Metropolitan Museum
of Art
New York
"New York Painting and
Sculpture: 1940-1970"

1977

Museum of Contemporary
Art
Chicago
"A View of a Decade"

1981

Royal Academy of Arts
London
"A New Spirit in Painting"

1982

Martin Gropius Haus
Berlin
"Zeitgeist"

Stedelijk Museum
Amsterdam
" '60-'80: Attitudes/
Concepts/Images–A
Selection from Twenty
Years of Visual Arts"

1983

Whitney Museum of
American Art
New York
"Minimalism to
Expressionism: Painting
and Sculpture Since 1965
from the Permanent
Collection"

1985

The Museum of Modern Art
New York
"Contrasts of Form:
Geometric Abstract Art
1910-1985"

BIBLIOGRAPHY

Alloway, Lawrence
SYSTEMIC PAINTING
(exhibition catalogue). New
York: The Solomon R.
Guggenheim Museum, 1966.

Fried, Michael
THREE AMERICAN PAINTERS:
KENNETH NOLAND, JULES
OLITSKI, FRANK STELLA
(exhibition catalogue).
Cambridge, Massachusetts:
Fogg Art Museum,
Harvard University, 1965.

Fried, Michael
TOWARD A NEW
ABSTRACTION (exhibition
catalogue). New York: The
Jewish Museum, 1963.

Geldzahler, Henry
NEW YORK PAINTING AND
SCULPTURE: 1940-1970
(exhibition catalogue). New
York: The Metropolitan
Museum of Art, 1971.

INDIAN BIRDS: PAINTED
METAL RELIEFS (exhibition
catalogue). New York: Leo
Castelli Gallery, 1979.

Leider, Philip
STELLA SINCE 1970
(exhibition catalogue). Fort
Worth, Texas: Fort Worth
Art Museum, 1978.

Rubin, William S.
FRANK STELLA (exhibition
catalogue). New York: The
Museum of Modern Art,
1970.

Rubin, William S.
FRANK STELLA: 1970-1987
(exhibition catalogue). New
York: The Museum of
Modern Art, 1987.

FRANK STELLA

Study for *Watson and the Shark I*   1990 *

Watson and the Shark I   1991

JESSICA STOCKHOLDER   *No Title*   1990*

Born in Seattle, 1959; studied at the University of Victoria, British Columbia (BFA, 1982), Yale University, New Haven (MFA, 1985); lives in New York.

ONE-ARTIST EXHIBITIONS

1985

Malinda Wyatt Gallery
New York

1987

Contemporary Art Gallery
Vancouver

1988

Mercer Union
Toronto

1989

Mattress Factory
Pittsburgh

1990

American Fine Arts
New York

GROUP EXHIBITIONS

1985

Artists Space
New York
"Selection from the Artists Files"

1988

John Gibson Gallery
New York
"Artists and Curators"

1989

American Fine Arts
New York

Galerie Barbara Farber
Amsterdam
"A Climate of Site"

1990

Andrea Rosen Gallery
New York
"The Stendhal Syndrome: The Cure"

Consortium
Dijon
"Le choix des femmes"

Galerie Isabella Kacprzak
Cologne
"For Mary Heilmann"

Jack Tilton Gallery
New York
"Detritus"

Whitney Museum of American Art at Equitable Center
New York
"Contingent Realms: Four Contemporary Sculptors"

BIBLIOGRAPHY

Bankowsky, Jack
"The Obligatory Bed Piece." ARTFORUM, 19 (October 1990), pp. 140-145.

Nickas, Robert
"The State of Things: Questions to Three Object-Conscious Artists." FLASH ART, no. 151 (March-April 1990), pp. 131-33.

Parks, Addison
"Going It Alone with Sculpture." THE CHRISTIAN SCIENCE MONITOR, November 29, 1990.

Ruzicka, Joseph
"Jessica Stockholder at American Fine Arts Co." ART IN AMERICA, 78 (September 1990), p. 196.

Saltz, Jerry
"Mis-appropriation: Jessica Stockholder's Sculpture with No Name." ARTS MAGAZINE, 64 (April 1990), pp. 21-22.

Schaffner, Ingrid
"Jessica Stockholder: American Fine Arts Co." SCULPTURE, 9 (July-August 1990), pp. 57-58.

Siegel, Jeanne
"Jessica Stockholder." ARTS MAGAZINE, 64 (Summer 1990), p. 77.

Smith, Roberta
"Jessica Stockholder." THE NEW YORK TIMES, March 2, 1990.

Weinberg, Adam D.
CONTINGENT REALMS: FOUR CONTEMPORARY SCULPTORS (exhibition catalogue). New York: Whitney Museum of American Art at Equitable Center, 1990.

JESSICA STOCKHOLDER

Untitled Seepage "Sandwashed Sundried & Shrinkwrapped" 1991*

Recording Forever Pickled   1990*

285

PHILIP TAAFFE

Necromancer   1990*

Born in Elizabeth, New Jersey, 1955; studied at the Cooper Union, New York (BFA, 1977); lives in Naples.

ONE-ARTIST EXHIBITIONS

1982

Roger Litz Gallery
New York

1984

Galerie Ascan Crone
Hamburg

Pat Hearn Gallery
New York

1986

Galerie Ascan Crone
Hamburg

Pat Hearn Gallery
New York

Galerie Paul Maenz
Cologne

1987

Mario Diacono Gallery
Boston

Pat Hearn Gallery
New York

1988

Donald Young Gallery
Chicago

1989

Mary Boone Gallery
New York

Pat Hearn Gallery
New York

GROUP EXHIBITIONS

1983

Studio Sandro Chia
New York
"Turn It Over"

1984

Cable Gallery
New York
"Sex"

1985

Charlottenborg Exhibition
Hall
Copenhagen
"A Brave New World,
A New Generation"

Wacoal Art Center
Tokyo
"Vernacular Abstraction"

1986

Fundación Amelio
Ercolano, Italy
"Terrae Motus"

John Good Gallery
New York
"Recent Abstract Painting"

1987

The Aldrich Museum
of Contemporary Art
Ridgefield, Connecticut
"Post Abstract Abstraction"

Sala de Exposiciones,
Fundación Caja de Pensiones
Madrid
"Art and Its Double:
A New York Perspective"

Städtische Kunsthalle
Düsseldorf
"Similia/Dissimilia: Modes of
Abstractions in Painting,
Sculpture, and Photography
Today" (traveled)

Whitney Museum of
American Art
New York
"1987 Biennial Exhibition"

Whitney Museum of
American Art at
Equitable Center
New York
"Generations of Geometry"

BIBLIOGRAPHY

Cameron, Dan
ART AND ITS DOUBLE:
A NEW YORK PERSPECTIVE
(exhibition catalogue).
Madrid: Fundación Caja de
Pensiones, 1987.

Cameron, Dan
"The Other Philip Taaffe."
ARTS MAGAZINE, 60
(October 1985), pp. 18-20.

Cortez, Diego
PHILIP TAAFFE (exhibition
catalogue). Hamburg:
Galerie Ascan Crone, 1986.

Diacono, Mario
PHILIP TAAFFE (exhibition
catalogue). Boston: Mario
Diacono Gallery, 1987.

PARKETT, no. 26
(December 1990)
Collaborative issue by
Günther Förg and Philip
Taaffe.

Saltz, Jerry
BEYOND BOUNDARIES: NEW
YORK'S NEW ART. New York:
Alfred van der Marck
Editions, 1986.

Smith, Roberta
VERNACULAR ABSTRACTION
(exhibition catalogue).
Tokyo: Wacoal Art Center,
1985.

Solomon, Thomas
A BRAVE NEW WORLD, A NEW
GENERATION (exhibition
catalogue). Copenhagen:
Charlottenborg Exhibition
Hall, 1985.

Sussman, Elisabeth
"The Last Picture Show."
In ENDGAME: REFERENCE
AND SIMULATION IN RECENT
PAINTING AND SCULPTURE
(exhibition catalogue).
Boston: The Institute of
Contemporary Art, 1986.

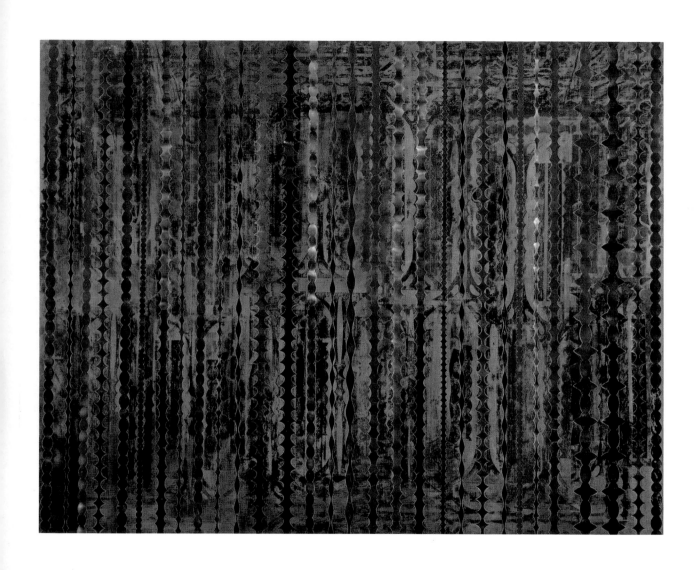

PHILIP TAAFFE   *Easter Choir*   1990

Desert Flowers 1990

MARK TANSEY

Constructing the Grand Canyon 1990

Born in San Jose, California, 1949; studied at the Art Center College of Design, Los Angeles (BA, 1972), Hunter College, New York (1975-78); lives in New York.

ONE-ARTIST EXHIBITIONS

1984

Grace Borgenicht Gallery
New York

John Berggruen Gallery
San Francisco

1985

Contemporary Arts Museum
Houston

1986

Curt Marcus Gallery
New York

1987

Curt Marcus Gallery
New York

1990

Curt Marcus Gallery
New York

Kunsthalle Basel

Seattle Art Museum
(traveled)

GROUP EXHIBITIONS

1981

The New Museum of
Contemporary Art
New York
"Not Just for Laughs"

1983

Whitney Museum of
American Art
New York
"1983 Biennial Exhibition"

1984

The Museum of Modern Art
New York
"An International Survey
of Recent Painting and
Sculpture"

1985

The Museum of
Contemporary Art
Los Angeles
"The Car Show"

1986

Venice
"XLII Biennale di Venezia"

1987

Kassel, West Germany
"Documenta 8"

Los Angeles County
Museum of Art
"Avant-Garde in the
Eighties"

1989

Modern Art Museum of
Fort Worth
"Ten + Ten: Contemporary
Soviet and American
Painters" (traveled)

Whitney Museum of
American Art
New York
"Image World: Art and
Media Culture"

1990

Whitney Museum of
American Art, Downtown
at Federal Reserve Plaza
New York
"The Charade of Mastery:
Deciphering Modernism in
Contemporary Art"

BIBLIOGRAPHY

Armstrong, Richard
"Mark Tansey: Grace
Borgenicht Gallery."
ARTFORUM, 21 (February
1983), pp. 75-76.

Cone, Michèle
"Mark Tansey." FLASH ART,
no. 129 (Summer 1986),
p. 69.

Joselit, David
"Milani, Innerst, Tansey."
FLASH ART, no. 134 (May
1987), pp. 100-01.

Joselit, David
"Wrinkles in Time." ART IN
AMERICA, 75 (July 1987),
pp. 106-11, 137.

Kuspit, Donald
"Mark Tansey: Curt Marcus
Gallery." ARTFORUM, 25
(September 1986), p. 132.

Larson, Kay
"Shrinking History." NEW
YORK, October 5, 1987,
p. 101.

Larson, Kay
"Ways With Wit." NEW
YORK, November 15, 1982,
pp. 98, 101.

Mahoney, Robert
"New York in Review." ARTS
MAGAZINE, 64 (Summer
1990), p. 92.

Pincus-Witten, Robert
"Entries: Concentrated Juice
and Kitschy Kitschy
Koons." ARTS MAGAZINE, 63
(February 1989), pp. 34-39.

Sims, Patterson
MARK TANSEY: ART AND
SOURCE (exhibition
catalogue). Seattle: Seattle
Art Museum, 1990.

MARK TANSEY   *Bridge Over the Cartesian Gap*   1990*

CY TWOMBLY

Winter's Passage (Luxor)   1985–90

Born in Lexington, Virginia, 1928; studied at Washington and Lee University, Lexington, Virginia, the Boston Museum School (1948-49), Art Students League, New York (1951), Black Mountain College, North Carolina (1951-52); lives in Rome.

ONE-ARTIST EXHIBITIONS

1951

Kootz Gallery
New York

1955

Stable Gallery
New York

1958

Galleria La Tartaruga
Rome

1960

Leo Castelli Gallery
New York

1965

Museum Haus Lange
Krefeld

1966

Stedelijk Museum
Amsterdam

1973

Kunstmuseum Basel

Städtische Galerie im
Lenbachhaus
Munich

1975

Institute of Contemporary
Art, University of
Pennsylvania
Philadelphia (traveled)

1979

Whitney Museum of
American Art
New York

1986

DIA Art Foundation
New York

1987

Whitechapel Art Gallery
London

1988

Musée National d'Art
Moderne, Centre
Georges Pompidou
Paris

1989

Gagosian Gallery
New York

The Menil Collection
Houston

1990

Thomas Ammann Fine Art
Zurich

GROUP EXHIBITIONS

1953

Stable Gallery
New York
"Rauschenberg: Paintings
and Sculpture/Cy Twombly:
Paintings and Drawings"

1967

Whitney Museum of
American Art
New York
"1967 Annual Exhibition of
Contemporary American
Painting"

1978

Venice
"XXXVIII Biennale di
Venezia"

1981

Royal Academy of Arts
London
"A New Spirit in Painting"

1982

Kassel, West Germany
"Documenta 7"

1986

Whitechapel Art Gallery
London
"In Tandem: The Painter-
Sculptor in the Twentieth
Century"

1988

Nationalgalerie
Berlin
"Positionen Heutiger
Kunst—Positions of
Present-Day Art"

BIBLIOGRAPHY

Barthes, Roland
CY TWOMBLY: PAINTINGS
AND DRAWINGS 1954-1977
(exhibition catalogue). New
York: Whitney Museum of
American Art, 1979.

Bastian, Heiner
CY TWOMBLY: BILDER—
PAINTINGS 1952-1976.
Frankfurt, Berlin, and
Vienna: Verlag Ullstein,
Propyläen Verlag, 1978.

Bastian, Heiner
CY TWOMBLY: DAS
GRAPHISCHE WERK
1953-1984. A CATALOGUE
RAISONNÉ OF THE PRINTED
GRAPHIC WORK. Munich and
New York: Edition
Schellmann, 1984.

Bastian, Heiner
CY TWOMBLY: ZEICHNUNGEN
1953-1973. Frankfurt,
Berlin, and Vienna: Verlag
Ullstein, Propyläen Verlag,
1973.

Bastian, Heiner
JOSEPH BEUYS, ROBERT
RAUSCHENBERG, CY
TWOMBLY, ANDY WARHOL:
SAMMLUNG MARX. Munich:
Prestel Verlag, 1979.

Lambert, Yvon, and Roland
Barthes
CY TWOMBLY: CATALOGUE
RAISONNÉ DES OEUVRES SUR
PAPIER, VI: 1973-1976.
Milan: Edizione Multhipla,
1979.

CY TWOMBLY   *Rotalla*   1986–90*

Untitled   1983–90

ALEX WEBB   *Miami Beach, Florida*   1989

Born in San Francisco, 1952; studied at Apeiron Photography Workshop, Millerton, New York (1972), Harvard University, Cambridge, Massachusetts (BA, 1974); lives in New York.

ONE-ARTIST EXHIBITIONS

1983

Galerie Magnum
Paris

1986

California Museum of Photography, University of California, Riverside

Canon Photo Gallery
Amsterdam

1987

Museo dell'Automobile
Turin

1989

Sala de Exposiciones del Canal de Isabel II
Madrid

GROUP EXHIBITIONS

1980

Fogg Art Museum, Harvard University
Cambridge, Massachusetts
"Color Photography"

1983

California Museum of Photography, University of California, Riverside
"Color in the Streets"

The Carpenter Center for the Visual Arts, Harvard University
Cambridge, Massachusetts
"Grave Relics"

1984

The Photographer's Gallery
London
"Alex Webb, Harry Gruyeart"

1986

Walker Art Center
Minneapolis
"On the Line: The New Color Photojournalism" (traveled)

1987

The Museum of Contemporary Photography, Columbia College, Chicago
"This and Other Worlds: Susan Meiselas, Gilles Peress, Eugene Richards, Alex Webb"

Museum of Photographic Arts
San Diego
"Masters of the Street: Part Three"

1988

Photographic Resource Center at Boston University
"Leopold Godowsky Jr. Color Photography Awards"

1989

Museum of Photographic Arts
San Diego
"Haiti: Revolution in Progress"

1990

Catherine Edelman Gallery
Chicago
"Five from Magnum"

BIBLIOGRAPHY

Grundberg, Andy
"Photojournalism: It's Back with a New Face." MODERN PHOTOGRAPHY (June 1980), pp. 94-101.

Johnstone, M.
"The Active Streets." ARTWEEK, April 16, 1983, p. 11.

Kozloff, Max
"Picturing the Killing Fields." ART IN AMERICA, 78 (June 1990), pp. 144-51, 199-201, 205.

Webb, Alex
HOT LIGHT/HALF-MADE WORLDS: PHOTOGRAPHS FROM THE TROPICS. New York: Thames and Hudson, 1986.

Webb, Alex
In "India: Ritual and the River." APERTURE, no. 105 (Winter 1986), pp. 58-63.

Webb, Alex
UNDER A GRUDGING SUN: PHOTOGRAPHS FROM HAITI LIBERE 1986-1988. New York: Thames and Hudson, 1989.

Weinberg, Adam D.
ON THE LINE: THE NEW COLOR PHOTOJOURNALISM (exhibition catalogue). Minneapolis: Walker Art Center, 1986.

ALEX WEBB

Fort Pierce, Florida   1989

St. Augustine, Florida   1989

CARRIE MAE WEEMS   *Untitled*   1990

*Born in Portland, Oregon, 1953;
studied at the California Institute
of the Arts, Valencia (BA, 1981),
University of California, San
Diego (MFA, 1984), University
of California, Berkeley (M.A.,
1991); lives in Northampton,
Massachusetts.*

ONE-ARTIST EXHIBITIONS

1989

Museum of Art, Rhode Island
School of Design
Providence

1990

CEPA Gallery
Buffalo

P.P.O.W.
New York

GROUP EXHIBITIONS

1980

Los Angeles Women's
Building
"Women's Work"

1981

Barnsdall Art Gallery
Los Angeles
"Multi-Cultural Focus"

1986

The New Museum of
Contemporary Art
New York
"Past, Present, Future"

1987

Centro Cultural de la Raza
San Diego
"Visible Differences"

Johnson Library Center,
Hampshire College
Amherst, Massachusetts

1988

Alternative Museum
New York
"Prisoners of Image,
1800-1988"

The Houston Center for
Photography
"The Other"

1990

MIT List Visual Arts
Center
Cambridge, Massachusetts
"Trouble in Paradise"

The New Museum of
Contemporary Art at
Marine Midland Bank
New York
"Spent: Currency, Security,
and Art on Deposit"

Randolph Street Gallery
Chicago
"Who Counts?"

The Studio Museum in
Harlem
New York
"Urban Home"

BIBLIOGRAPHY

Friis-Hansen, Dana
TROUBLE IN PARADISE
(exhibition catalogue).
Cambridge, Massachusetts:
MIT List Visual Arts
Center, 1990.

Jenkins, Rupert, and
Chris Johnson
"Disputed Identities." SAN
FRANCISCO CAMERAWORK,
17 (Fall 1990), pp. 5-9.

Jones, Kellie
"In Their Own Image."
ARTFORUM, 29 (November
1990), pp. 133-38.

Schwendenwien, Jude
"A Look at Privilege,
Presumption." HARTFORD
COURANT, November 18,
1990, p. G6.

Wallis, Brian
"Questioning Documentary."
APERTURE, no. 112 (Fall
1988), pp. 60-71.

Weems, Carrie Mae
"Making Art, Making Money:
13 Artists Comment."
ART IN AMERICA, 78
(July 1990), p. 140.

CARRIE MAE WEEMS

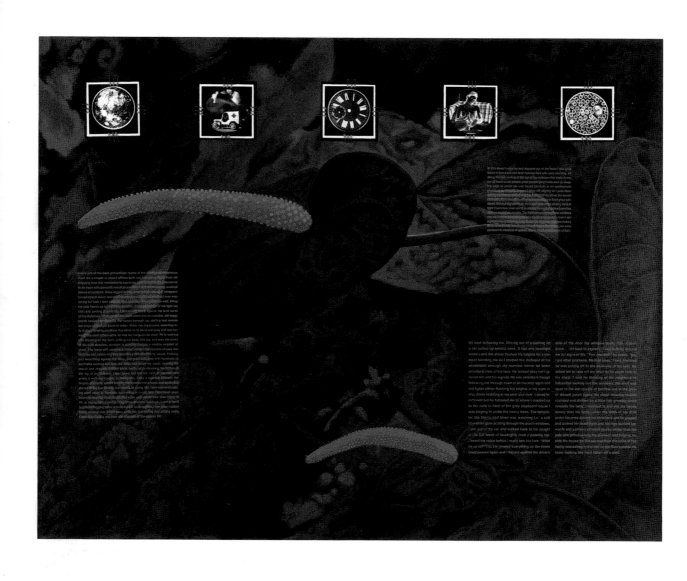

Born in Redbank, New Jersey, 1954; lives in New York.

ONE-ARTIST EXHIBITIONS

1982

Alexander Milliken Gallery
New York

1983

Hal Bromm Gallery
New York

Civilian Warfare
New York

1985

Institute of Contemporary
Art, University of
Pennsylvania
Philadelphia

1984

Galerie Anna Friebe
Cologne

Gracie Mansion Gallery
New York

1986

Cartier Foundation
Paris

Galerie Anna Friebe
Cologne

Gracie Mansion Gallery
New York

1987

Ground Zero Gallery
New York

1989

P.P.O.W.
New York

1990

P.P.O.W.
New York

University Galleries, Illinois
State University
Normal (traveled)

GROUP EXHIBITIONS

1980

Club 57
New York
"Erotic Show"

1982

Gracie Mansion Gallery
New York
"Famous Show"

Alexander Milliken Gallery
New York
"Fast"

1983

Brooklyn Terminal
New York
"The Terminal Show"

Monique Knowlton Gallery
New York
"Intoxication"

1984

University Art Museum,
University of California
Santa Barbara
"Neo York"

Whitney Museum of
American Art at
Philip Morris
New York
"Modern Masks"

Whitney Museum of
American Art
New York
"1985 Biennial Exhibition"

1986

Aspen Museum of Art and
the University of Colorado
at Boulder Art Gallery
"Of the Street"

1989

Artists Space
New York
"Witnesses: Against
Our Vanishing"

University Art Galleries,
Wright State University
Dayton, Ohio
"The Assembled Photograph"

BIBLIOGRAPHY

Blinderman, Barry
DAVID WOJNAROWICZ:
TONGUES OF FLAME
(exhibition catalogue).
Normal: University
Galleries, Illinois State
University, 1990.

Frank, Peter, and
Michael McKenzie
NEW, USED, & IMPROVED:
ART FOR THE EIGHTIES. New
York: Abbeville Press, 1987.

Goldin, Nan, and
David Wojnarowicz
WITNESSES: AGAINST OUR
VANISHING (exhibition
catalogue). New York:
Artists Space, 1989.

Kardon, Janet
DAVID WOJNAROWICZ:
PAINTINGS AND SCULPTURE.
Philadelphia: Institute of
Contemporary Art,
University of Pennsylvania,
1985.

Lubowsky, Susan
MODERN MASKS (exhibition
catalogue). New York:
Whitney Museum of
American Art at Philip
Morris, 1984.

Wallis, Brian, ed.
BLASTED ALLEGORIES: AN
ANTHOLOGY OF WRITINGS BY
CONTEMPORARY ARTISTS.
New York: The New
Museum of Contemporary
Art; Cambridge,
Massachusetts: The MIT
Press, 1987.

Wojnarowicz, David
SOUNDS IN THE DISTANCE.
London: Aloes Books, 1982.

When I put my hands on your body on your flesh I feel the history of that body. Not just the beginning of its formation in that distant lake but all the way beyond its ending. I feel the warmth and texture and simultaneously I see the flesh unwrap from the layers of fat and disappear. I see the fat disappear from around the muscle. I see the muscle disappearing from around the organs and displacing itself from the bones. I see the organs gradually fade into transparency leaving a gleaming skeleton gleaming like ivory that slowly revolves until it becomes dust. I am consumed in the sense of your weight the way your flesh occupies momentary space the fullness of it beneath my palms. I am amazed at how perfectly your body fits to the curves of my hands. If I could attach our blood vessels so we could become each other I would. If I could attach our blood vessels in order to anchor you to the earth to this present time to me I would. If I could open your body and slip up inside your skin and look out your eyes and forever have my lips fused with yours I would. It makes me weep to feel the history of you of your flesh beneath my hands in a time of so much loss. It makes me weep to feel the movement of your flesh beneath my palms as you twist and turn over to create a series of gestures to reach up around my neck to draw me nearer. All these memories will be lost in time like tears in the rain.

Film and Video

REDEFINING FILM AND VIDEO ART
John G. Hanhardt

The film and video selections for the 1991 Biennial Exhibition illustrate the reflections of contemporary artists on a number of important issues in our society, ranging from feminism to the representation of cultures. These media artists are in fact contributing to the discourses that are redefining cultural practices. One crucial discourse concerns the changing definition of representation, in particular how the self and other are encoded within social and cultural images and institutions. This investigation is renegotiating the boundaries between gender and sexuality through a deconstruction of the binary opposition between homosexuality and heterosexuality, a deconstruction that questions the very invention of those terms. The politics of history also informs a powerful struggle to invest theory with history and vice versa, revealing in the process how and why we frame social and political ideologies, whether from the left or right. In addition to the ideological dimensions of representation, genre and formal issues are being readdressed with new vigor in works ranging from documentary and dance to the feature-length narrative film.

In recent film and video, the concept of innovation has taken on a broader meaning. It now serves to redefine the notion of the avant-garde as both a genre and as an issue of periodization within film history. In other words, the traditional constitution of the avant-garde film as a specific canon of works is being broadened by feminists and by African-American, Asian-American, Native American, and Latino media and film artists. Moreover, as artists combine both media in their productions, the separation of film from video is no longer rigid. Thus, on a theoretical as well as material level, the film and media arts are experiencing a profound process of change.

There is a sense of introspection in much of this work, reflecting a two-year period of transition to the final decade of the century. For many, this historical marker portends a transition to a renewed social consciousness, an expectation that may appear utopian after a decade in which the growth of a Neo-Conservative free-market economy was accompanied by a sense of diminished possibilities within domestic politics. The opening up of Eastern Europe and the Soviet Union to freedom of speech, press, and thought has been apposed in this country by a resurgent anti-intellectualism and state censorship. This development has been in part directed against a dramatic new intellectual movement that is reexamining our Euro-centric notion of American culture. This challenging agenda, which posits a redefinition of the United States as a site of multiple cultures, as well as gay and lesbian communities, has had an important impact on much of the alternative media culture. Artists working in all formats of film and video are inserting themselves into these debates by forging new forms of distribution and exhibition in the spaces that exist within and between mainstream institutions.

How we represent ourselves and others is the fundamental theme that runs through all the work presented here. Lawrence Andrews, Victor Masayesva, Jr., Tony Cokes and Donald Trammel, and Hans Breder introduce this theme in powerful and original ways. Andrews' *Strategies for the development of / Redefining the purpose served / Art in the age of . . . aka the making of the towering inferno* explores the traditional contrast between our definition of work and creativity within the art school and within the social space of the workplace. In Andrews' videotape, the definitions of "physical" or "skilled" that attach themselves to labor as well as to the practice of art making become issues with complex social ramifications. Victor Masayesva, Jr., in his videotape *Siskyavi: The Place of Chasms*, treats the self-image of

Native American culture by contrasting how Euro-American institutions, namely the museum, employ empirical and interpretive methods to define Native American artifacts. With great sensitivity, Masayesva goes to the heart of a centuries-long difference between the two cultures by focusing on Native Americans' perceptions of their own culture, amplifying and interpreting the "voice" of a Native American people.

Like other people of color, African-Americans have historically been excluded from positions of wealth and power. In Tony Cokes and Donald Trammel's *Fade to Black*, African-American experience and history, popular culture and life-styles, words and music, are edited together to offer a powerful reexamination of racism in daily life. Hans Breder's *From Here and There Too: Moscow Postcards 1989* interprets the representation of a culture going through revolutionary change. This image-processed diary of Moscow offers a personal and poetic response to the idiosyncrasies of a culture experiencing renewed freedom of expression.

The exploration of self-representation includes the issue of how the self is culturally defined—what informs our desires and beliefs. In this context, artists are considering how gender and sexuality are transcribed both within the bourgeois family and in the broader perceptions of society. In *Belladonna*, Ida Applebroog and Beth B offer a haunting mix of texts from Sigmund Freud, Josef Mengele, and Joel Steinberg, spoken on screen by different people. As the spectral imagery and the composition of the shots impart rhythm to the articulation of the text, the work becomes a powerful and profound exploration of the dark side of human nature. The family unit and its influence on an individual's formative years are powerfully studied in Su Friedrich's searching *Sink or Swim*. The voice-over text, together with found and filmed footage of Friedrich's family, constructs an evocative self-examination and confessional. In *A Spy in the House That Ruth Built*, Vanalyne Green looks at baseball as a means to explore the cultural construction of sexuality. Green has created an engaging and witty interpretation of sports, the different metaphors men and women assign to it, and the relationship women have to the male-dominated spectacle of professional sports.

How public figures come under scrutiny even as their personae are being fashioned by the media becomes the central question in Aimee (Rankin) Morgana's *The Man in the Mirror*. This work examines Michael Jackson through a variety of found footage and written texts that reveal how Jackson is constructed on television and how the public projects onto that manufactured persona its own desires and dreams. In *Memories from the Department of Amnesia*, Janice Tanaka goes back to her mother's difficult experiences as a Japanese-American, through which she struggles to achieve self-understanding. Tanaka's use of a variety of image-processing techniques enhances this richly poetic and complex work.

The construction of sexuality within a culture is determined in large measure by socially defined norms that have been institutionally implemented. *The Deadman* by Peggy Ahwesh and Keith Sanborn transposes a prose piece (*Le Mort*) by the French author Georges Bataille into a contemporary American landscape. The actors present a frenzy of death and sexuality within a narrative of confrontation and a despairing testing of the limits of sexual definition. These same limits, as encoded by society, are the playful subject of Ericka Beckman and Mike Kelley's *Blind Country*. Through a colorful mise-en-scène of performance, objects, and sexual identity, this parody creatively removes the veneer of respectability that frames the rules we live by. In Zeinabu irene Davis' *Cycles*, the images of a female identity informed by African and Caribbean culture and music are edited together in a subtle and powerful intercultural evocation of the menstrual cycle. Popular culture has given each generation an image of the "typical" American family; these images are wittily excavated in Lewis Klahr's *Tales of the Forgotten Future, Part Two* and *Part Three*. Animated collages of pop recordings and found images taken from comic books, pulp fiction, design magazines, and advertisements expose an erotic and violent subtext hidden within cultural nostalgia.

The epistemology of gay sensibility is a powerful force within contemporary culture. Visual and literary artists are confronting the representation of sexuality and the social codes—as constructed by late nineteenth-century science and society—that define heterosexuality as the norm and homosexuality as the deviant other. Cinema, which emerged in the last century, became a primary vehicle for promulgating heterosexuality and defining normal life within the structure of the bourgeois family. Today the traditional exclusion of homosexuality from society, culture, and history is under critical and theoretical attack, an attack given greater urgency by the need to stop the spread of AIDS. Film and media artists are playing a leading role in this effort.

The tragedy of AIDS underlies any representation of gay and lesbian life today. Tom Kalin's *They are lost to vision altogether* looks at the devastation caused by AIDS, the people it has affected, the federal government's response, and the misrepresentation of the disease in the media. This is an angry work that confirms the significant contribution politically engaged art makes to our culture. Another important example is Marlon Riggs' *Tongues Untied*, a poignant and virtuoso articulation of the experiences of oppression and ecstasies of liberation for a black gay man. A different aspect of the gay world is documented by Jennie Livingston's *Paris Is Burning*. Although transvestite display and dressing up have long been a part of gay culture, in recent years in Harlem there has developed a spectacular form of this self-expression, called voguing. Livingston's film offers a landmark look at the people and the theater of this transvestite phenomenon that is now influencing popular culture.

The feature-length film has been defined by the traditional narrative codes and strategies of the bourgeois cinema or by the strategies of high modernism. These approaches have been turned inside out in Yvonne Rainer's remarkable and witty new film, *Privilege*, which challenges socially constructed ideas about menopause and female sexuality. The innovative mix of texts and languages, performance styles and filmic references, makes this a major addition to the feature film genre. The feature film is also a place for personal reflection, storytelling, and the representation of different life-styles. Growing up in the shadow of Hollywood, Gregg Araki has been a leading director in alternative cinema. Araki's *the long weekend (o' despair)* portrays a post-punk generation of young people on the margins of Los Angeles who act out their alienation and search for extreme experiences to offset their ennui. The visual style of the black-and-white cinematography, coupled with the dialogue and music, gives this work a definite cutting edge.

From the beginning of the cinema, dance has been recorded and interpreted on film. Today, the dance genre represents an important component of the independent film and video movements. Few artists have been more successful in translating the choreography and grammar of dance than Charles Atlas. His video *Because We Must*, featuring the choreography of Michael Clark, is a powerful rendition of the mise-en-scène of the performance that preserves the choreographer's extraordinary presentation of sexuality and gender mixing.

The politics of history—how it is recorded and manipulated to construct and explain our actions and policies—has been a subject of increasing interest to media artists. For many years, Juan Downey has been producing a series of videotapes that investigates the semiotics of culture and the codes of historical representation. His most recent work, *Hard Times and Culture, Part I*, establishes, through a mix of genres and styles, parallels between fin-de-siècle Vienna and New York City in the 1980s. Another major new work, Steve Fagin's *The Machine That Killed Bad People*, examines American policy in the Philippines, US support of Ferdinand Marcos, and the frustrated hopes for the Aquino regime through a postmodern spectacle of global media and the invention of history. All of this becomes, in Fagin's blend of performances and home videos of Marcos, an exploration of the "unreal politic" of American foreign policy.

Francesc Torres is a leading video artist whose multimedia installations and single-channel tapes reflect on the ideologies of power and war. His latest videotape, *Sur del Sur*, looks at Spanish history and the exploration-exploitation of the Americas through a mix of post-production techniques that create a poetic and disturbing text of imperialistic power. The role of media in contemporary history has been the subject of many projects by Antonio Muntadas. His *Video Is Television?* looks at the pervasive spread of capitalism as a media spectacle, powerfully invoked by a graphic mix of his statements on media with images of retail displays of television monitors. The

treatment of Japanese-Americans during World War II is a disturbing part of American history which contributes, as does the subsequent rise of Japan as a world economic power, to how Asian-Americans see themselves and are viewed through mass media in our society today. Rea Tajiri's *History and Memory* is a powerful new work that examines the cultural identity of Japanese-Americans through images of American pop culture.

This year's Biennial selection also includes an important group of films and videos that explore the phenomenology of image making. These works, often based on the material foundations of celluloid and electronic images, are created as poetic texts in direct dialogue with the modernist tradition of image making. Peter Hutton's *New York Portrait Part III* continues his landmark series of haunting renditions of the city. This latest installment shows a New York suffused with risk and violence, shadows and darkness, in black-and-white images that reveal buildings, fireworks, and the texture of the streets. Another form of diary filmmaking is Warren Sonbert's *Friendly Witness*, a bravura piece of editing that links images he shot around the world in a cascading display against a soundtrack of pop and classical music.

Water and Power marks a major development in Pat O'Neill's work on the construction of individual moving images on 35mm film. It reveals O'Neill's uncanny eye for exploring the perceptual and poetic space of the recorded image. The relationship of word to image has always been central to the videotapes and video installations of Gary Hill. In addition to an installation, Hill is represented by his latest videotape, *Site/Recite (A Prologue)*. This videotape combines a voice-over text that moves from spoken word to spoken word with a camera that moves from object to object through shifts in focus; thus Hill fashions a revealing and inventive interplay of image and spoken word.

Language, performance, and the construction of a richly detailed mise-en-scène inform the ambitious 35mm feature-length film by Meredith Monk. *Book of Days* is a remarkable evocation of a medieval site filled with the movements of her performers and a powerful vocal soundtrack. It constitutes an extraordinary cinematic affirmation of Monk's aesthetic and her ability to fashion compelling images and move the action with grace and economy. Like Meredith Monk, Joan Jonas has made an important contribution to the arts through her performances, multimedia installations, and videotapes. In *Volcano Saga*, her mix of ancient and contemporary mythologies with an evocation of place is articulated in a subtle use of image processing, allowing her to combine images and scenes in her own distinctive vocabulary.

The Film and Video section tours under the auspices
of The American Federation of Arts.

Second Floor Film/Video Gallery

PEGGY AHWESH AND
KEITH SANBORN

LAWRENCE ANDREWS

IDA APPLEBROOG
AND BETH B

GREGG ARAKI

CHARLES ATLAS

ERICKA BECKMAN AND
MIKE KELLEY

HANS BREDER

TONY COKES AND
DONALD TRAMMEL

ZEINABU IRENE DAVIS

JUAN DOWNEY

STEVE FAGIN

SU FRIEDRICH

VANALYNE GREEN

GARY HILL

PETER HUTTON

JOAN JONAS

TOM KALIN

LEWIS KLAHR

JENNIE LIVINGSTON

VICTOR MASAYESVA, JR.

MEREDITH MONK

AIMEE (RANKIN) MORGANA

ANTONIO MUNTADAS

PAT O'NEILL

YVONNE RAINER

MARLON RIGGS

WARREN SONBERT

REA TAJIRI

JANICE TANAKA

FRANCESC TORRES

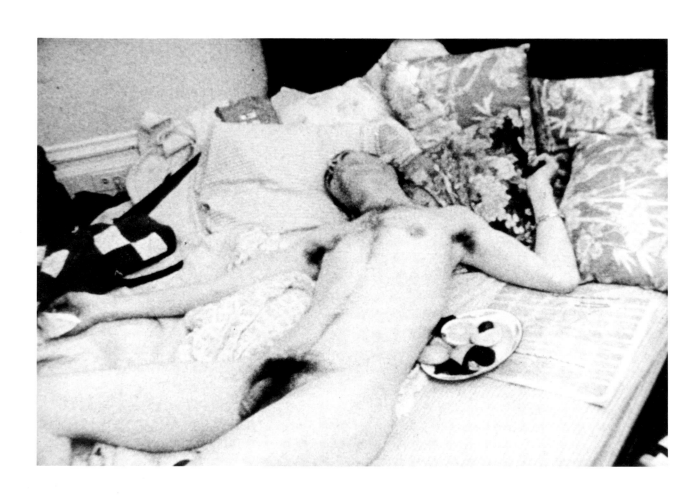

PEGGY AHWESH AND KEITH SANBORN   *The Deadman* 1989

PEGGY AHWESH
Born in Pittsburgh, 1954; studied at Antioch College, Yellow Springs, Ohio (BFA, 1978), Graduate Center of the City University of New York (1984-88); lives in New York.

ONE-ARTIST EXHIBITIONS
1983
London Film Makers Co-op

1984
Hallwalls
Buffalo

1985
University of Wisconsin, Milwaukee

1988
Filmforum
Los Angeles

1989
Collective for Living Cinema
New York

1990
The Carnegie Museum of Art
Pittsburgh

The Museum of Modern Art
New York

Pleasure Dome
Toronto

GROUP EXHIBITIONS
1985
The Kitchen
New York
"Super 8 Motel"

1988
Pacific Film Archive, University Art Museum, University of California, Berkeley
"Recent Film Works by Women"

1989
Hallwalls
Buffalo
"The Politics and Poetics of Feminism, Sexuality and Reproductive Freedom"

San Francisco Cinematheque
"In Bataille's Dark Chamber: 'The Deadman'" (with Sanborn) (traveled)

1990
Filmtheater Desmet
Amsterdam
"A Passage Illuminated: De Amerikaanse Avant-Garde 1980-90" (with Sanborn) (traveled)

LACE
Los Angeles
"Opaque Projections: Childhood and Memory"

London International Film Festival

Other Cinema
San Francisco
"Agony, Ecstasy and Excess" (with Sanborn)

BIBLIOGRAPHY
Dargis, Manohla
"On 'The Deadman.'" ARTFORUM, 28 (May 1990), pp. 29-30.

Durant, Mark
"Woman with a Movie Camera." ARTWEEK, November 14, 1987, pp. 8-9.

Margulies, Ivone
"After the Fall: Peggy Ahwesh's Vérité." MOTION PICTURE, 3 (Winter 1989-90), pp. 31-33.

Montgomery, Jennifer
"Her Logic Is in Contradiction: The Films of Peggy Ahwesh." CINEMATOGRAPH, no. 3 (Fall 1988), pp. 39-42.

KEITH SANBORN
Born in Wichita, Kansas, 1952; studied at Rice University, Houston (BA, 1974), Columbia University, New York (MA, 1975), State University of New York, Buffalo (MA, 1980); lives in New York.

ONE-ARTIST EXHIBITIONS
1979
Media Study/Buffalo

1983
The Funnel Film Centre
Toronto

London Film Makers Co-op

The National Film School
Beaconsfield, England

1984
Rice Media Center
Houston

1986
San Francisco Cinematheque

1988
Millennium
New York

1989
San Francisco State University

GROUP EXHIBITIONS
1984
Hallwalls
Buffalo
"A Tribute to Hollis Frampton"

1987
P.S. 122
New York
"Cement Beach"

San Francisco Cinematheque
"Another View"

West Orange, New Jersey
Thomas A. Edison Black Maria Film Festival (traveled)

1988
The American Museum of the Moving Image
Astoria, New York
"Independent America: New Film 1978-1988"

Boston Film/Video Foundation
"Exposures: The Body Brought to Light"

1989
Pacific Film Archive, University Art Museum, University of California, Berkeley
"Smile, Be Happy"

San Francisco Cinematheque (with Ahwesh)

1990
Copenhagen
Det Danske Filmværksted (with Ahwesh)

BIBLIOGRAPHY
Bataille, George
THE DEAD MAN. Keith Sanborn (as Jayne Austen), transl. Las Vegas: Ediciones La Calavera, 1988.

Muse, John
"The Body Lost and Found." CINEMATOGRAPH, no. 3 (Fall 1988), pp. 9-22.

Sanborn, Keith
"Modern, All Too Modern." CINEMATOGRAPH, no. 3 (Fall 1988), pp. 107-16.

Sanborn Keith
SUPER 8/BERLIN: THE ARCHITECTURE OF DIVISION (exhibition catalogue). Buffalo: Hallwalls, 1984.

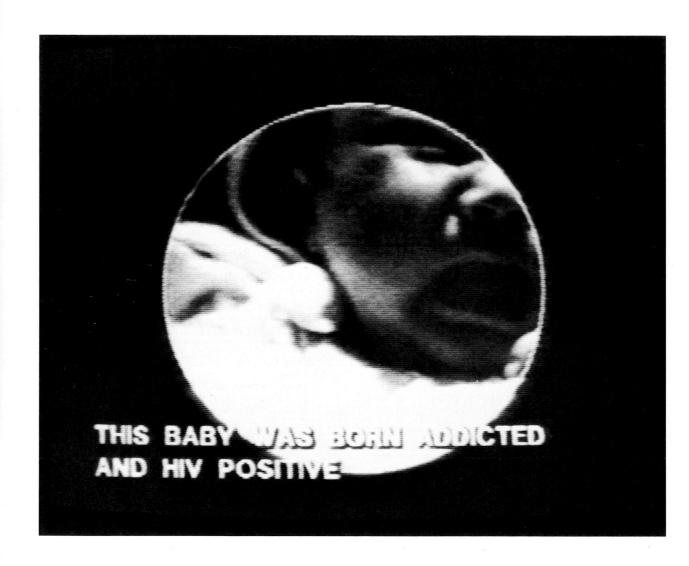

LAWRENCE ANDREWS

Strategies for the development of/Redefining the purpose served/Art in the age of . . .
aka the making of the towering inferno   1989

Born in Providence, Rhode Island, 1964; studied at the Corcoran School of Art, Washington, D.C. (1982), San Francisco Art Institute (BFA, 1987); lives in San Francisco.

ONE-ARTIST EXHIBITIONS

1987

Western Addition Cultural Center
San Francisco

1989

New Langton Arts
San Francisco

1990

Rene Coelho Gallery
Amsterdam

GROUP EXHIBITIONS

1988

San Francisco Museum of Modern Art
"1988 SECA Video Invitational"

San Francisco State University
"Countervisions: Pioneers in Bay Area Art"

SF Camerawork
San Francisco
"Digital Photography"
(traveled)

1989

The Brooklyn Museum
New York
"Video 101: An Introduction to American Video Art"

The Kitchen
New York
"Twentysomething"

Long Beach Museum of Art
Long Beach, California
"Icono Negro: The Black Aesthetic in Video Art"

Los Angeles
1989 American Film Institute Video Festival

Video Inn
Vancouver
"Crossed Borders"

West Berlin
39. Internationale Filmfestspiele Berlin

1990

Long Beach Museum of Art
Long Beach, California
"Open Channels V"

Moscow
Soviet/American Festival

Time Based Arts
Amsterdam
"Six Pack"

BIBLIOGRAPHY

Brew, Kathy
"Sermon on the Monitor (It's Been a Long Time Coming)."
SHIFT MAGAZINE, 2 (1988), pp. 2-4.

Durant, Mark Alice
"Representational Conflict, Cultural Resistance."
ARTWEEK, July 1, 1989, p. 3.

Fitzsimons, Connie
"In Living Color: Representations of Race and Civil Rights." HIGH PERFORMANCE, 12 (Summer 1989), pp. 72-73.

Fitzsimons, Connie
"L.A. Freewaves: Celebrating the Existence of Independent Video."
ARTWEEK, December 7, 1989, pp. 18-21.

Payne, Robert
"No Simplistic Answers."
ARTWEEK, February 22, 1990, p. 16.

IDA APPLEBROOG AND BETH B   *Belladonna*   1989

IDA APPLEBROOG
Born in New York, 1929;
studied at the New York
Institute of Applied Arts and
Sciences (1948-50), School
of The Art Institute of Chicago
(1965-68); lives in New York.

ONE-ARTIST EXHIBITIONS

1973

Newport Harbor Art Museum
Newport Beach, California

1978

Whitney Museum of
American Art
New York

1984

The Chrysler Museum
Norfolk, Virginia

1986

Institute of Contemporary
Art, University of
Pennsylvania
Philadelphia

1987

Wadsworth Atheneum,
Hartford

1989

Ronald Feldman Fine Arts
New York

1990

Contemporary Arts Museum
Houston

GROUP EXHIBITIONS

1983

Hirshhorn Museum and
Sculpture Garden,
Smithsonian Institution
Washington, D.C.
"Directions 83"

1984

The Museum of Modern Art
New York
"An International Survey of
Recent Painting and
Sculpture"

1987

Kassel, West Germany
"Documenta 8"

1989

Cincinnati Art Museum
"Making Their Mark:
Women Artists Today. A
Documentary Survey,
1970-1985" (traveled)

1990

Museum of Contemporary
Hispanic Art, The New
Museum of Contemporary
Art, and The Studio
Museum in Harlem
New York
"The Decade Show:
Frameworks of Identity in
the 1980s"

BIBLIOGRAPHY

McCormick, Carlo
IDA APPLEBROOG:
NOSTRUMS, BELLADONNA
(exhibition catalogue). New
York: Ronald Feldman Fine
Arts, 1989.

Schor, Mira
"Medusa Redux, Ida
Applebroog and the Spaces
of Post-Modernity."
ARTFORUM, 28 (March 1990),
pp. 116-22.

Zeitlin, Marilyn,
Thomas Sokolowski, and
Lowery Sims
IDA APPLEBROOG: HAPPY
FAMILIES, A FIFTEEN-YEAR
SURVEY (exhibition
catalogue). Houston:
Contemporary Arts
Museum, 1990.

BETH B
Born in New York, 1955;
studied at San Diego State
University (1972), University of
California, Irvine (1973-75),
School of Visual Arts,
New York (BFA, 1976); lives
in New York.

ONE-ARTIST EXHIBITIONS

1977

Stedelijk Museum
Amsterdam

1980

Film Forum
New York

1981

Museum of Art, Carnegie
Institute
Pittsburgh

National Film Theatre,
British Film Institute
(traveled)

1982

Walker Art Center
Minneapolis

1983

Hirshhorn Museum and
Sculpture Garden,
Smithsonian Institution
Washington, D.C.

1987

The Museum of Fine Arts
Houston

1988

International Museum of
Photography at George
Eastman House
Rochester, New York

GROUP EXHIBITIONS

1979

The Kitchen
New York
"Filmworks"

1980

New York
"The Times Square Show"

1982

New York Film Festival

1983

Film in the Cities
St. Paul, Minnesota
"Coastal Waves: New Films
from San Francisco and
New York"

1987

West Berlin
37. Internationale
Filmfestspiele Berlin

1990

Los Angeles
1990 American Film
Institute Video Festival
(with Ida Applebroog)

Long Beach Museum of Art
Long Beach, California
"The Mother Child Reunion"
(with Ida Applebroog)

The Museum of Modern Art
New York
"Myths" (with Ida
Applebroog)

BIBLIOGRAPHY

Corliss, Richard
"Cinema: To Be Young,
Gifted and Broke." TIME,
March 14, 1983.

Hoberman, J.
"No Wavelength: The Para-
Punk Underground."
THE VILLAGE VOICE, May 21,
1979, pp. 42-43.

MacDonald, Scott
"Interview with Beth and
Scott B." OCTOBER, no. 24
(Spring 1983), pp. 3-36.

GREGG ARAKI

*Born in Los Angeles, 1959;
studied at the University of
California, Santa Barbara (BA,
1982), University of Southern
California, Los Angeles (MFA,
1984); lives in Los Angeles.*

ONE-ARTIST EXHIBITIONS

1988

Independent Feature
Project
Los Angeles

Roxie Cinema
San Francisco

1989

Kino Einzeit
West Berlin

Nuart Theater
Los Angeles

University of California,
Santa Barbara

Walker Art Center
Minneapolis

1990

Anthology Film Archives
New York

Euclid Theater
Toronto

GROUP EXHIBITIONS

1987

Festival Internazionale del
Film Locarno

Festival International du
Nouveau Cinéma et de la
Vidéo de Montréal

1988

Edinburgh International
Film Festival

Tokyo
International Asian
American Film Festival

The 12th San Francisco
International Lesbian and
Gay Film Festival

1989

American Film Institute/
Los Angeles Film Festival

National Film Theatre,
British Film Institute
London
"Dangerous to Know"
(traveled)

Sydney International Film
Festival

1990

Munich
Filmfest München

San Remo, Italy
La Mostra Internazionale
del Film d'Autore

BIBLIOGRAPHY

Knode, Helen
"Being and Somethingness."
LA WEEKLY, January 13-19,
1989, p. 40.

Lee, Craig
"Introducing Gregg Araki."
L.A. STYLE, 5 (August 1989),
pp. 59, 185.

Rosenbaum, Jonathan
"Critic's Choice: 'the long
weekend (o' despair).'"
[Chicago] READER,
November 17, 1989,
section 2, p. 36.

Swanger, Hugh
"Lost and Found."
NEW YORK NATIVE, July 31,
1989, p. 30.

Thomas, Kevin
"The Revelations of 'Three
Bewildered People.'"
LOS ANGELES TIMES, January
17, 1989, part VI, p. 3.

Timmons, Stuart
"Bewildered, Bothered, and
Brilliant." THE ADVOCATE,
February 2, 1988, pp. 38, 62.

Wasley, Aidan
"Film Festival Shows Depth,
Diversity." THE JAPAN
TIMES, December 22, 1990,
p. 15.

CHARLES ATLAS

Because We Must 1989

Born in Saint Louis, 1949; studied at Swarthmore College, Swarthmore, Pennsylvania (1965-66); lives in New York.

ONE-ARTIST EXHIBITIONS

1979

The Museum of Modern Art
New York

1980

Center Screen
Cambridge, Massachusetts

The Kitchen
New York

1981

Festival de Danse
Châteauvallon, France

1982

Anthology Film Archives
New York

1983

Musée National d'Art
Moderne, Centre
Georges Pompidou
Paris

1985

Institute of Contemporary
Arts
London

Walker Art Center
Minneapolis

1987

The Museum of
Contemporary Art
Los Angeles

1989

Museu da Imagem e do
Som
São Paulo

GROUP EXHIBITIONS

1981

London
Filming Dance Festival

1982

Musée National d'Art
Moderne, Centre
Georges Pompidou
Paris
"Ciné-Vidéo-Danse"

1984

Paris
Festival d'Automne

1985

Whitney Museum of
American Art
New York
"1985 Biennial Exhibition"
(traveled)

1986

Palais de Beaux-Arts
Brussels
"Au coeur du maelstrom"

1987

Kassel, West Germany
"Documenta 8"

The Museum of
Contemporary Art,
Los Angeles and the
Stedelijk Museum,
Amsterdam
"The Arts for Television"
(traveled)

1989

Centre de Cultura
Contemporània
Barcelona
"II Mostra de Vídeo/Dansa"

Festival International du
Nouveau Cinéma et de la
Vidéo de Montréal

1990

The 14th San Francisco
International Lesbian and
Gay Film Festival

BIBLIOGRAPHY

Becker, Nancy F.
"Filming Cunningham
Dance: A Conversation with
Charles Atlas." DANCE
THEATRE JOURNAL, 1
(Spring 1983), pp. 21-25.

Korteweg, Ariejan
"Charles Atlas geeft in
videofilms eigenzinnig:
vorm aan beeldverhall."
DE VOLKSRANT, September
15, 1989, p. 10.

Louppe, Laurence
"La vidéo-danse au bord de
la fiction." ART PRESS,
no. 83 (July-August 1984),
pp. 50-51.

Tee, Ernie
"The Irreality of Dance." In
THE ARTS FOR TELEVISION
(exhibition catalogue). Los
Angeles: The Museum of
Contemporary Art;
Amsterdam: Stedelijk
Museum, 1987, pp. 54-64.

Ulrich, Allan
"Tracking a Dancer with an
Obsessive Camera." SAN
FRANCISCO EXAMINER, June
26, 1987, p. D7.

ERICKA BECKMAN AND MIKE KELLEY

Blind Country   1989

ERICKA BECKMAN
Born in Hempstead, New York, 1951; studied at Washington University, Saint Louis (BFA, 1974), Independent Study Program, Whitney Museum of American Art, New York (1975), California Institute of the Arts, Valencia (MFA, 1976); lives in New York.

MIKE KELLEY
See page 131.

ONE-ARTIST EXHIBITIONS

1983

The Kitchen
New York

1984

Institute of Contemporary Arts
London

LACE
Los Angeles

1985

The New Museum of Contemporary Art
New York

1986

Walker Art Center
Minneapolis

1987

Lege Riumte Gallery
Bruges, Belgium

1988

Bess Cutler Gallery
New York

National Gallery of Art
Washington, D.C.

1989

Hirshhorn Museum and Sculpture Garden, Smithsonian Institution
Washington, D.C.

The Institute of Contemporary Art
Boston

GROUP EXHIBITIONS

1983

New York Film Festival

Whitney Museum of American Art
New York
"1983 Biennial Exhibition" (traveled)

1985

Kunstmuseum Bern
"Das Poetisch ABC"

Musée National d'Art Moderne, Centre Georges Pompidou
Paris
"Alibi"

1986

Palais de Beaux-Arts
Brussels
"Au coeur du maelstrom"

1988

Halle Sud
Geneva
"Reprise des vues"

Hallwalls
Buffalo
"New Installations"

The Renaissance Society at The University of Chicago and the Newport Harbor Art Museum, Newport Beach, California
"CalArts: Skeptical Belief(s)"

1989

The Museum of Contemporary Art
Los Angeles
"A Forest of Signs: Art in the Crisis of Representation"

1990

The Hague
World-Wide Video Festival

BIBLIOGRAPHY

Banes, Sally
"Imagination and Play: The Films of Ericka Beckman." MILLENNIUM FILM JOURNAL, no. 13 (Fall-Winter 1983-84), pp. 98-112.

Beckman, Ericka
"Drawings for 'You the Better.'" In CAVE CANEM, John Miller, ed. New York: Cave Canem Books, 1983.

Dika, Vera
"Cinema: A Feminist Fairy Tale." ART IN AMERICA, 75 (April 1987), pp. 31-33.

Hoberman, J.
"A Kind of Close Encounter." THE VILLAGE VOICE, December 13, 1983, p. 76.

Joselit, David
"Mind over Matter." THE BOSTON PHOENIX, September 7, 1990, section III, p. 9.

Rickey, Carrie
"Popcorn and Canvas." ARTFORUM, 22 (December 1983), pp. 64-69.

Schwendenwien, Jude
"Ericka Beckman/Bess Cutler Gallery." ARTFORUM, 27 (October 1988), pp. 145-46.

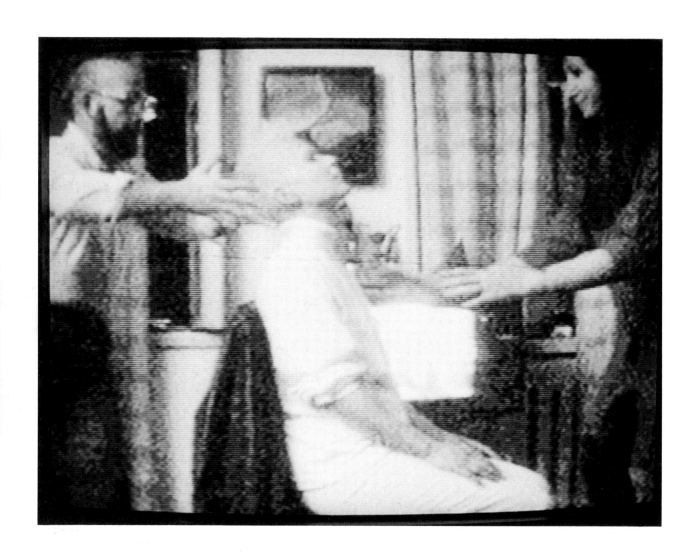

HANS BREDER

From Here and There Too: Moscow Postcards 1989   1990

Born in Herford, Germany, 1935; studied at the Hochschule für Bildende Künste, Bielefeld (1957-59), Hochschule für Bildende Künste, Hamburg (1959-64); lives in Iowa City.

ONE-ARTIST EXHIBITIONS

1967

Richard L. Feigen and Co.
New York

1972

Galerie Marcel Liatowitsch
Basel

1976

Internationaal Cultureel
Centrum
Antwerp

1979

Galerie Wolfgang Förster
Münster, West Germany

1982

Galerie Hachmeister and
Schnake
Münster, West Germany

1983

P.S. 1, Institute for Art
and Urban Resources
Long Island City, New York

1987

Schreiber Cutler
Contemporary Art
New York

1988

Galerie Hachmeister
Münster, West Germany

1989

Schreiber Cutler
Contemporary Art
New York

1990

Ruth Siegel Gallery
New York

GROUP EXHIBITIONS

1967

Whitney Museum of
American Art
New York
"Recent Acquisitions"

1969

The Jewish Museum
New York
"Superlimited: Books,
Boxes and Things"

1972

Max Hutchinson Gallery
New York
"Hybrids"

1977

The Museum of Modern Art
New York
"Signals"

1982

Kölnischer Kunstverein
Cologne
"Videokunst in Deutschland,
1963-1982"

1984

International
Bauausstellung Berlin
"Die Zukunft der Metropolen"

1986

LACE
Los Angeles
"Video and Language: Video
as Language" (traveled)

1987

Sydney
The 2nd Australian Video
Festival

1989

Kuznetzky Most Exhibition
Hall
Moscow
"Painting Beyond the Death
of Painting: American
Imagistic and Abstract
Work"

Whitney Museum of
American Art
New York
"1989 Biennial Exhibition"
(traveled)

BIBLIOGRAPHY

Foster, Stephen C., and
Estera Milman
"The Media as Medium:
Hans Breder's Berlin
Work." KANSAS QUARTERLY,
17 (Summer 1985), pp. 17-24.

Henry, Gerrit
"Hans Breder at Schreiber
Cutler." ART IN AMERICA,
77 (January 1989), p. 153.

Kuspit, Donald
"New York Reviews."
ARTFORUM, 27 (May 1989),
pp. 149-150.

Pozzi, Lucio
"Che ve ne sembra
dell'America? Lettera da
New York." IL GIORNALE
DELL'ARTE, no. 74 (January
1990).

Rapaport, Herman
"Hans Breder and the Auras
of Video." ART CRITICISM, 4
(1987), pp. 48-50.

TONY COKES AND DONALD TRAMMEL   *Fade to Black*   1990

TONY COKES
Born in Richmond, Virginia, 1956; studied at Goddard College, Plainfield, Vermont (BA, 1979), Independent Study Program, Whitney Museum of American Art, New York (1983-84), Virginia Commonwealth University, Richmond (MFA, 1985); lives in New York.

DONALD TRAMMEL
Born in Detroit, 1951; studied at Michigan State University, East Lansing (BA, 1971); lives in New York.

TONY COKES

ONE-ARTIST EXHIBITIONS

1979

Pratt Center, Goddard College
Plainfield, Vermont

1985

Anderson Gallery, Virginia Commonwealth University
Richmond

GROUP EXHIBITIONS

1983

Virginia Museum of Fine Arts
Richmond
"The Next Juried Show"

1984

Washington Project for the Arts
Washington, D.C.
"History as Content"

Whitney Museum of American Art
New York
"Re-Viewing Television: Interpretations of the Mass Media, Part I; Video Artists Look at TV"

1987

Artists Space
New York
"Buying In and Selling Out"

1988

The American Museum of the Moving Image
Astoria, New York
"Images of Vietnam: The Struggle for Memory"

The Bronx Museum of the Arts, Satellite Gallery, Hostos Community College
New York
"Ancient History: Three Video Installations"

1989

Washington Project for the Arts
Washington, D.C.
"The Blues Aesthetic: Black Culture and Modernism" (traveled)

BIBLIOGRAPHY

Hanhardt, John G.
RE-VIEWING TELEVISION: INTERPRETATIONS OF THE MASS MEDIA, PART I; VIDEO ARTISTS LOOK AT TV (Program notes: The New American Filmmakers Series, 20). New York: Whitney Museum of American Art, 1984.

Horrigan, Bill
NEW WORKS (Program notes: American Film Institute Video Festival). Los Angeles: American Film Institute, 1988.

Payne, Robert
"Pirate Video: [A]Mass[ed] Media at LACE." ARTWEEK, December 28, 1989, p. 15.

Thompson, Richard
"Dismything Objectivity: Buffalo's Video Festival of New Journalism." THE INDEPENDENT, 13 (June 1990), pp. 12-14.

Walworth, Dan
"Buying In and Selling Out" (program notes). New York: Artists Space, 1987.

TONY COKES AND DONALD TRAMMEL

GROUP EXHIBITIONS

1990

Los Angeles
1990 American Film Institute Video Festival

1991

The Kitchen
New York
"New Works 90, New World '91"

LACE
Los Angeles
"Black Men in America: Changing Reality?"

ZEINABU IRENE DAVIS

Cycles 1989

*Born in Philadelphia, 1961;
studied at Brown University,
Providence (BA, 1983),
University of California, Los
Angeles (MA, 1985; MFA,
1988); lives in Yellow Springs,
Ohio.*

GROUP EXHIBITIONS

1986

8th Havana International
Festival of New Latin
American Cinema

Turin, Italy
4th International Youth
Film Festival

1988

Artemisia Gallery
Chicago
"Slow Fade to Black: A
Video Installation"

1989

Carbondale, Illinois
Big Muddy Film and Video
Festival

Cinema De Amicis di Milano
Milan, Italy
"Black Cinema USA"
(traveled)

Creteil, France
Festival International de
Films de Femmes

National Black
Programming Consortium
Columbus, Ohio
"Prized Pieces: International
Video and Film Festival"

Spaces Art Gallery
Cleveland
"Outside/In Video Series"

Uppsala, Sweden
Uppsala International Film
Festival

Vancouver
"In Visible Colours: An
International Women of
Colour and Third World
Film/Video Festival and
Symposium"

1990

Anthology Film Archives
New York
"Changing the Subject:
Recent Film and Video by
Women of Color"

Athens, Ohio
Athens International Film
and Video Festival

Montreal
Sixième Festival de Films et
Vidéos de Femmes

1991

Ouagadougou, Burkina
Faso, West Africa
12e Festival Panafricain du
Cinéma et de la Télévision

Whitney Museum of
American Art
New York
"The Return of Visual
Pleasure"

BIBLIOGRAPHY

Allen, Austin
"Borrowing Landscapes."
DIALOGUE: ARTS IN THE
MIDWEST, 13 (November-
December 1990), pp. 14-16.

Davis, Zeinabu irene
"The Future of Black Film:
The Debate Continues."
BLACK FILM REVIEW, 5
(1989), pp. 6, 8, 26, 28.

Davis, Zeinabu irene
"Interview with Independent
Filmmaker Julie Dash."
BLACK FILM REVIEW, 6
(1990), pp. 12-17, 20-21.

Davis, Zeinabu irene
"Woman with a Mission:
Zeinabu irene Davis on
Filmmaking." HOT WIRE, 7
(January 1991), pp. 18-19, 56.

Springer, Christina
"Waiting and Dreaming,
Praying and Cleaning."
SOJOURNER, 15 (April 1990),
pp. 1-3.

Swanholm, Mark
"Focusing Voice and
Vision." ANTIOCH FORUM
(Winter 1990-91), pp. 1, 9.

Ventura, Jan
"Women's Work." LA WEEKLY,
April 7-13, 1989, p. 69.

JUAN DOWNEY   *Hard Times and Culture, Part I*   1990

Born in Santiago, Chile, 1940; studied at the Catholic University of Chile, Santiago (B. Arch. 1961), Atelier 17, Paris (1963-65), Pratt Institute, Brooklyn, New York (1967-69); lives in New York.

ONE-ARTIST EXHIBITIONS

1968

Judson Memorial Church Gallery
New York

1970

Howard Wise Gallery
New York

1974

The Kitchen
New York

1976

Long Beach Museum of Art
Long Beach, California

1977

Everson Museum of Art
Syracuse, New York

1978

Whitney Museum of American Art
New York

1983

P.S. 1, Institute for Art and Urban Resources
Long Island City, New York

1985

San Francisco Museum of Modern Art

1989

The Institute of Contemporary Art
Boston

1990

International Center of Photography
New York

GROUP EXHIBITIONS

1974

Kennedy Center for the Performing Arts
Washington, D.C.
"Art Now '74"

Kölnischer Kunstverein
Cologne
"Projekt '74"

1977

Kassel, West Germany
"Documenta 6"

1980

Venice
"XXXIX Biennale di Venezia"

1984

The Museum of Modern Art
New York
"A Survey: Artist's TV Lab, WNET/Thirteen"

1985

Whitney Museum of American Art
New York
"1985 Biennial Exhibition" (traveled)

1988

The Bronx Museum of the Arts
New York
"The Latin Spirit"

The Jewish Museum
New York
"Time and Memory: Video Art and Identity"

Whitney Museum of American Art
New York
"Eye for I: Video Self-Portraits" (traveled)

1990

Musée National d'Art Moderne, Centre Georges Pompidou
Paris
"Passages de l'image" (traveled)

BIBLIOGRAPHY

Boyle, Deirdre
"Juan Downey's Recent Videotapes." AFTERIMAGE, 6 (Summer 1978), pp. 10-11.

Downey, Juan
"Travelogues of Video Trans Americas." In VIDEO ART: AN ANTHOLOGY, Ira Schneider and Beryl Korot, eds. New York: Harcourt Brace Jovanovich, 1976, pp. 38-39.

Downey, Juan, et al.
FESTIVAL DOWNEY: VIDEO PORQUE TE VE (exhibition catalogue). Santiago, Chile: Visuala Galería, 1987.

Hagen, Charles
"Juan Downey, 'Information Withheld.'" ARTFORUM, 22 (February 1984), pp. 76-77.

Hoy, Anne H.
JUAN DOWNEY: THE THINKING EYE (exhibition brochure). New York: International Center of Photography, 1987.

Stanislaus, Grace
FINIS TERRAE/THE ENDS OF THE EARTH: THE TERRITORIES OF JUAN DOWNEY, ISMAEL FRIGERIO, JORGE TACLA (exhibition catalogue). Miami: Frances Wolfson Art Gallery, Miami-Dade Community College, 1988.

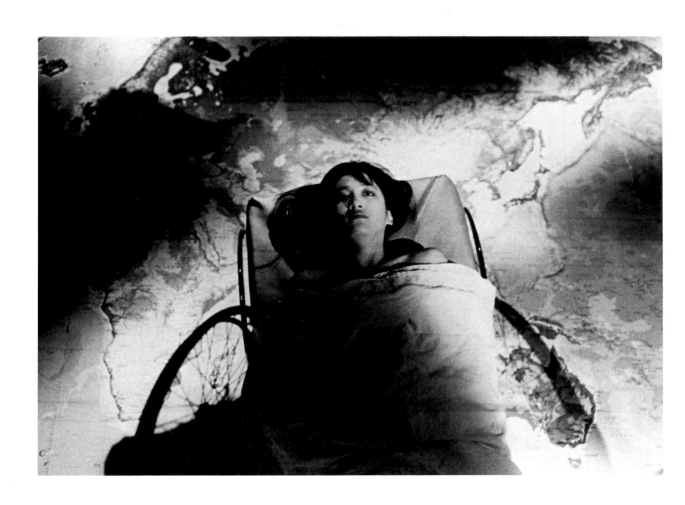

STEVE FAGIN   *The Machine That Killed Bad People*   1990

Born in Chicago, 1946; studied at the University of Illinois, Chicago (BA, 1970), Northwestern University, Evanston, Illinois (MA, 1973); lives in La Jolla.

ONE-ARTIST EXHIBITIONS

1985

Anthology Film Archives
New York

1986

The Museum of Modern Art
New York

San Francisco Cinematheque

Video Free America
San Francisco

1987

Hallwalls
Buffalo

1988

Institute of Contemporary
Arts
London

Pacific Film Archive
University of California,
Berkeley

1990

Collective for Living
Cinema
New York

Intermedia Arts Minnesota
Minneapolis

Wexner Center for the
Visual Arts, Ohio State
University
Columbus

GROUP EXHIBITIONS

1978

Edinburgh International
Film Festival

1985

The Hague
World-Wide Video Festival

The Museum of Modern Art
New York
"West Coast Video"

Rotterdam Film Festival

1986

Los Angeles
1986 American Film Institute
Video Festival

1987

La Jolla Museum of
Contemporary Art
"Mediated Narrative"
(traveled)

Whitney Museum of
American Art
New York
"1987 Biennial Exhibition"
(traveled)

1988

The American Museum of
the Moving Image
Astoria, New York
"Video Biopics"

1990

Festival International du
Nouveau Cinéma et de la
Vidéo de Montréal

BIBLIOGRAPHY

Mellencamp, Patricia
"Excursions in Catastrophe:
Power and Contradiction in
the Phillipines." AFTERIMAGE,
17 (April 1990), pp. 8-11.

Morse, Margaret
"Waking and Shaking."
AFTERIMAGE, 13 (November
1985), pp. 15-17.

Skoller, Jeffrey
"An Interview with Steve
Fagin." CINEMATOGRAPH,
no. 4 (1991), pp. 184-192.

Wollen, Peter
"An Interview with Steve
Fagin." OCTOBER, no. 41
(Summer 1987), pp. 75-100.

SU FRIEDRICH   *Sink or Swim*   1990

*Born in New Haven, 1954;
studied at The University of
Chicago (1971-72, 1975), Oberlin
College, Oberlin, Ohio (BA,
1974); lives in New York.*

ONE-ARTIST EXHIBITIONS

1984

Arsenal
West Berlin

Millennium
New York

1985

The Funnel Film Centre
Toronto

Museum of Art,
Carnegie Institute
Pittsburgh

1986

Walker Art Center
Minneapolis

1987

The Museum of Modern Art
New York

Whitney Museum of
American Art
New York

1988

Anthology Film Archives
New York

1990

National Gallery of Canada
Ottawa

GROUP EXHIBITIONS

1982

Collective for Living
Cinema
New York
"10 Years of Living Cinema"
(traveled)

1985

The Museum of Modern Art
New York
"New Directors/New Films"

1986

Montreal
Deuxième Festival de Films
et Vidéos de Femmes

1987

Toronto
Festival of Festivals

Wells College
Aurora, New York
"Robert Flaherty Film
Seminar"

1988

Atlanta Film Festival

Collective for Living
Cinema
New York
"Sexism, Colonialism,
Misrepresentation: A
Corrective Film Series and
Conference"

Creteil, France
Festival International de
Film de Femmes

1989

Whitney Museum of
American Art
New York
"1989 Biennial Exhibition"
(traveled)

1990

London International
Film Festival

New York Film Festival

BIBLIOGRAPHY

Gever, Martha
"Girl Crazy: Lesbian
Narratives in 'She Must Be
Seeing Things' and
'Damned If You Don't.'"
THE INDEPENDENT, 11 (July
1988), pp. 14-18.

Jenkins, Bruce
"Gently Down the Stream."
MILLENNIUM FILM JOURNAL,
nos. 16-18 (Fall-Winter
1986-87), pp. 195-99.

Katz, John Stuart
"Reflections in a Golden
'I.'" INTERNATIONAL
DOCUMENTARY (Fall 1990),
pp. 31-33.

MacDonald, Scott
"Daddy Dearest: Su
Friedrich Talks About
Filmmaking, Family,
and Feminism." THE
INDEPENDENT, 13
(December 1990),
pp. 28-34.

MacDonald, Scott
"Su Friedrich:
Reappropriations." FILM
QUARTERLY, 41 (Winter
1987-88), pp. 34-42.

Sykora, Katharina
"When Form Takes as Many
Risks as the Content."
FRAUEN UND FILM, no, 46
(February 1989), pp. 100-06.

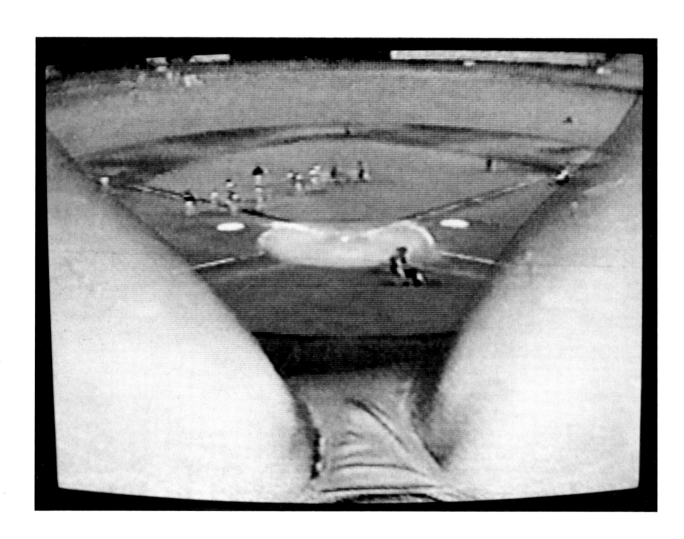

VANALYNE GREEN   *A Spy in the House That Ruth Built*   1989

Born in Fort Knox, Kentucky, 1948; studied at the California Institute of the Arts, Valencia (BA, 1974); lives in Chicago.

ONE-ARTIST EXHIBITIONS

1978

Los Angeles Institute of Contemporary Art

1979

Franklin Furnace
New York

1980

Nexus Gallery
Philadelphia

1981

Federal Hall National Memorial
New York

1982

Boston Film/Video Foundation

1983

Taller Latino Americano
New York

1984

The Kitchen
New York

1989

The Museum of Modern Art
New York

GROUP EXHIBITIONS

1986

The New Museum of Contemporary Art
New York
"The Art of Memory/The Loss of History"

West Orange, New Jersey
Thomas A. Edison Black Maria Film Festival
(traveled)

1987

Whitney Museum of American Art
New York
"Social Engagement: Women's Video in the '80s"

1988

Artists Space
New York
"Unacceptable Appetites"

The Museum of Modern Art
New York
"Committed to Print"

Whitney Museum of American Art, Downtown at Federal Reserve Plaza
New York
"Identity: Representations of the Self"

1989

Los Angeles
1989 American Film Institute Video Festival

1990

The Hague
World-Wide Video Festival

Museum of Contemporary Hispanic Art, The New Museum of Contemporary Art, and The Studio Museum in Harlem
New York
"The Decade Show: Frameworks of Identity in the 1980s"

Wells College
Aurora, New York
"Robert Flaherty Film Seminar"

BIBLIOGRAPHY

Chris, Cynthia
"Diamonds Are Forever." AFTERIMAGE, 18 (September 1990), p. 20.

Green, Vanalyne
"Mother Baseball." M/E/A/N/I/N/G, no. 1 (December 1986), pp. 35-39.

Hoptman, Laura
"The Hunger." AFTERIMAGE, 16 (Summer 1988), pp. 21-22.

Katz, John Stuart
"Reflections in a Golden 'I.'" INTERNATIONAL DOCUMENTARY (Fall 1990), pp. 31-33.

Raven, Arlene
"A Hunger Artist." In CROSSING OVER: FEMINISM AND ART OF SOCIAL CONCERN. Ann Arbor, Michigan: UMI Research Press, 1988, pp. 57-62.

Rice, Shelley
"Vanalyne Green." ARTFORUM, 20 (January 1982), pp. 81-82.

PETER HUTTON

Born in Detroit, 1944; studied at the San Francisco Art Institute (BFA, 1969); lives in Annandale-on-Hudson, New York.

ONE-ARTIST EXHIBITIONS

1972

Millennium
New York

1976

Carpenter Center for the
Visual Arts, Harvard
University
Cambridge, Massachusetts

1979

Film Forum
New York

1980

Akademie der Künste
West Berlin

1982

Arsenal
West Berlin

1984

Magyar Filmgyártó Vállalat
Balázs Béla Stúdió
Budapest

1987

The Museum of Modern Art
New York

1989

Anthology Film Archives
New York

1990

Pacific Film Archive,
University Art Museum,
University of California,
Berkeley

San Francisco Cinematheque

GROUP EXHIBITIONS

1973

The Museum of Modern Art
New York
"Diary Films"

1975

Whitney Museum of
American Art
New York
"Images"

1978

Paris
Festival International du
Jeune Cinéma

1981

West Berlin
31. Internationale
Filmfestspiele Berlin

1983

Collective for Living
Cinema
New York
"10 Years of Living Cinema"
(traveled)

1985

Whitney Museum of
American Art
New York
"1985 Biennial Exhibition"
(traveled)

1987

ETC. Miedzynarodowe
Seminarium Sztuki
Warszawa
Warsaw

1988

The American Museum of
the Moving Image
Astoria, New York
"Independent America: New
Film 1978-1988"

1990

Filmtheater Desmet
Amsterdam
"A Passage Illuminated: De
Amerikaanse Avant-Garde
1980-90" (traveled)

The High Museum of Art
Atlanta
"Berlinart: Foreign
Filmmakers See Berlin"

BIBLIOGRAPHY

Green, Gary, and Pat Sims
"Satori Interview: Peter
Hutton." SATORI, 2 (Spring
1989), pp. 12-15.

Grindon, Leger
"The Films of Peter
Hutton." MILLENNIUM FILM
JOURNAL, nos. 4-5 (Summer-
Fall 1979), pp. 175-78.

Gunning, Tom
"The Image and Its Eclipse:
The Films of Peter
Hutton." SPIRAL, no. 4
(July 1985), pp. 7-10.

Hoberman, J.
"Peter Hutton: A Tale of
Two Cities." ARTFORUM, 25
(October 1986), pp. 93-97.

Jost, Jon
"Independents: Image
Conscious." AMERICAN
FILM, 11 (December 1985),
pp. 72-73.

JOAN JONAS

Ron Vawter and Tilda Swinton in *Volcano Saga*   1989

Born in New York, 1936; studied at Mount Holyoke College, South Hadley, Massachusetts (BA, 1958), School of the Museum of Fine Arts, Boston (1958-61), Columbia University, New York (MFA, 1965); lives in New York.

PERFORMANCES

1972

Tiber River
Rome
"Delay, Delay"

1973

Leo Castelli Gallery
New York
"Organic Honey's Vertical Roll" (traveled)

1974

The Kitchen
New York
"Funnel" (traveled)

1979

Sonnabend Gallery
New York
"Upsidedown and Backwards" (traveled)

1980

University Art Museum, University of California, Berkeley
"Joan Jonas: Performance/Video/Installation"

1981

The Performing Garage
New York
"Double Lunar Dogs" (traveled)

1982

Arsenal
West Berlin
"He Saw Her Burning" (traveled)

1986

Museum of Art, Carnegie Institute
Pittsburgh
"Volcano Saga" (traveled)

1990

Wave Hill
New York
"Variations on a Scene"

Whitney Museum of American Art
New York
"Fortune Telling Is Illegal"

GROUP EXHIBITIONS

1972

Kassel, West Germany
"Documenta 5"

1974

Kunsthalle Köln
Cologne
"Projekt '74"

1976

Institute of Contemporary Art, University of Pennsylvania
Philadelphia
"Stage Sets"

1979

Kunstmuseum Bern
"American Art from The Museum of Modern Art"

1981

Contemporary Arts Museum
Houston
"Other Realities: Installations for Performance"

Tokyo
International Video Art Festival

1982

Stedelijk Museum
Amsterdam
"'60-'80: Attitudes/Concepts/Images—A Selection from Twenty Years of Visual Arts"

1985

Whitney Museum of American Art
New York
"1985 Biennial Exhibition" (traveled)

1988

Deutscher Akademischer Austauschdienst
West Berlin
"Balkon mit Facher" (traveled)

Whitney Museum of American Art at Equitable Center
New York
"Video Art: Expanded Forms"

BIBLIOGRAPHY

Adams, Brooks
"Joan Jonas' Elysian Fields." CONTEMPORANEA, no. 22 (November 1990), pp. 78-81.

Crimp, Douglas
"Joan Jonas's Performance Works." STUDIO INTERNATIONAL, 142 (July-August 1976), pp. 10-12.

Douglas Crimp, ed.
SCRIPTS AND DESCRIPTIONS 1968-1982 (exhibition catalogue). Eindhoven, The Netherlands: Stedelijk Museum; Berkeley: University Art Museum, University of California, 1982.

Jonas, Joan, with Rosalind Krauss
"Seven Years." THE DRAMA REVIEW, 19 (March 1975), pp. 13-16.

Junker, Howard
"Joan Jonas: The Mirror Staged." ART IN AMERICA, 69 (February 1981), pp. 86-95.

Krauss, Rosalind
"Video: The Aesthetics of Narcissism." OCTOBER, 1 (Spring 1976), pp. 51-64.

White, Robin
"Joan Jonas" (interview). VIEW, 2 (April 1979).

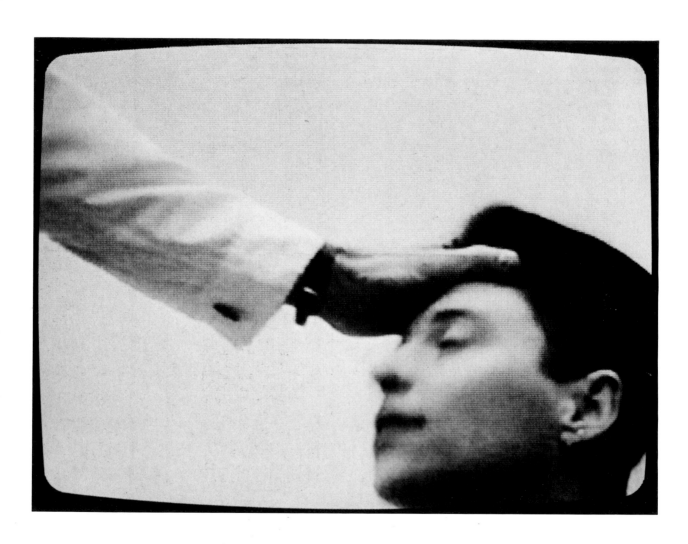

TOM KALIN

They are lost to vision altogether 1989

Born in Chicago Heights, Illinois, 1962; studied at the University of Illinois, Champaign-Urbana (BFA, 1984), School of The Art Institute of Chicago (MFA 1987), Independent Study Program, Whitney Museum of American Art, New York (1987-88); lives in New York.

GROUP EXHIBITIONS

1985

Evansville Museum of Art
Indiana
"37th Annual Midstates Exhibition"

1986

Photo Centre Gallery
"Exhibition of Graduate Photography, Portfolio 1986, by the School of The Art Institute of Chicago"
Hong Kong (traveled)

1987

Los Angeles
1987 American Film Institute Video Festival

1988

CAGE
Cincinnati
"Gender Benders"

Centro Colombo Americano
Medellín, Colombia
"American Art 1988"
(traveled)

The Kitchen
New York
"New Works"

Los Angeles
1988 American Film Institute Video Festival

Neue Gesellschaft für Bildende Kunst
West Berlin
"Vollbild"

Randolph Street Gallery
Chicago
"The Whole World Is Still Watching"

1989

LACE
Los Angeles
"Against Nature"

West Berlin
39. Internationale Filmfestspiele Berlin

Whitney Museum of American Art
New York
"AIDS Media: Counter-Representations"

Whitney Museum of American Art
New York
"Image World: Metamedia"

1990

The 14th Atlanta Film and Video Festival

Institute of Contemporary Arts
London
"New Activist Videos"

New Langton Arts
San Francisco
"A History of Loss"

BIBLIOGRAPHY

Furlong, Lucinda
AIDS MEDIA: COUNTER-REPRESENTATIONS (Program notes: New American Film and Video Series, 47). New York: Whitney Museum of American Art, 1989.

Horrigan, Bill
NEW WORKS (Program notes: American Film Institute Video Festival). Los Angeles: American Film Institute, 1988.

Sadownick, Doug
"ACT UP Makes a Spectacle of AIDS." HIGH PERFORMANCE, 13 (Spring 1990), pp. 26-31.

Tormollan, Carole
"John Greyson/Tom Kalin/Barbara Hammer." NEW ART EXAMINER, 15 (December 1987), p. 63.

Treichler, Paula A.
"Seduced and Terrorized: AIDS and Network Television." ARTFORUM, 28 (October 1989), pp. 147-51.

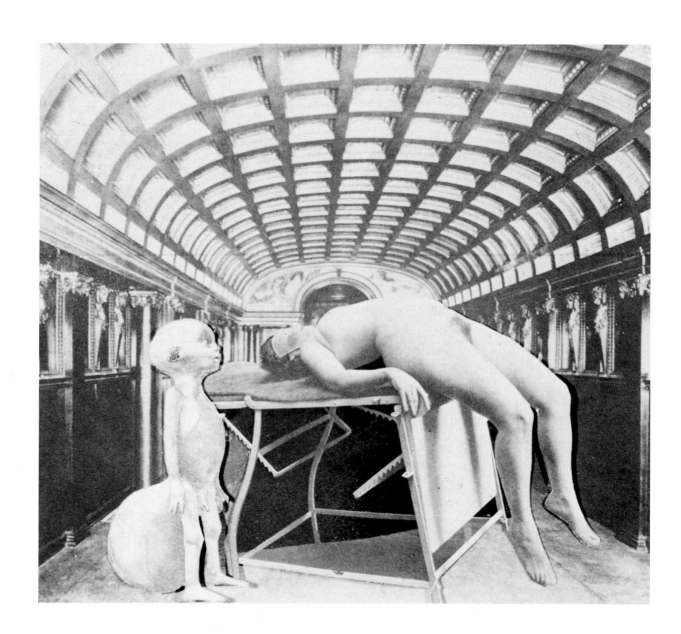

LEWIS KLAHR   *Tales of the Forgotten Future, Part Two, Five O'Clock Worlds: The Organ Minder's Gronkey*   1990

Born in New York, 1956; studied at the State University of New York, College at Purchase (1974-76), Center for Media Study, State University of New York, Buffalo (1977-78), State University of New York, Empire State College, Saratoga Springs (BS, 1979); lives in New York.

ONE-ARTIST EXHIBITIONS

1983

Millennium
New York

1984

Films Charas
New York

1985

Bromfield Gallery
Boston

1987

Boston Film/Video
Foundation

Hallwalls
Buffalo

1988

Collective for Living
Cinema
New York

1989

The Museum of Modern Art
New York

San Francisco Cinematheque

1990

Filmforum
Los Angeles

GROUP EXHIBITIONS

1985

Ann Arbor, Michigan
The 15th Annual Ann
Arbor 8mm Film Festival
(traveled)

The Kitchen
New York
"Super 8 Motel"

West Berlin
Interfilm 3

1987

Doylestown, Pennsylvania
Buck's County Film
Festival (traveled)

1988

The American Museum of
the Moving Image
Astoria, New York
"Independent America: New
Film 1978-1988"

Exit Art
New York
"First International Forum of
Super 8"

1989

Oberhausen, West Germany
Internationale Westdeutsche
Kurzfilmtage Oberhausen

1990

Collective for Living
Cinema
New York
"Breaking the Fall"

Pleasure Dome
Toronto
"The Super-8 Underground:
Closet Fantasies and Caustic
Visions"

RAPP Arts Center
New York
"Conspiracies"

BIBLIOGRAPHY

Arthur, Paul
"In Two Dimensions: Lewis
Klahr's 'In the Month of
Crickets,' Pat O'Neill's
'Water and Power.'" MOTION
PICTURE, 3 (Winter 1989-90),
pp. 21-23.

Beroes, Stephanie
"Interviews, New York: Lewis
Klahr." CINEMATOGRAPH,
2 (1986), pp. 74-76.

Chomont, Tom
"New York Letter." THE
INDEPENDENT EYE, 2 (Fall
1989), pp. 31-32.

Dargis, Manohla
"Counter Currents: Out of
the Past." THE VILLAGE
VOICE, February 28, 1989,
pp. 62-63.

Gunning, Tom
"Towards a Minor Cinema:
Fonoroff, Herwitz, Ahwesh,
Lapore, Klahr, and
Solomon." MOTION
PICTURE, 3 (Winter
1989-90), pp. 2-5.

Thomas, Kevin
"Special Screening: Lewis
Klahr's Vintage Graphics
Tell 'Future.'" LOS ANGELES
TIMES, September 17, 1990,
p. F11.

JENNIE LIVINGSTON

Paris Is Burning 1990

Born in Dallas, 1962; studied at Yale University, New Haven (BA, 1983); lives in New York.

ONE-ARTIST EXHIBITIONS

1990

Hirshhorn Museum and Sculpture Garden, Smithsonian Institution Washington, D.C.

1991

Film Forum
New York

GROUP EXHIBITIONS

1990

Baltimore Film Forum at the Baltimore Museum of Art
"Independents Weekend '90"

The 14th San Francisco International Lesbian and Gay Film Festival

New York
Margaret Mead Film Festival

New York
The New Festival

The 7th Annual Los Angeles International Gay and Lesbian Film and Video Festival

Toronto
Festival of Festivals

1991

41. Internationale Filmfestspiele Berlin

Park City, Utah
Sundance Film Festival

BIBLIOGRAPHY

Ehrenstein, David
"A Passion for Fashion: 'Paris Is Burning' Chronicles the Fantasy World of Vogueing." THE ADVOCATE, December 4, 1990, pp. 68-69.

Howell, John
"Exits and Entrances: On Voguing." ARTFORUM, 27 (February 1989), pp. 9-11.

Livingston, Jennie
"The Fairer Sex." APERTURE, no. 121 (Fall 1990), pp. 6-10.

Parkerson, Michelle
" 'Paris Is Burning.' "
BLACK FILM REVIEW, 6, no. 3 (1991), pp. 26-28.

Reynaud, Bérénice
"A Cult Is Born: Le vogueing a déjà 'son' film." LIBÉRATION, August 23, 1990, p. 26.

Sheehan, Henry
"Art of Autonomy: 'Paris Is Burning' Reveals the Sociosexual Roots of 'Voguing.' " [Los Angeles] READER, July 6, 1990, pp. 29-30.

VICTOR MASAYESVA, JR.

Siskyavi: The Place of Chasms 1990

Born on the Hopi Reservation, Arizona, 1951; studied at Princeton University, New Jersey (BFA, 1976), University of Arizona, Tucson (1976-78); lives in northern Arizona.

ONE-ARTIST EXHIBITIONS

1986

The Museum of Modern Art
New York

1988

Cooper Union
New York

1989

Amon Carter Museum
Fort Worth

Haus der Kulturen der Welt
West Berlin

Mesa Community College
Phoenix

1990

Andrew Smith Gallery
Santa Fe

Evergreen State College
Olympia, Washington

911 Contemporary Arts
Center
Seattle

GROUP EXHIBITIONS

1984

New York
Native American Film and
Video Festival

1986

Arsenal
West Berlin
"Neue im Kino Video
Projektionen"

Wells College
Aurora, New York
"Robert Flaherty Film
Seminar"

1987

Artists Space
New York
"We the People"

1988

Long Beach Museum of Art
Long Beach, California
"Foreign Exchange"

Los Angeles
1988 American Film
Institute Video Festival

Oklahoma City
Red Earth Festival

1989

Anderson Ranch Arts
Center for Photographic
Education
Snowmass, Colorado
"The Political Landscape"

The Museum of Modern Art
New York
"Video and the Computer"

1990

Arizona Center for the
Media Arts
Tucson
"Native Visions"

BIBLIOGRAPHY

Boyle, Deirdre
AMERICAN DOCUMENTARY
VIDEO: SUBJECT TO CHANGE
(exhibition brochure). New
York: The Museum of
Modern Art, 1988.

Renov, Michael
"Itam Hakim, Hopiit." In
ANTHROPOS '87/THE
BARBARA MYERHOFF FILM
FESTIVAL (exhibition
catalogue). Los Angeles:
University of Southern
California, 1987, p. 51.

Sands, Kathleen
"Seeing with a Native Eye."
AMERICAN INDIAN
QUARTERLY, 14 (Fall 1990),
pp. 387-96.

Weatherford, Elizabeth, and
Emelia Seubert
NATIVE AMERICANS ON FILM
AND VIDEO. New York:
Museum of the American
Indian/Heye Foundation,
1988, II, pp. 36-37, 42-43.

MEREDITH MONK

Born in New York, 1942; studied at Sarah Lawrence College, Bronxville, New York (BA, 1964); lives in New York.

PERFORMANCES

1969

The Solomon R. Guggenheim Museum, Minor Latham Playhouse, and The House
New York
"Juice: A Theater Cantata"

1970

Connecticut College
New London
"Needlebrain Lloyd and the Systems Kid: A Live Movie"

1971

The House, The Performing Garage, and Wooster Parking Lot
New York
"Vessel: An Opera Epic"

1972-76

Kennedy Center for the Performing Arts
Washington, D.C.
"The Travelogue Series: Paris/Chacon/Venice/Milan" (in collaboration with Ping Chong) (traveled)

1973

Brooklyn Academy of Music
New York
"Education of the Girlchild: An Opera" (traveled)

1976

La Mama Annex
New York
"Quarry: An Opera" (traveled)

1981

The Public Theater
New York
"Specimen Days: A Civil War Opera" (traveled)

1983

Schaubühne am Lehniner Platz
West Berlin
"The Games" (in collaboration with Ping Chong) (traveled)

1985

Carnegie Hall
New York
"Carnegie Hall Concert"

1991

Houston Grand Opera
"ATLAS: an opera in three parts" (traveled)

GROUP EXHIBITIONS

1975

Venice
"Biennale-teatro di Venezia"

1980

New York
Dance Film Festival

1981

Neuberger Museum, State University of New York, College at Purchase
"Soundings"

1982

New York
American Film Festival

1983

Toronto
"Video Culture/Canada"

1989

The Chicago International Film Festival

New York Film Festival

West Berlin
39. Internationale Filmfestspiele Berlin

1990

Cannes Film Festival

Castro Theater
San Francisco
"On Screen: A Celebration of Women in Film"

BIBLIOGRAPHY

Banes, Sally
"Meredith Monk: Homemade Metaphors." In TERPSICHORE IN SNEAKERS: POST-MODERN DANCE. Boston: Houghton Mifflin Company, 1980, pp. 148-65.

Berger, Mark
"Meredith Monk: A Metamorphic Theater." ARTFORUM, 11 (May 1973), pp. 60-63.

Hanhardt, John G. MEREDITH MONK (Program notes: The New American Filmmakers Series, 22). New York: Whitney Museum of American Art, 1985.

Lynch, Joan Driscoll
"'Book of Days': An Anthology of Monkwork." MILLENNIUM FILM JOURNAL, nos. 23-24 (Winter 1990-91), pp. 38-47.

Spector, Nancy
"The Anti-Narrative: Meredith Monk's Theater." PARKETT, 23 (March 1990), pp. 110-18.

Westwater, Angela
"Meredith Monk: An Introduction." ARTFORUM, 11 (May 1973), pp. 57-59.

AIMEE (RANKIN) MORGANA   *The Man in the Mirror*   1990

Born in Chicago, 1958; studied at Southern Illinois University, Carbondale (BA, 1978), San Francisco Art Institute (MFA, 1984), Independent Study Program, Whitney Museum of American Art, New York (1984-85); lives in New York.

ONE-ARTIST EXHIBITIONS

1984

Walter/McBean Gallery, San Francisco Art Institute

1985

The New Museum of Contemporary Art
New York
(window installation)

Postmasters Gallery
New York

1987

Postmasters Gallery
New York

1988

Michael Kohn Gallery
Los Angeles

Postmasters Gallery
New York

1989

The Institute of Contemporary Art
Boston

1991

American Fine Arts
New York

Pat Hearn Gallery
New York

GROUP EXHIBITIONS

1986

Artists Space
New York
"The Fairy Tale"

1987

Whitney Museum of American Art at Philip Morris
New York
"The Viewer as Voyeur"

1988

The New Museum of Contemporary Art
New York
"Girls Night Out"

1989

La Foret Museum
Tokyo
"Pop Culture and American Art"

University Art Galleries, Wright State University
Dayton, Ohio
"Art and Technology"

Whitney Museum of American Art
New York
"Image World: Metamedia"

Whitney Museum of American Art, Downtown at Federal Reserve Plaza
New York
"The Desire of the Museum"

1990

Le Frac Bourgogne
Dijon
"Le choix de femmes"

New Langton Arts
San Francisco
"Television Exposé"

Simon Watson Gallery
New York
"Total Metal"

BIBLIOGRAPHY

Kelley, Mike
"Foul Perfection: Thoughts on Caricature." ARTFORUM, 27 (January 1989), pp. 92-99.

Liu, Catherine
"In the Realm of the Senses." FLASH ART, no. 142 (October 1988), pp. 100-01, 123.

McGrath, Patrick
"Aimee Rankin at Postmasters." ART IN AMERICA, 76 (December 1988), pp. 146-47.

Rankin, Aimee
"Dream Quest in the Magic Kingdom: No país das maravilhas." LUSITANIA, 1 (Fall 1990), pp. 98-107.

Rankin, Aimee
"The Legacy of the Real, or the Limits of Representation." In DISCUSSIONS IN CONTEMPORARY CULTURE, NO. 1, Hal Foster, ed. Seattle: Bay Press, 1987, pp. 92-98.

Rankin, Aimee
"A Project for Artforum: Art or the Caress." ARTFORUM, 39 (December 1990), pp. 122-23.

ANTONIO MUNTADAS

Video Is Television?   1989

Born in Barcelona, 1942; studied at the University of Barcelona (1959-62), Escuela Técnica Superior Ingenieros Industriales, Barcelona (MA, 1967); lives in New York.

ONE-ARTIST EXHIBITIONS

1976

Museo de Arte
Contemporáneo de Caracas

1978

The Museum of Modern Art
New York

1980

and/or
Seattle

1985

Los Angeles Institute of
Contemporary Art

1987

Hall Gallery, Massachusetts
College of Art
Boston

Musée d'Art Moderne
Villeneuve d'Ascq, France

1988

Centro de Arte Reina Sofía
Madrid

1989

Walter Phillips Gallery
Banff, Alberta

1990

The Israel Museum
Jerusalem

Kent Fine Arts
New York

GROUP EXHIBITIONS

1975

Espace Cardin
Paris
"Deuxième rencontre
ouverte de vidéo"

1976

Venice
"XXXVII Biennale di
Venezia"

1977

Kassel, West Germany
"Documenta 6"

1980

The Solomon R.
Guggenheim Museum
New York
"New Images from Spain"
(traveled)

1981

São Paulo
"VI Bienal de São Paulo"

1985

Alternative Museum
New York
"Disinformation: The
Manufacture of Consent"

LACE
Los Angeles
"Public Domain"

1989

Kent Fine Arts
New York
"Public Domain"

Whitney Museum of
American Art
New York
"Image World: Metamedia"

1990

The New Museum of
Contemporary Art and the
Public Art Fund, Inc.
New York
"Rhetorical Image"

BIBLIOGRAPHY

McGee, Micki
"Born-Again Broadcasting."
AFTERIMAGE, 16 (May
1989), pp. 19-20.

Mendel, Mark
MUNTADAS: MEDIA
LANDSCAPE (exhibition
brochure). Andover,
Massachusetts: The
Addison Gallery of
American Art, Phillips
Academy, 1982.

Mercader, Antoni, ed.
MUNTADAS: 10 PROYECTAS/10
TEXTOS (exhibition
catalogue). Madrid: Galería
Vandrés, 1980.

Morgan, Robert C., Kathy
Rae Huffman, Eugeni
Bonet, Antonio Muntadas,
and Marshall Reese
MUNTADAS (exhibition
catalogue). Madrid: Galería
Fernando Vijande, 1985.

Rivas, F.
MUNTADAS (exhibition
catalogue). Antwerp:
Internationaal Cultureel
Centrum, 1976.

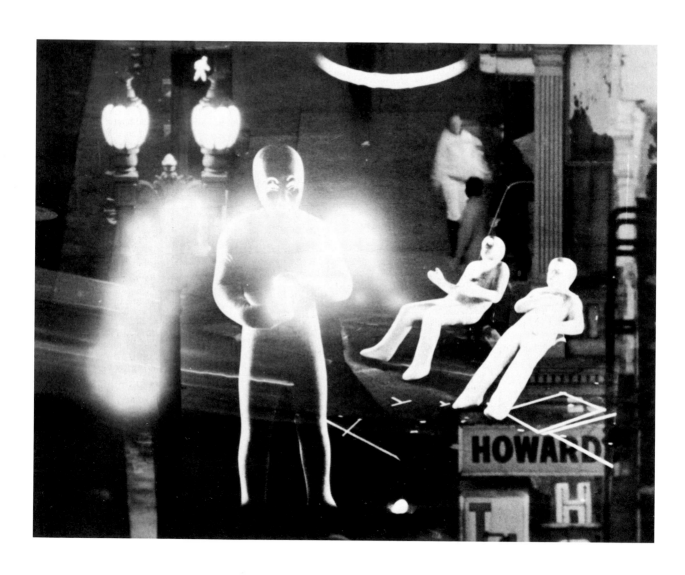

PAT O'NEILL

*Born in Los Angeles, 1939;
studied at the University of
California, Los Angeles (BFA,
1962; MFA, 1964); lives in
Los Angeles.*

ONE-ARTIST EXHIBITIONS

1974

Millennium
New York

1977

Walker Art Center
Minneapolis

1979

The Kitchen
New York

The Museum of Modern Art
New York

1982

Le Cinéma Parallèle
Montreal

LACE
Los Angeles

1985

Musée National d'Art
Moderne, Centre
Georges Pompidou
Paris

1986

Archives du Film
Expérimental
Avignon

1989

Pacific Film Archive,
University Art Museum,
University of California,
Berkeley

1990

The Carnegie Museum
of Art
Pittsburgh

GROUP EXHIBITIONS

1972

Ann Arbor, Michigan
Ann Arbor Film Festival
(traveled)

1973

Edinburgh International
Film Festival

1977

Kölnischer Kunstverein
Cologne
"Film as Film" (traveled)

Los Angeles County
Museum of Art
"The Poetic Eye"

1978

Center Screen
Cambridge, Massachusetts
"New Personal
Documentaries"

1981

Cineteca Italiano
Milan
"Cinema Independente
Americano e Francese"

1985

Musée National d'Art
Moderne, Centre
Georges Pompidou
Paris
"Cinéma Immatériel"

1989

New York Film Festival

Whitney Museum of
American Art
New York
"Image World: Metamedia"

1990

Park City, Utah
Sundance Film Festival

BIBLIOGRAPHY

Arthur, Paul
"Water and Power's Dazzling
Dialectic." MONTAGE
(March 1990), pp. 6-7.

Brinkman, Christine, and
Grahame Weinbren
"Selective Transparencies:
Pat O'Neill's Recent
Films." MILLENNIUM FILM
JOURNAL, no. 6 (Spring
1980), pp. 51-72.

Camper, Fred
"Natural Industry."
[Chicago] READER,
November 9, 1990, section
1, pp. 10, 42.

Hammen, Scott
"Four Films by Pat O'Neill."
AFTERIMAGE, 2 (March
1975), pp. 2-3.

Perlberg, Deborah
"Pat O'Neill/Film Forum."
ARTFORUM, 17 (September
1978), pp. 82-83.

Sitney, P. Adams
"'Saugus Series.'"
MILLENNIUM FILM JOURNAL,
nos. 16-18 (Fall-Winter
1986-87), pp. 158-61.

Swarthout, Miles
"Patrick O'Neill Interviewed
by Miles Swarthout. 1971."
FILM CULTURE, nos. 53-55
(Spring 1972), pp. 126-33.

YVONNE RAINER

Privilege 1990

*Born in San Francisco, 1934;
lives in New York.*

ONE-ARTIST EXHIBITIONS

1976

Städtisches Museum
Mönchengladbach,
West Germany

1977

Arsenal
West Berlin

1981

Bleecker Street Cinema
New York

1982

Institute of Contemporary
Arts
London

1985

Thalia Cinema
New York

1986

Whitney Museum of
American Art
New York

1988

Museum of Fine Arts
Boston

1990

The Performance Space
Sydney

San Francisco Cinematheque

1991

Film Forum
New York

GROUP EXHIBITIONS

1974

Cannes Film Festival

1975

Edinburgh International
Film Festival

1977

West Berlin
27. Internationale
Filmfestspiele Berlin

1980

Rotterdam Film Festival

1981

Whitney Museum of
American Art
New York
"1981 Biennial Exhibition"

1985

Toronto
Festival of Festivals

1986

Creteil, France
Festival International de
Film de Femmes

1987

Whitney Museum of
American Art
New York
"1987 Biennial Exhibition"
(traveled)

1990

New York Film Festival

1991

Park City, Utah
Sundance Film Festival

BIBLIOGRAPHY

Easterwood, Kurt, Susanne
Fairfax, and Laura Poitras
YVONNE RAINER: DECLARING
STAKES (exhibition
catalogue). San Francisco:
San Francisco Cinematheque,
1990.

de Lauretis, Teresa
"Strategies of Coherence:
Narrative Cinema, Feminist
Poetics, and Yvonne
Rainer." In TECHNOLOGIES
OF GENDER: ESSAYS ON
THEORY, FILM, AND FICTION.
Bloomington: Indiana
University Press, 1987,
pp. 107-26.

Mayne, Judith
"Screentests." In THE
WOMAN AT THE KEYHOLE.
Bloomington: Indiana
University Press, 1990,
pp. 75-85.

Rainer, Yvonne
THE FILMS OF YVONNE
RAINER. Bloomington:
Indiana University Press,
1989.

Rainer, Yvonne
"Thoughts on Women's
Cinema: Eating Words,
Voicing Struggles." THE
INDEPENDENT, 10 (April
1987), pp. 14-16.

Reynaud, Bérénice
"Impossible Projections."
SCREEN, 28 (Autumn 1987),
pp. 40-52.

MARLON RIGGS

Tongues Untied 1989

Born in Fort Worth, 1957; studied at Harvard University, Cambridge, Massachusetts (BA, 1978), Graduate School of Journalism, University of California, Berkeley (MA, 1981); lives in Oakland.

ONE-ARTIST EXHIBITIONS

1988

Pacific Film Archive, University Art Museum, University of California, Berkeley

1989

The Museum of Modern Art
New York

Richmond Art Center
Richmond, California

1990

Center for the Study of Black Literature and Culture, University of Pennsylvania
Philadelphia

Museum of Fine Arts
Boston

The Painted Bride Art Center
Philadelphia

San Francisco Black Coalition on AIDS

Southeastern Center for Contemporary Art
Winston-Salem,
North Carolina

GROUP EXHIBITIONS

1986

The Oakland Festival of the Arts

1987

Leipzig International Film Festival

1988

Philadelphia International Public Television Festival

1989

Los Angeles
1989 American Film Institute Video Festival

The Second Annual New York City Lesbian and Gay Experimental Film Festival

Whitney Museum of American Art
New York
"Image World: Metamedia"

1990

The Brooklyn Museum
New York
"African-American Video Visions"

40. Internationale Filmfestspiele Berlin

The 14th Atlanta Film and Video Festival

Intermedia Arts Minnesota
Minneapolis
"Endangered: Art and Performance by Men of Color"

Riga, Latvia
"Robert Flaherty Film Seminar"

BIBLIOGRAPHY

Banneker, Revon Kyle
"Marlon T. Riggs Untied."
BLK, April 17, 1990, p. 10.

Benjamin, Jody A.
"Riggs Films the Gay Side of Black Experience." THE CITY SUN, July 3, 1990, p. 36.

Ferrise, Susan
"Racism." THE OAKLAND TRIBUNE, August 3, 1986, p. B1.

Freeman, Mark
"Blackness and Difference." SAN FRANCISCO WEEKLY, March 14, 1990.

Simmons, Ron
"Other Notions." BLACK FILM REVIEW, 5 (Summer 1989), p. 20.

WARREN SONBERT

Born in New York, 1947; studied at New York University (BA, 1969); lives in San Francisco.

ONE-ARTIST EXHIBITIONS

1971

The Museum of Modern Art
New York

1976

Österreichisches
Filmmuseum
Vienna

1981

San Francisco Cinematheque

1983

Whitney Museum of
American Art
New York

1986

Collective for Living
Cinema
New York

Deutsches Filmmuseum
Frankfurt

1989

Filmforum
Los Angeles

1990

Arsenal
Berlin

The Museum of Modern Art
New York

Paris Cinémathèque

GROUP EXHIBITIONS

1970

National Film Archive
London
First International
Experimental Film Festival

1977

West Berlin
27. Internationale
Filmfestspiele Berlin

1980

Moderna Museet
Stockholm
"New American Cinema"

1984

The Kitchen
New York
"Best Films of the Year"

1985

Musée National d'Art
Moderne, Centre
Georges Pompidou
Paris
"Le cinéma expérimental
américain (1905-1984)"

1987

Whitney Museum of
American Art
New York
"1987 Biennial Exhibition"
(traveled)

1988

The Public Theater
New York

1989

New York Film Festival

Telluride, Colorado
Telluride Film Festival

1990

Wellington, New Zealand
Wellington Film Festival

BIBLIOGRAPHY

Camper, Fred
"Pulling Apart, Coming
Together." [Chicago] READER,
October 12, 1990, p. 33.

Carroll, Noel
"Causation: The Ampliation of
Movement and Avant-Garde
Film." MILLENNIUM FILM
JOURNAL, nos. 10-11 (Fall-
Winter 1981-82), pp. 61-82.

Hanhardt, John G.
WARREN SONBERT (Program
notes: The New American
Filmmakers Series, 10).
New York: Whitney Museum
of American Art, 1983.

Sitney, P. Adams
"Point of View: Rear-Garde."
AMERICAN FILM, 10 (July-
August 1985), pp. 13, 61.

Sonbert, Warren
"Narrative Concerns."
POETICS JOURNAL, 5 (May
1985), pp. 107-10.

Sterritt, David
"The Best of Independent
Films Are There If You
Look for Them."
CHRISTIAN SCIENCE
MONITOR, December 27,
1990, p. 11.

Born in Chicago, 1958; studied at the California Institute of the Arts, Valencia (BFA, 1980; MFA, 1982); lives in New York.

GROUP EXHIBITIONS

1983

Artists Space
New York
"And His Normal Reaction Of Saying Oh This Is Great You Don't Miss Me, Oh This Is Great, And That Laugh!!!"

1987

The New Museum of Contemporary Art
New York
"Social Studies: Recent Work on Video and Film"

The Renaissance Society at The University of Chicago and the Newport Harbor Art Museum, Newport Beach, California
"CalArts: Skeptical Belief(s)"

1988

Christine Burgin Gallery
New York
"Films"

The Kitchen
New York
"New Works"

Montbéliard, France
4ᵉ Manifestation Internationale de Vidéo et de TV de Montbéliard

New York
The 6th Asian American International Video Festival

1989

LACE
Los Angeles
"[A]Mass[ed] Media"

Long Beach Museum of Art
Long Beach, California
"Reconstructed Realms"

West Berlin
39. Internationale Filmfestspiele Berlin

Whitney Museum of American Art
New York
"Image World: Metamedia"

Whitney Museum of American Art
New York
"1989 Biennial Exhibition" (traveled)

1990

Artists Space
New York
"Disarming Genres"

The Brooklyn Museum
New York
"New Histories"

New American Makers
San Francisco
"Personal Statements"

BIBLIOGRAPHY

James, Caryn
"Avant-Garde Films in a Struggle to Stay Avant." THE NEW YORK TIMES, June 29, 1989, p. C17.

Kruger, Barbara
"Kim Ingraham, Rea Tajiri." ARTFORUM, 26 (October 1987), pp. 133-34.

Lord, Catherine, et al.
CALARTS: SKEPTICAL BELIEF(S) (exhibition catalogue). Chicago: The Chicago Renaissance Society at The University of Chicago; Newport Beach, California: Newport Harbor Art Museum, 1987.

Olander, William
SOCIAL STUDIES: RECENT WORK ON VIDEO AND FILM (exhibition brochure). New York: The New Museum of Contemporary Art, 1987.

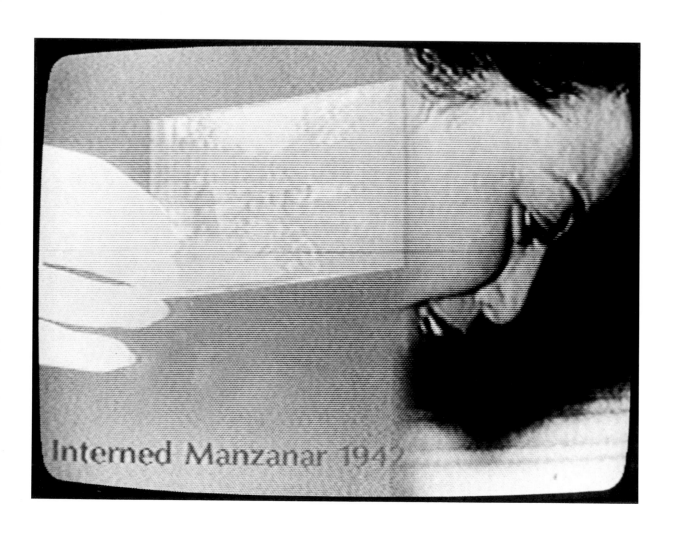

Interned Manzanar 1942

JANICE TANAKA   *Memories from the Department of Amnesia*   1989

*Born in Hollywood, 1940;
studied at Southwest College,
Chicago (AAS, 1975), School of
The Art Institute of Chicago
(BFA, 1979; MFA, 1981); lives
in Boulder, Colorado.*

ONE-ARTIST EXHIBITIONS

1982

Anthology Film Archives
New York

Long Beach Museum of Art
Long Beach, California

1984

Boston Film/Video
Foundation

Center for New Television
Chicago

1985

Elvehjem Museum of Art,
University of Wisconsin,
Madison

1988

The Los Angeles Center for
Photographic Studies

1991

The Carnegie Museum
of Art
Pittsburgh

GROUP EXHIBITIONS

1981

Kennedy Center for the
Performing Arts, American
Film Institute
Washington, D.C.
National Video Festival

1982

The Museum of Modern Art
New York
"Chicago Video"

1983

9th Annual Ithaca Video
Festival (traveled)

1985

Walter Phillips Gallery
Banff, Alberta
"Visualization Collage"

1986

Chicago
"Women in the Director's
Chair Film/Video Festival"

1988

The Hague
World-Wide Video Festival

1990

Laguna Gloria Art Museum
Austin
"The Territory"

Long Beach Museum of Art
Long Beach, California
"The Mother Child Reunion"

Museum of Fine Arts
Boston
"Women's Work"

BIBLIOGRAPHY

Koehler, Robert
"Breakthrough TV: A
Thinking Person's
Festival." LOS ANGELES
TIMES, October 31, 1990.

Straayer, Chris
"Sexuality and Video
Narrative." AFTERIMAGE, 16
(May 1989), pp. 8-11.

Sturken, Marita
"Video in the United States:
Notes on the Evolution of
an Art Form." In VIDÉO,
René Payant, ed. Montreal:
Artextes, 1986, pp. 55-65.

FRANCESC TORRES

Sur del Sur   1990

Born in Barcelona, 1948; studied at Escola Missana, Barcelona (1965-67), École des Beaux-Arts, Paris (1967-68); lives in New York.

ONE-ARTIST EXHIBITIONS

1975

Artists Space
New York

1977

112 Greene Street
New York

1978

Whitney Museum of
American Art
New York

1980

Elise Meyer Gallery
New York

1982

Herbert F. Johnson
Museum of Art, Cornell
University
Ithaca, New York

1984

Damon Brandt Gallery
New York

1986

La Jolla Museum of
Contemporary Art

1988

Künstforum, Nationalgalerie
West Berlin

University Gallery,
University of Massachusetts,
Amherst

1990

Capp Street Project
San Francisco

GROUP EXHIBITIONS

1973

N.A.M.E. Gallery
Chicago
"Chicago"

1978

Los Angeles Institute of
Contemporary Art
"Artwords/Bookworks"

1981

The New Museum of
Contemporary Art
New York
"Alternatives in Retrospect"

1984

The Museum of
Contemporary Art
Los Angeles
"Automobile and Culture"

Stedelijk Museum
Amsterdam
"The Luminous Image"
(traveled)

1985

Alternative Museum
New York
"Disinformation: The
Manufacture of Consent"

1986

The Bronx Museum of
the Arts
New York
"Disarming Images"
(traveled)

1988

The Museum of Modern Art
New York
"Committed to Print"

1989

Whitney Museum of
American Art
New York
"1989 Biennial Exhibition"
(traveled)

BIBLIOGRAPHY

Ancona, Victor
"Francesc Torres:
Sociopsychological Video."
VIDEOGRAPHY, 6 (October
1981), pp. 64-71, 73.

Hanhardt, John G.
"Landscapes of History: The
Art of Francesc Torres." In
FRANCESC TORRES: PLUS
ULTRA (exhibition catalogue).
West Berlin: Nationalgalerie,
1988, pp. 3-10.

Posner, Helaine, Francesc
Torres, Mar Villaepesa, and
Marilyn A. Zeitlin
BELCHITE/SOUTH BRONX:
A TRANS-CULTURAL AND
TRANS-HISTORICAL
LANDSCAPE (exhibition
catalogue). Amherst:
University Gallery,
University of Massachusetts,
Amherst, 1988.

Rice, Shelley
"Francesc Torres: The
Tyranny of the Past."
AFTERIMAGE, 10 (December
1982), pp. 4-7.

Zaya, Octavio
"Entrevista a Francesc
Torres." HARTÍSIMO (Fall
1985), pp. 117-28.

WORKS IN THE EXHIBITION

Dimensions are in inches;
height precedes width precedes depth.

PAINTING   SCULPTURE   PHOTOGRAPHY

VITO ACCONCI

Convertible Clam Shelter, 1990
Fiberglass, galvanized steel, clam shells, audio, and electric
lights, two parts, 120 x 96 x 36 each, dimensions variable.
James Corcoran Gallery, Santa Monica

CARLOS ALFONZO

Cimetière Marin, 1990
Oil on linen, 84 x 120. Estate of the artist

Figurat, 1990
Oil on linen, 96 x 84. Collection of Peter Menendez

JENNIFER BARTLETT

Air, 1990
Oil on canvas, 84 x 84. Paula Cooper Gallery, New York

Earth, 1990
Oil on canvas, 84 x 84. Paula Cooper Gallery, New York

Fire, 1990
Oil on canvas, 84 x 84. Collection of Matthew and Iris Strauss

Water, 1990
Oil on canvas, 84 x 84. Collection of Laila and
Thurston Twigg-Smith

NAYLAND BLAKE

Restraint #6 (Ankle, Shelf, Mirror), 1989
Steel and leather, 47 x 24 x 10. Collection of Alan Power

Work Station #5, 1989
Stainless steel, 54½ x 24½ x 55½. Collection of Dare and
Themistocles Michos

Still Life, 1990
Sony Video 8 TV recorder and shelf, 8½ x 5 x 5. Collection of
Richard Kuhlenschmidt and Betty-Jo Tilley

Magic, 1990–91
Puppet, box, and armature, 36 x 6½ x 9. Collection of
Jay Gorney

CHUCK CLOSE

Bill, 1990
Oil on canvas, 72 x 60. The Pace Gallery, New York

April, 1990–91
Oil on canvas, 100 x 84. Collection of Eli and Edythe L. Broad

JOHN COPLANS

Self-Portrait, 1990
Three gelatin silver prints, 123 x 48 overall. Collection of Laila
and Thurston Twigg-Smith

Self-Portrait, 1990
Four gelatin silver prints, 45 x 114 overall. Galerie Lelong,
New York

JESSICA DIAMOND

No Inside, No Outside, 1990
Latex paint on wall, dimensions variable. American Fine Arts,
New York

*New Economic Shorthand: Totally Unequal
(In the Red Version)*, 1991
Latex paint on wall, dimensions variable. American Fine Arts,
New York

*New Economic Shorthand: What Money?
(In the Red Version)*, 1991
Latex paint on wall, dimensions variable. American Fine Arts,
New York

CARROLL DUNHAM

Floating Shape, 1989–90
Acrylic, vinyl, and graphite on linen, 77¼ x 99¼.
Mottahedan Collection

Shape with Entrance, 1990
Acrylic, vinyl, and graphite on linen, 94¼ x 158¾.
Mottahedan Collection

JEANNE DUNNING

Head 2, 1989
Laminated Cibachrome print mounted on plexiglass, 28¼ x 19.
Collection of Patti Gilford

Head 6, 1989
Laminated Cibachrome print mounted on plexiglass, 30 x 19.
Collection of the artist; courtesy Feature, New York

Head 8, 1990
Laminated Cibachrome print mounted on plexiglass, 30 x 19.
Collection of the artist; courtesy Feature, New York

Head 10, 1990
Laminated Cibachrome print mounted on plexiglass, 25½ x 18.
Feature, New York (work exhibited in Group Material, *AIDS Timeline*)

Neck, 1990
Laminated Cibachrome print mounted on plexiglass, 33 x 28.
Collection of Refco Group, Ltd., Chicago

ERIC FISCHL

In the Temple, 1989
Oil on linen, 105 x 48. Collection of Stefan Edlis and
Gael Neeson

On the Stairs of the Temple, 1989
Oil on linen, 115¼ x 140½. Collection of Boris and
Sophie Leavitt

BILL FONTANA

Vertical Water, 1991
Four Sennheiser MD-211 and 2 MKH-20 microphones for
sound recording, courtesy Sennheiser Electronic, Wedemark,
Germany; compact disc player, compact disc (edition of three);
eight BOSE series 102 loudspeakers and two BOSE Acoustic
Wave Cannons, courtesy BOSE Corporation, Framingham,
Massachusetts; two audio amplifiers; two equalizers. Gallery
Paule Anglim, San Francisco

DAWN FRYLING

No Title, 1990
Painted wood frames, glass, and halide lights,
dimensions variable. Collection of the artist; courtesy Gallery
Paule Anglim, San Francisco

ADAM FUSS

Untitled, 1991
Unique photogram, Cibachrome print, 40 x 30. Robert Miller
Gallery, New York

Untitled, 1991
Unique photogram, Cibachrome print, 29¾ x 39¾.
Private collection

Untitled, 1991
Unique photogram, Cibachrome print, 40 x 30.
Private collection

Untitled, 1991
Unique photogram, Cibachrome print, 40 x 30. Collection of
Thomas Walther

Untitled, 1991
Unique photogram, Cibachrome print, 40 x 30. Private
collection

JOSEPH GLASCO

Big Green, 1990
Acrylic and paper on canvas, 141 x 98. Collection of the artist

001, 1990
Acrylic on canvas, 84 x 60. Collection of the artist

ROBERT GOBER

Untitled, 1990
Wax, cotton, wood, leather, and human hair, 9 x 16½ x 45.
Museum Boymans-van Beuningen, Rotterdam

Untitled, 1990
Beeswax and human hair, 24 x 15½ x 12. Collection of
Lise Spiegel Wilks

FELIX GONZALEZ-TORRES

Untitled (Death by Gun), 1990
Stack of offset print on paper, endless copies, 9 x 33 x 44.
Andrea Rosen Gallery, New York

Untitled (Lover Boys), 1991
355 pounds of wrapped candies and paint on wall,
dimensions variable. Andrea Rosen Gallery, New York

GROUP MATERIAL

AIDS Timeline, 1989–91
Mixed-media installation, dimensions variable. Organized by
Group Material

PETER HALLEY

Double Elvis, 1990
Day-Glo, acrylic, and Roll-A-Tex on canvas, 97½ x 190.
Cooperfund, Inc., Oakbrook, Illinois

303, 1991
Day-Glo, acrylic, and Roll-A-Tex on canvas, 88½ x 91½.
Sonnabend Gallery, New York

KEITH HARING

Matador, 1989
Enamel and acrylic on canvas, 72 x 96. Estate of the artist;
courtesy Tony Shafrazi Gallery, New York

Untitled, 1989
Enamel and acrylic on canvas, 72 x 96. Estate of the artist;
courtesy Tony Shafrazi Gallery, New York

GARY HILL

Between Cinema and a Hard Place, 1991
Three ¾-inch videotape players; three ¾-inch videotapes,
black-and-white and color, sound; computer controlled
audio/video switching matrix; variable number of monitors,
dimensions variable. Collection of the artist

RONI HORN

Thicket No. 2, 1990
Plate aluminum with epoxy resin inlay, two units,
4¼ x 25¾ x 51¼ each. Mary Boone Gallery, New York

Thicket No. 3: Kafka's Palindrome, 1991
Plate aluminum with epoxy resin inlay, 4¼ x 49 x 42.
Mary Boone Gallery, New York

WENDY JACOB

Wall, Fourth Floor, 1991
Rubber, latex, and wood, with electric motor, 204 x 54 x 36.
Robbin Lockett Gallery, Chicago

Wall, Lower Gallery, 1991
Rubber, latex, and wood, with electric motor, 120 x 57⅜ x 136½.
Robbin Lockett Gallery, Chicago

LUIS JIMENEZ

Border Crossing—Cruzando El Rio Bravo, 1989
Acrylic urethane on fiberglass, 127 x 34 x 54. Collection of
the artist; courtesy Betty Moody Gallery, Houston

Steelworker—Hunky, 1990
Acrylic urethane on fiberglass, 146 x 83 x 37½. Collection of
the artist; courtesy Adair Margo Gallery, El Paso

JASPER JOHNS

Untitled, 1990
Oil on canvas, 75 x 50. Collection of the artist

Untitled, 1990
Oil on canvas, 31⅝ x 41. Collection of the artist

LARRY JOHNSON

Untitled (Jesus + I), 1990
Ektacolor print, 61 x 84½. Collection of Judy and Stuart
Spence; courtesy Stuart Regen Gallery, Los Angeles

Untitled (Winter Me), 1990
Ektacolor print, 61 x 86½. Collection of Richard Prince

ALEX KATZ

Black Brook 4, 1989
Oil on canvas, 126 x 96. Marlborough Gallery, New York

Black Brook 10, 1990
Oil on canvas, 126 x 96. Marlborough Gallery, New York

MIKE KELLEY

*Empathy Displacement: Humanoid Morphology
(2nd and 3rd Remove)*, 1990
Acrylic on panels and found, handmade stuffed dolls in painted
wood boxes

#1: panel, 36 x 24; box, 4¼ x 9⅛ x 13⅝. Collection of
Mike Finney

#2: panel, 86¼ x 26; box, 6 x 9½ x 33⅛. Private collection

#7: panel, 24 x 19; box, 4 x 7⅞ x 9⅛. Collection of
Alan Hergott and Curt Shepard

#9: panel, 49¼ x 16⅛; box, 3½ x 6¾ x 18½. Collection of
Byron R. Meyer

#11: panel, 34 x 19; box, 5 x 7¾ x 13⅛. Collection of
Douglas S. Cramer

#14: panel, 84¼ x 14; box, 5¾ x 5¾ x 28⅞. Collection of the
artist; courtesy Rosamund Felsen Gallery, Los Angeles

#15: panel, 65 x 31⅛; box, 4½ x 12 x 26.
Collection of Duke Comegys

Untitled, 1990
Yarn on cotton blanket, 1¾ x 85¾ x 89¾.
Galerie Jablonka, Cologne

ELLSWORTH KELLY

Green Curve with White Panel, 1989
Oil on canvas, two panels, 90½ x 125 overall. Collection of the
artist; courtesy Leo Castelli Gallery, New York

Orange Red Relief (for Delphine Seyrig), 1991
Oil on canvas, two panels, 120 x 98½ overall. Collection of the
artist; courtesy Blum Helman Gallery, New York

MARY KELLY

Interim Part II: Pecunia, 1989
Silkscreen on galvanized steel, twenty units, 16 x 6½ x 11½ each;
16 x 6½ x 360 overall. Vancouver Art Gallery

LOUISE LAWLER

*Standing Before You, Rather Behind You, To Tell You of
Something I Know Nothing About*, 1991
Photographs, words, paint, paperweights, and pedestals,
dimensions variable. Collection of the artist; courtesy Metro
Pictures, New York

ROY LICHTENSTEIN

Interior with African Mask, 1991
Oil and magna on canvas, 114 x 146. Private collection

Interior with Mirrored Wall, 1991
Oil and magna on canvas, 126 x 160½. Private collection

GLENN LIGON

Untitled (I Do Not Always Feel Colored), 1990
Oil stick and gesso on wood, 80 x 30. Max Protetch Gallery,
New York

*Untitled (I Feel Most Colored When I Am Thrown Against a
Sharp White Background)*, 1990
Oil stick and gesso on wood, 80 x 30. Collection of the artist

Untitled (I Remember the Very Day I Became Colored), 1990
Oil stick and gesso on wood, 80 x 30. Collection of George Wolfe

DONALD LIPSKI

Blood #1, 1991
Glass, liquids, and metal hardware, 12 x 132 x 8.
Rhona Hoffman Gallery, Chicago

Dirt Ball, 1991
Rope and leather belting, 132 diameter. Galerie Lelong,
New York

Untitled #91–8, 1991
Oak table and cotton string, 39 x 55 x 36. Galerie Lelong,
New York

SALLY MANN

Fallen Child, 1989
Gelatin silver print, 20 x 24. Collection of the artist; courtesy
Houk Friedman Gallery, New York

The 42-Pound Squash, 1989
Gelatin silver print, 20 x 24. Collection of the artist; courtesy
Tartt Gallery, Washington, D.C.

Gorjus, 1989
Gelatin silver print, 20 x 24. Collection of the artist; courtesy
Houk Friedman Gallery, New York

Hay Hook, 1989
Gelatin silver print, 20 x 24. Collection of the artist; courtesy
Houk Friedman Gallery, New York

Naptime, 1989
Gelatin silver print, 20 x 24. Collection of the artist; courtesy
Houk Friedman Gallery, New York

Sorry Game, 1989
Gelatin silver print, 20 x 24. Collection of the artist; courtesy
Tartt Gallery, Washington, D.C.

CHRISTIAN MARCLAY

Tape Fall, 1989–91
Recorded magnetic tape, Revox player, and two speakers, dimensions variable. Tom Cugliani Gallery, New York

Bone Yard, 1990
750 cast hydrostone telephone receivers, dimensions variable. Galerie Isabella Kacprzak, Cologne, and Tom Cugliani Gallery, New York

Sound Sheet, 1990
Vinyl flexi-discs, 171 x 99. Tom Cugliani Gallery, New York

DAVID McDERMOTT AND PETER McGOUGH

Les Recréations Scientifiques, 1884, 1990
Platinum palladium prints in wood frames with gold labels, twenty photographs, 27 x 23¾ each, framed. Robert Miller Gallery, New York

Pail in Equilibrium on a Stick, 1884, from *Les Recréations Scientifiques, 1884*, 1990
Collection of Lunn Ltd., Paris

A Siphon Formed with a Small Band of Cloth, 1884, from *Les Recréations Scientifiques, 1884*, 1990
Robert Miller Gallery, New York

Spiral of Cardboard Put in Rotation by the Ascending Movement of a Current of Warm Air, 1884, from *Les Recréations Scientifiques, 1884*, 1990
Fraenkel Gallery, San Francisco

JOHN MILLER

Natural History, 1989
Acrylic on Styrofoam, wood, papier-mâché, modeling paste, and plastic model, 19 x 56 x 44. Metro Pictures, New York

Untitled, 1989
Graphite on paper, 13⅛ x 13¼. Collection of Pamela Lee

Echo and Narcissus, 1990
Acrylic on mannequins and clothing, with mirror: male, 72 x 34 x 29; female, 60 x 7 x 30; mirror, 72 x 20. Metro Pictures, New York

RICHARD MISRACH

Dead Animals #79, 1989
Dye coupler print, 40 x 50. Collection of the artist; courtesy Fotomann, Inc., New York

Dead Animals #86, 1989
Dye coupler print, 40 x 50. Collection of the artist; courtesy Fraenkel Gallery, San Francisco

Dead Animals #327, 1989
Dye coupler print, 40 x 50. Collection of the artist; courtesy Jan Kesner Gallery, Los Angeles

Playboy #38, 1990
Dye coupler print, 50 x 40. Collection of the artist; courtesy Fraenkel Gallery, San Francisco

Playboy #90, 1990
Dye coupler print, 40 x 50. Collection of the artist; courtesy Fotomann, Inc., New York

JOAN MITCHELL

Champs, 1990
Oil on canvas, 110¼ x 70¾. Galerie Jean Fournier, Paris

Champs, 1990
Oil on canvas, 110¼ x 141¾. Galerie Jean Fournier, Paris

ED MOSES

Spectra Tres Ojos, 1989
Oil and acrylic on canvas, 78 x 132. Collection of Laila and Thurston Twigg-Smith

Kudjur, 1990–91
Oil and acrylic on canvas, 78 x 132. Louver Gallery, New York

CELIA ALVAREZ MUÑOZ

Ella y El, 1990
Maple cabinet, Cibachrome photographs, letterpress type, fabric, ribbon, buttons, dijos, and found objects, 32 x 54 x 4. The Barrett Collection

Tu y Yo, 1990
Fujichrome photographs, letterpress type, and oak frame on museum board, with latex interior wall paint on wall, 60 x 84. Collection of the artist; courtesy Adair Margo Gallery, El Paso

ELIZABETH MURRAY

Hobo, 1990
Oil on canvas, two parts, 88 x 74 x 3 overall. Collection of
Laila and Thurston Twigg-Smith

Sorry Dogs, 1990
Oil on canvas, 76¼ x 99¾ x 11¾. Paula Cooper Gallery,
New York

BRUCE NAUMAN

Andrew Head/Andrew Head Stacked, 1990
Cast wax, 22 x 8 x 9. Daniel Weinberg Gallery, Santa Monica

Raw Material—"MMMM," 1990
Video installation, dimensions variable. Daniel Weinberg
Gallery, Santa Monica

CADY NOLAND

Crate of Beer, 1989
Crate with beer cans, 15 x 11 x 12½. Collection of Kathleen and
Roland Augustine

This Piece Has No Title Yet, 1989
Mixed media, dimensions variable. Collection of Elaine and
Werner Dannheisser

Open Sore (Diana Balton with Cady Noland), 1990
Plexiglass, wood, and electric light, dimensions variable.
Collection of Wilhelm Schürmann; courtesy Luhring Augustine
Hetzler Gallery, Santa Monica

PHILIP PEARLSTEIN

Model Posing with Unfinished Painting, 1990
Oil on canvas, 60 x 96. Hirschl & Adler Modern, New York

Fox, Fish, Models, and Wooden Lady, 1991
Oil on canvas, 96 x 72. Hirschl & Adler Modern, New York

ELLEN PHELAN

Meadow Hampshire—Lifting Clouds, 1989
Oil on linen, 67½ x 108¾. Collection of Evelyn and
Leonard Lauder

Summer Light—Morning (Second Version), 1989
Oil on linen, 72 x 72. Susanne Hilberry Gallery, Birmingham,
Michigan, and Barbara Toll Fine Arts, New York

RONA PONDICK

Double Bed, 1989
Plastic, rope, plastic pillows, and baby bottles, 9 x 73 x 162.
Fiction/Nonfiction Gallery, New York, and Asher/Faure Gallery,
Los Angeles

Chairman, 1990
Plastic, wax, comics, and shoes, 17¼ x 21½ x 16.
Collection of Dr. Jack E. Chachkes

Seat, 1990
Plastic, wax, lace, and shoes, 17¼ x 16½ x 16. Private collection

REBECCA PURDUM

Footnote and Fumbling, 1990
Oil on canvas, 108 x 108. Private collection; courtesy
Jack Tilton Gallery, New York

Ribbon, 1990
Oil on canvas, 108 x 108. Jack Tilton Gallery, New York

ALAN RATH

Voyeur II, 1989
Tripod, aluminum, steel, acrylic, electronics, and two cathode
ray tubes, 83 x 68 x 25. Dorothy Goldeen Gallery, Santa Monica

Hound, 1990
Wood, steel, aluminum, electronics, and two cathode ray tubes,
18 x 76 x 26. Dorothy Goldeen Gallery, Santa Monica

Magic Mushrooms, 1990
Wood, plastic, electronics, and speakers, 73 x 33 x 22.
Collection of Henry and Lisille Matheson

ROBERT RAUSCHENBERG

Appalachian Double Latch Spring Glut, 1989
Assembled metal parts, 64¼ x 33¼ x 11¼.
Knoedler & Company, New York

Yellow Visor, 1989
Assembled metal parts, 58 x 49¾ x 10. Knoedler & Company,
New York

TIM ROLLINS + K.O.S.

The Temptation of Saint Antony: The Nicolaitans, 1990
Blood, water, isopropyl alcohol, Xerograph on rag paper,
twelve sheets, 11 x 8½ each, framed. Collection of
Marc and Livia Straus

The Temptation of Saint Antony: The Trinity, 1990
Blood, water, and Xerograph on rag paper mounted on linen,
three panels, 68 x 191 overall. Thomas Ammann Fine Art,
Zurich

ALLEN RUPPERSBERG

Kunstkammer, 1991
Graphite on paper, silkscreen on movie screens, color
photographs, black-and-white photograph, found drawing,
and posters, dimensions variable. Christine Burgin Gallery,
New York

The Gift and the Inheritance (The World Within the Word), 1989
Graphite on paper, 21½ x 27. Collection of Emily Fisher Landau

DAVID SALLE

E.A.J.A., 1990
Oil and acrylic on canvas, 102 x 123. Collection of
Mr. and Mrs. Israel Lapciuc

Mingus in Mexico, 1990
Oil and acrylic on canvas, 96 x 122½. Collection of
Douglas S. Cramer

JOSEPH SANTORE

The Frayed Rope, 1988–89
Oil on canvas, 113 x 86. Edward Thorp Gallery, New York

The Yellow Painting, 1989–90
Oil on canvas, 113 x 102. Edward Thorp Gallery, New York

THOMAS LANIGAN SCHMIDT

Incomplete Caress, 1989–90
Upholstery, office and household staples, holographic tape,
theatrical cells, and various brands of plastic bags on plywood,
48 x 48. Collection of the artist; courtesy Holly Solomon
Gallery, New York

Olympio (The Naked Macho), 1989–90
Upholstery, rugs, holographic tape, theatrical cells, contact
paper, Xerox acetate, Scotch tape, and Magic Markers on
plywood, 48 x 72. Museé d'Art Contemporain,
Fondation Edelman, Lausanne, Switzerland

Platonic Love (Mozart and Candy Cubism), 1989–90
Upholstery, office and household staples, holographic tape,
theatrical cells, and various brands of plastic bags on plywood,
48 x 48. Collection of David Brenman Richardson

JULIAN SCHNABEL

Self-Portrait with Champagne Glass, 1987–90
Patinated bronze, 155 x 45 x 31. The Pace Gallery, New York

Golem, 1989
Patinated bronze, 156 x 83 x 68. The Pace Gallery, New York

Esso Ess, 1990
Patinated bronze with wax, 125 x 141 x 59.
Galerie Bruno Bischofberger, Zurich

JIM SHAW

My Mirage, 1986–90
Mixed media on paper, 107 pieces, approximately 17 x 14 each.
Various collections

My Mirage was originally assembled and presented at the
University Art Museum, University of California, Berkeley, in
conjunction with Intersection for the Arts, San Francisco, and
made possible in part by grants from the Paul L. and Phyllis
Wattis Foundation, the National Endowment for the Arts,
The LEF Foundation, the California Arts Council, and Art
Matters, Inc.

Devotional Art, 1987, from *My Mirage*, 1986–90
Gouache on paperboard, 17 x 14. Whitney Museum of
American Art, New York; Purchase, with funds from
Mr. and Mrs. William A. Marsteller   90.11

My Mirage Logo #3, 1989, from *My Mirage*, 1986–90
Silkscreen on paperboard, 17 x 14. Collection of the artist;
courtesy Linda Cathcart Gallery, Santa Monica

Bubblegum Cards (Fronts), 1990, from *My Mirage*, 1986–90
Gouache on paperboard, 17 x 14. Collection of Linda and
Jerry Janger

CINDY SHERMAN

Untitled, 1989
Color photograph, 95 x 64. Collection of Elaine and
Werner Dannheisser

Untitled, 1990
Color photograph, 82 x 48. Collection of PaineWebber Group
Inc., New York

LAURIE SIMMONS

Bending Globe, 1990
Color photograph, 53 x 89. Metro Pictures, New York

Sitting Accordion, 1990
Color photograph, 53 x 89. Metro Pictures, New York

Sitting Microscope, 1991
Black-and-white photograph, 53 x 89. Metro Pictures,
New York

LORNA SIMPSON

Double Negative, 1990
Four color Polaroids, three plastic plaques,
113½ x 21 overall. The High Museum of Art, Atlanta;
Purchase, with funds from the National Endowment for
the Arts and Edith G. and Philip A. Rhodes

Untitled, 1991
Four gelatin silver prints, 45 x 135 overall. Josh Baer Gallery,
New York

KIKI SMITH

Untitled, 1990
Beeswax and pigment, two figures, approximately
60 x 24 x 14 each. Collection of the artist; courtesy
Fawbush Gallery, New York

Untitled, 1991
Paper and wood, 23 x 20 x 12. Collection of the artist; courtesy
Fawbush Gallery, New York

PHILIP SMITH

Epiphany II, 1990
Oil and wax on canvas, 75 x 98. Collection of Mr. and Mrs.
Jay I. Kislak

Roman Conversations, 1990
Oil and wax on canvas, 78 x 98. Private collection

PAT STEIR

Sixteen Waterfalls of Dreams, Memories, and Sentiment, 1990
Oil on canvas, 78½ x 15⅛. Robert Miller Gallery, New York

Wolf Waterfall, 1990
Oil on canvas, 173 x 92. Robert Miller Gallery, New York

Curtain Waterfall, 1991
Oil on canvas, approximately 146 x 116½. Robert Miller
Gallery, New York

FRANK STELLA

Watson and the Shark I, 1991
Aluminum on iron base, 151 x 192 x 138 overall.
Collection of the artist; courtesy Knoedler & Company, New York

JESSICA STOCKHOLDER

Recording Forever Pickled #2, 1991
Mixed-media construction, dimensions variable.
American Fine Arts, New York

PHILIP TAAFFE

Desert Flowers, 1990
Mixed media on linen, 61 x 79. Gagosian Gallery, New York

Easter Choir, 1990
Mixed media on linen, 91 x 115. Gagosian Gallery, New York

MARK TANSEY

Constructing the Grand Canyon, 1990
Oil on canvas, 85 x 126½. Walker Art Center, Minneapolis;
Gift of Penny and Mike Winton, 1990

Derrida Queries de Man, 1990
Acrylic on canvas, 83¾ x 63¾. Collection of Penny and
Mike Winton

Wheel (in collaboration with Fritz Buehner), 1990
Plywood and wood veneer, 38 x 48 x 48. Curt Marcus Gallery,
New York

CY TWOMBLY

Untitled, 1983–90
Painted bronze, 68¾ x 10⅝ x 9. Collection of the artist;
courtesy Thomas Ammann Fine Art, Zurich

Winter's Passage (Luxor), 1985–90
Bronze, 20⅞ x 41 x 18¾. Collection of the artist; courtesy
Thomas Ammann Fine Art, Zurich

ALEX WEBB

Fort Pierce, Florida, 1989
Pearl surface Cibachrome print, 20 x 30. Collection of the artist

Immokalee, Florida, 1989
Pearl surface Cibachrome print, 20 x 30. Collection of the artist

Miami Beach, Florida, 1989
Pearl surface Cibachrome print, 20 x 30. Collection of the artist

Migrant Workers, Immokalee, Florida, 1989
Pearl surface Cibachrome print, 20 x 30. Collection of the artist

St. Augustine, Florida, 1989
Pearl surface Cibachrome print, 20 x 30. Collection of the artist

CARRIE MAE WEEMS

Untitled, 1990
Gelatin silver print, 28¼ x 28¼. P.P.O.W. Gallery, New York

Untitled, 1990
Three gelatin silver prints, 28¼ x 28¼ each.
P.P.O.W. Gallery, New York

Untitled, 1990
Gelatin silver print, 28¼ x 28¼. P.P.O.W. Gallery, New York

Untitled, 1990
Gelatin silver print, 28¼ x 28¼. P.P.O.W. Gallery, New York

DAVID WOJNAROWICZ

He Kept Following Me, 1990
Acrylic on board with photographs, 48 x 60. Private collection;
courtesy P.P.O.W. Gallery, New York

Sex Series, 1990
Eight gelatin silver prints, 15 x 18 each.
P.P.O.W. Gallery, New York

When I Put My Hands on Your Body, 1990
Gelatin silver print with silkscreen, 26 x 38.
Collection of the artist; courtesy P.P.O.W. Gallery, New York

VITO ACCONCI

Adaptable Wall Bra, 1990
Steel rebar, plaster, canvas, steel cable, audio, and electric
lights, 288 x 96 x 60, dimensions variable. James Corcoran
Gallery, Santa Monica

Convertible Clam Shelter, 1990
Fiberglass, galvanized steel, clam shells, audio, and electric
lights, two parts, 120 x 96 x 36 each, dimensions variable.
James Corcoran Gallery, Santa Monica

CARLOS ALFONZO

Told, 1990
Oil on linen, 96 x 84. Estate of the artist

CHUCK CLOSE

Judy, 1989–90
Oil on canvas, 72 x 60. Modern Art Museum of Fort Worth;
Gift of Anne Burnett Tandy in memory of Ollie Lake Burnett,
by exchange

JOHN COPLANS

Self-Portrait, 1990
Two gelatin silver prints, 48 x 120 overall. Galerie Lelong,
New York

JESSICA DIAMOND

Food for Thought, 1990
Installation at Artspace, San Francisco

CARROLL DUNHAM

Shape with Incline, 1990
Acrylic, vinyl, and graphite on linen, 77¾ x 103¾.
Collection of Michael and B.Z. Schwartz

ERIC FISCHL

The Tire Store, 1989
Oil on linen, 109 x 75. Collection of the artist

DAWN FRYLING

Flour Slots, 1990
Wood, plexiglass, and flour, 63 x 54½ x 24. Collection of the
artist; courtesy Gallery Paule Anglim, San Francisco

Toast (Units 3 and 4), 1990
Wood and bread, 15½ x 39 x 4¾. Collection of the artist;
courtesy Gallery Paule Anglim, San Francisco

JOSEPH GLASCO

004, 1990
Acrylic and paper on canvas, 96 x 84. Collection of the artist

ROBERT GOBER

Untitled, 1990
Wax, cotton, wood, leather, and human hair, 10¾ x 20½ x 5⅝.
Hirshhorn Museum and Sculpture Garden, Smithsonian
Institution, Washington, D.C.; Joseph H. Hirshhorn Purchase
Fund, 1990

FELIX GONZALEZ-TORRES

*Untitled (Somewhere Better Than This Place/Nowhere Better
Than This Place)*, 1990
Two stacks of offset print on paper, endless copies,
26 x 56 x 29 overall. Collection of Estelle Schwartz

Untitled (U.S.A. Today), 1990
300 pounds of wrapped candies, dimensions variable.
Collection of Elaine and Werner Dannheisser

PETER HALLEY

The Moment Passed, 1989
Day-Glo, acrylic, and Roll-A-Tex on canvas, 97¾ x 95.
Collection of Douglas S. Cramer

The Terminator, 1990
Day-Glo, acrylic, and Roll-A-Tex on canvas, 97½ x 95.
Private collection; courtesy Galerie Jablonka, Cologne

KEITH HARING

Brazil, 1989–90
Enamel and acrylic on canvas, 72 x 72. Estate of the artist

GARY HILL

Beacon, 1990
Installation at the Stedelijk Museum, Amsterdam

RONI HORN

Asphere VII, 1989
Solid forged and machined stainless steel, 12 x 12⅝ diameter.
Private collection

WENDY JACOB

Untitled, 1990 (two views)
Rubber, latex, and wood, with electric motor, 90 x 40 x 26.
Robbin Lockett Gallery, Chicago

Untitled, 1990 (two views)
Rubber, latex, and wood, with electric motor, 124 x 63¾.
Andrea Rosen Gallery, New York

LUIS JIMENEZ

Fiesta—Jarabe, 1989–91
Acrylic urethane on fiberglass, 114½ x 96 x 59.
General Services Administration, Washington, D.C.

JASPER JOHNS

Untitled, 1990
Oil on canvas, 18 x 18. Collection of the artist

LARRY JOHNSON

Untitled (Dead + Buried), 1990
Ektacolor print, 61 x 84½. Stuart Regen Gallery, Los Angeles,
and 303 Gallery, New York

ALEX KATZ

Black Brook 11, 1990
Oil on canvas, 108 x 138. Marlborough Gallery, New York

ELLSWORTH KELLY

Blue Panel with Green Curve, 1989
Oil on canvas, two panels, 99½ x 86¼ overall.
Collection of Douglas S. Cramer

LOUISE LAWLER

(Bought from Leo Castelli in 1963 and Bought from Martha Jackson around 1960) Bought from Count Panza di Biumo in 1985, 1989
Cibachrome print, 50¼ x 37¼. Collection of the artist; courtesy
Metro Pictures, New York

Detail, 1990
Cibachrome print, 40 x 54. Collection of the artist; courtesy
Metro Pictures, New York

Glass and Local Storms, 1990
Cibachrome print, 41 x 52. Collection of the artist; courtesy
Metro Pictures, New York

ROY LICHTENSTEIN

Interior with Built-in Bar, 1991
Painted and printed paper on board, 25½ x 42½.
Private collection

DONALD LIPSKI

White, No Tracer, 1990
Rope, 132 diameter. Installation at the National Garden
Festival, Dunston Staithe, Gateshead, England, 1990

CHRISTIAN MARCLAY

Tape Fall, 1989–90
Recorded magnetic tape, Revox player, and ladder, dimensions
variable. Tom Cugliani Gallery, New York

JOHN MILLER

Untitled, 1990
Acrylic on figurine, Styrofoam sphere, papier-mâché, plastic
objects, and wood base: 32 x 24 x 117; base, 31 x 22 x 22.
Metro Pictures, New York

JOAN MITCHELL

River, 1989
Oil on canvas, 110½ x 157½. Robert Miller Gallery, New York

CELIA ALVAREZ MUÑOZ

Ella y El, 1990
Wood cabinet, photographs, and various objects, 32 x 54 x 4.
Tyler Museum of Art, Tyler, Texas

Stories Your Mother Never Told You, 1990
Mixed-media installation at Newhouse Center for
Contemporary Art, Snug Harbor Cultural Center, Staten Island

ELIZABETH MURRAY

Lonely Rivers, 1990
Oil on canvas, two parts, 88½ x 79¾ x 11½ overall.
Paula Cooper Gallery, New York

CADY NOLAND

Corral Gates (foreground), 1989
Mixed media, dimensions variable.
Installation at Galleria Massimo de Carlo, Milan, 1989

Frame Device and *Oozwald*, 1989
Mixed media, dimensions variable.
Installation at Galleria Massimo de Carlo, Milan, 1989

This Piece Has No Title Yet, 1989
Installation at The Mattress Factory, Pittsburgh

PHILIP PEARLSTEIN

Kiddie Car-Plane, Airplane, and Models, 1990
Oil on canvas, 60 x 72.
Collection of Mr. and Mrs. R. Crosby Kemper

ELLEN PHELAN

Island in the River—River Test, 1989
Oil on linen, 51¼ x 45⅝. The Brooklyn Museum, New York;
Gift of Edward A. Bragaline, by exchange

REBECCA PURDUM

Chin Up, 1990
Oil on canvas, 108 x 72. Jack Tilton Gallery, New York

ROBERT RAUSCHENBERG

Blue Gate Secret Spring Glut, 1989
Assembled metal parts and chain, 46¼ x 19¼ x 6½.
Knoedler & Company, New York

ALLEN RUPPERSBERG

The Gift and the Inheritance, 1989
Installation at Christine Burgin Gallery, New York, 1989

*The Gift and the Inheritance (Looking Backward 2000–1887
by Edward Bellamy)*, 1989
Graphite on paper, 22½ x 29. Christine Burgin Gallery,
New York

How to Remember a Better Tommorow, Sets and Props, 1989–90
Installation at John Weber Gallery, New York, 1990

DAVID SALLE

Ugolino's Room, 1990–91
Oil and acrylic on canvas, 87 x 114. Gagosian Gallery,
New York

JOSEPH SANTORE

Peonies, 1990
Oil on canvas, 42 x 41½. Edward Thorp Gallery, New York

CINDY SHERMAN

Untitled, 1989
Color photograph, 73¼ x 57.
Collection of Linda and Harry Macklowe

LORNA SIMPSON

Guarded Conditions, 1989
Eighteen color Polaroid prints and twenty-one plastic plaques,
91 x 131 overall. San Diego Museum of Contemporary Art,
La Jolla, California; Museum Purchase, Contemporary
Collectors Fund

1978–88, 1990
Four gelatin silver prints and thirteen plastic plaques, 49 x 68
overall. Josh Baer Gallery, New York

KIKI SMITH

Untitled, 1989
Ink on gampi paper, 70 x 24 x 24.
Collection of the artist; courtesy Fawbush Gallery, New York

Trough, 1990
Plaster, 60 x 24 x 30. Fawbush Gallery, New York

PHILIP SMITH

Court of Law, 1989
Oil and wax on canvas, 69½ x 97½.
Collection of Mr. and Mrs. S. Brooks Barron

FRANK STELLA

Raft of the Medusa, Part II and Part III, 1990
Aluminum on iron base, two parts: 101½ x 110 x 88,
112 x 91 x 88. Musée d'Art Contemporain, Fondation Edelman,
Lausanne, Switzerland

Study for Watson and the Shark I, 1990
Aluminum, 108½ x 97 x 99. Gagosian Gallery, New York

JESSICA STOCKHOLDER

No Title, 1990
Metal table, glass, enamel paint, newspaper, and tennis balls,
dimensions variable. Collection of Xavier Hufkens

Recorded Forever Pickled, 1990
Mixed-media construction. Installation at Le Consortium,
Dijon, 1990

Untitled Seepage "Sandwashed Sundried & Shrinkwrapped," 1991
Installation at Ezra and Cecile Zilkha Gallery, Wesleyan
University, Middletown, Connecticut, 1991

PHILIP TAAFFE

Necromancer, 1990
Mixed media on linen, 89 x 69. Gagosian Gallery, New York

MARK TANSEY

Bridge Over the Cartesian Gap, 1990
Oil on canvas, 87 x 108. Private collection

CY TWOMBLY

Rotalla, 1986–90
Bronze, 28 x 26¾ x 19¾. Collection of the artist; courtesy
Thomas Ammann Fine Art, Zurich

FILM AND VIDEO

PEGGY AHWESH AND KEITH SANBORN

The Deadman, 1989
16mm film, black-and-white, sound; 38 minutes
Lent by the artists; distributed by Drift Distribution,
New York

LAWRENCE ANDREWS

Strategies for the development of/Redefining the purpose served/Art in the age of . . . aka the making of the towering inferno, 1989
Videotape, black-and-white and color, sound; 23 minutes
Lent by the artist; distributed by Electronic Arts Intermix,
New York, and Video Data Bank, Chicago

IDA APPLEBROOG AND BETH B

Belladonna, 1989
Videotape, black-and-white and color, sound; 12 minutes
Lent by the artists; distributed by Drift Distribution,
New York, and Video Data Bank, Chicago

GREGG ARAKI

the long weekend (o' despair), 1989
16mm film, black-and-white, sound; 93 minutes
Lent by the artist

CHARLES ATLAS

Because We Must, 1989
Videotape, color, stereo sound; 53 minutes
Lent by the artist; distributed by Electronic Arts Intermix,
New York

ERICKA BECKMAN AND MIKE KELLEY

Blind Country, 1989
Videotape, color, sound; 20 minutes
Lent by the artists; distributed by Video Data Bank, Chicago

HANS BREDER

From Here and There Too: Moscow Postcards 1989, 1990
Videotape, color, sound; 26 minutes
Lent by the artist

TONY COKES AND DONALD TRAMMEL

Fade to Black, 1990
Videotape, black-and-white and color, sound; 33 minutes
Lent by the artists; distributed by Drift Distribution and
The Kitchen, New York, and Video Data Bank, Chicago

ZEINABU IRENE DAVIS

Cycles, 1989
16mm film, black-and-white, sound; 17 minutes
Lent by the artist; distributed by Women Make Movies,
New York

JUAN DOWNEY

Hard Times and Culture, Part I, 1990
Videotape, color, stereo sound; 34½ minutes
Lent by the artist; distributed by Electronic Arts Intermix,
New York

STEVE FAGIN

The Machine That Killed Bad People, 1990
Videotape, color, sound; 120 minutes
Lent by the artist; distributed by Drift Distribution and
The Kitchen, New York, Video Data Bank, Chicago, and
Kijkhuis, The Hague

SU FRIEDRICH

Sink or Swim, 1990
16mm film, black-and-white, sound; 48 minutes
Lent by the artist; distributed by Drift Distribution, New York,
and Canyon Cinema, San Francisco

VANALYNE GREEN

A Spy in the House That Ruth Built, 1989
Videotape, color, sound; 29½ minutes
Lent by the artist; distributed by Women Make Movies,
New York, and Video Data Bank, Chicago

GARY HILL

Site/Recite (A Prologue), 1989
Videotape, color, stereo sound; 4 minutes
Lent by the artist; distributed by Electronic Arts Intermix,
New York

PETER HUTTON

New York Portrait Part III, 1990
16mm film, black-and-white, silent; 16 minutes
Lent by the artist; distributed by Canyon Cinema, San Francisco

JOAN JONAS

Volcano Saga, 1989
Videotape, color, sound; 28 minutes
Lent by the artist; distributed by Electronic Arts Intermix,
New York, and Video Data Bank, Chicago

TOM KALIN

They are lost to vision altogether, 1989
Videotape, color, sound; 13 minutes
Lent by the artist; distributed by Video Data Bank, Chicago,
and V-Tape, Toronto

LEWIS KLAHR

*Tales of the Forgotten Future, Part Two, Five O'Clock Worlds:
The Organ Minder's Gronkey; Hi-Fi Cadets; Verdant Sonar*, 1990
Three Super-8 films/videotapes, color, sound; 16, 10, and 2½
minutes
Lent by the artist; distributed by The Kitchen, New York

*Tales of the Forgotten Future, Part Three, Mood Opulence:
Cartoon Far; Yesterday's Glue; Elevator Music*, 1990–91
Three Super-8 films/videotapes, color, sound; 7, 15, and 15
minutes
Lent by the artist; distributed by The Kitchen, New York

JENNIE LIVINGSTON

Paris Is Burning, 1990
16mm film, color, sound; 76 minutes
Lent by the artist

VICTOR MASAYESVA, JR.

Siskyavi: The Place of Chasms, 1990
Videotape, color, sound; 30 minutes
Lent by the artist; distributed by Electronic Arts Intermix,
New York

MEREDITH MONK

Book of Days, 1989
35mm film, black-and-white and color, sound; 74 minutes
Lent by the artist; distributed by The Stutz Company, Berkeley

AIMEE (RANKIN) MORGANA

The Man in the Mirror, 1990
Videotape, color, sound; 25 minutes
Lent by the artist

ANTONIO MUNTADAS

Video Is Television?, 1989
Videotape, color, sound; 5½ minutes
Lent by the artist; distributed by Electronic Arts Intermix,
New York

PAT O'NEILL

Water and Power, 1989
35mm film, color, sound; 57 minutes
Lent by the artist; distributed by The Stutz Company, Berkeley

YVONNE RAINER

Privilege, 1990
16mm film, black-and-white and color, sound; 103 minutes
Lent by the artist; distributed by Zeitgeist Films, New York

MARLON RIGGS

Tongues Untied, 1989
Videotape, black-and-white and color, sound; 55 minutes
Lent by the artist; distributed by Frameline, San Francisco

WARREN SONBERT

Friendly Witness, 1989
16mm film, black-and-white and color, sound; 32 minutes
Lent by the artist; distributed by Canyon Cinema, San Francisco

REA TAJIRI

History and Memory, 1991
Videotape, black-and-white and color, sound; 32 minutes
Lent by the artist; distributed by Electronic Arts Intermix,
New York, and Video Data Bank, Chicago

JANICE TANAKA

Memories from the Department of Amnesia, 1989
Videotape, black-and-white and color, stereo sound; 13 minutes
Lent by the artist; distributed by Electronic Arts Intermix,
New York

FRANCESC TORRES

Sur del Sur, 1990
Videotape, color, stereo sound; 15 minutes
Lent by the artist; distributed by Productora Andaluza de
Programas, Seville, Spain

Exhibition installation and catalogue preparation were coordinated by Emily Russell; with research by Shannah Ehrhart, Elizabeth Finch, Sharon Freedman, and Matthew Yokobosky, curatorial assistants. Elizabeth Cooley, Jennifer Cosgrove, Karena Elwell, Suzanne Lane, and Valerie von Volz assisted with library research. Lucinda Furlong, Assistant Curator, Film and Video, coordinated the Film and Video sections of the exhibition and catalogue.

This publication was organized at the Whitney Museum by Doris Palca, Head, Publications and Sales; Sheila Schwartz, Editor; Jane Philbrick, Associate Editor; Aprile Gallant, Production Assistant; and Debra Kelvin, Secretary/Assistant.

Design by Anthony McCall Associates, New York; typesetting by Trufont Typographers; printing by Schneidereith & Sons.

PHOTOGRAPH CREDITS

Numbers refer to pages:
© Atlantic Records: *19*;
Beth B: *321*; Ben Blackwell: *268*; Bruce Berman: *114, 116, 117*; Geoffrey Clements: *250*; Dennis Cowley: *152, 153*; James Dee: *34, 36, 37, 85*; Susan Einstein: *122, 124, 125*; Lee Fatherree: *190, 192, 193*; José A. Hergueta: *374*; Ginny Hood: *242, 244, 245*; Bill Jacobson: *246, 249*; Bob Jackson: *200*; Robert McKeever: *146, 148, 149*; Andrew Moore: *82*; Fredrik Nilsen: *252, 253*; Jerry Pantzer: *356*; © Douglas M. Parker Studio: *106, 108, 109, 130, 132, 133, 194, 196, 197*; Georg Rehsteiner: *266*; Schneider/Erdman, Inc.: *308*; Sixth Street Studio: *50*; Steven Sloman: *94, 96, 278*; Ivar Smedstad: *354*; Lee Stalsworth: *84*; Jim Strong, Inc.: *118*; Ellen Page Wilson: *262, 264, 265*; Dorothy Zeidman: *120, 121, 156, 157, 238, 240, 241, 280*; Zindman/Fremont: *62, 64, 65, 204, 205, 206, 209*

ISBN 0-87427-075-8
ISBN 0-393-30772-7 (trade paperback)
ISBN 1043-3260

Printed in the United States of America

© 1991 Whitney Museum of American Art
945 Madison Avenue
New York, New York 10021